A Tour of Fab

A Tour of Fabletown

Patterns and Plots
in Bill Willingham's *Fables*

NETA GORDON

McFarland & Company, Inc., Publishers
Jefferson, North Carolina

LIBRARY OF CONGRESS CATALOGUING-IN-PUBLICATION DATA

Names: Gordon, Neta, 1971– author.
Title: A tour of fabletown : patterns and plots in Bill
Willingham's Fables / Neta Gordon.
Description: Jefferson, North Carolina : McFarland &
Company, Inc., Publishers, 2016. | Includes index.
Identifiers: LCCN 2016008318 | ISBN 9780786499854
(softcover : acid free paper) ∞
Subjects: LCSH: Willingham, Bill—Criticism and interpretation. |
Willingham, Bill. Fables. | Comic books, strips, etc.—History
and criticism. | Graphic novels—History and criticism. |
Fairy tales—Adaptations—History and criticism. | Legends—
History and criticism.
Classification: LCC PN6727.W54 Z64 2016 | DDC 741.5/973—dc23
LC record available at https://lccn.loc.gov/2016008318

BRITISH LIBRARY CATALOGUING DATA ARE AVAILABLE

ISBN 978-0-7864-9985-4 (print)
ISBN 978-1-4766-2401-3 (ebook)

Front cover images of castle and city © 2016 Dmytro/iStock

Printed in the United States of America

*McFarland & Company, Inc., Publishers
Box 611, Jefferson, North Carolina 28640
www.mcfarlandpub.com*

For Martin, Mina, and Sasha

Acknowledgments

This project has been a joy to work on from start to finish, not least because of the encouragement I have received along the way. First, to the members of the Department of English Language and Literature at Brock University—Rob Alexander, James Allard, Lynn Arner, Gregory Betts, Natalee Caple, Tim Conley, Gale Coskan-Johnson, Ronald Cummings, Martin Danahay, Adam Dickinson, Leah Knight, Mathew Martin, Andrew Pendakis, Elizabeth Sauer, Barbara Seeber, Sue Spearey, and Carole Stewart—thanks for your collegiality, good sense, and good humor. In particular, thank you to the current chair of the department, Ann Howey, for creating an environment so conducive to scholarly conversation, and to Janet Sackfie, the department's administrative assistant, for supporting all the work we do with such expertise. Thank you to Nicholas Hay, an honors student at Brock who agreed to participate in a directed reading course on *Fables*, and whose thoughts on this text were illuminating and often a springboard to my own thinking. Finally, a thank you to Marilyn Rose, whose sudden passing this year was a loss felt by the entire Brock community: I will miss your mentorship, friendship, wit, and generosity.

Thanks also to Gene Kannenberg, Jr., for his help with communicating with DC Entertainment, and to Mandy Noack-Barr at DC for all her efforts. Also, thanks to Geoff Rousseau at Sketchbook Comics and Games in St. Catharines, Ontario, for keeping me in *Fables*.

Most importantly, to my family: Yael Seliger, Michael Gordon, Gilda Berger, Ruth Seliger, Amir Gordon, Shira Brym-Friedland, Ben Friedland, Sophie Friedland, Talia Gordon, and Eytan Gordon; thanks for your enduring enthusiasm for my work. To Mina and Sasha, the two smartest people I know, thanks for your love, laughter, and excitement about the idea that Mommy is writing a book about comics! And thank you to Martin, my partner and best reader, whose life-long love of comic books inspired me to read *Fables* in the first place.

Table of Contents

Preface

A Tour of Fabletown is a thematic introduction to Bill Willingham's comic book series *Fables*, the first issue of which was published in July 2002 and the last issue of which was published in July 2015. The goal of this study is to examine the series as a holistic piece and to consider the wide range of ideas that recur, exploring, for example, how *Fables* confronts the relatively closed moral system of the fairy tale, especially in terms of imagining avenues for redemption and change; how the tension between conservatism and radicalism that emerges in *Fables* reflects current anxieties about changing social roles and the politics of nationhood and community, especially with respect to notions of identity, difference, and belonging in an increasingly globalized world; and how the representation of the extraordinary and the magical reflects both a desire for limitations on occluded power and a celebration of the comforts of community.

This project emerged out of an interest in the way *Fables* operates as a contemporary adaptation of folk and fairy tale, particularly in the potential opposition between, on the one hand, tendencies in folk and fairy tale adaptation toward postmodern and feminist revision (see Bacchilega 1997, Shippey 2003, and Kukkonen 2013) and, on the other hand, the male readers usually thought to be the primary consumers of comic books (see Pustz 1999 and Phillips and Strobl 2013). Thus, a consideration of the source tales is often a starting point for analysis and many sections of this book include background information, generated by folklorists and fairy tale scholars, on the literary history and characteristic elements of, for example, a figure such as Snow White, or a tale type such as the Clever Animal Tale, or a standard feature of folk and fairy tales such as the Magical Object, or a canonical work such as the *Arabian Nights*. Also important was the work of such fairy tale scholars as D.L. Ashliman, Cristina Bacchilega, and Jack Zipes, especially their discussion of the way folk and fairy tales operate as a reflection of cultural fears and hopes, how they are

1

structured to both respond to and help organize notions of wish-fulfillment, and how—as Zipes notes—the folk and fairy tale persists as a repeatable cultural meme with contemporary cultural relevance (2006, 2). Willingham's predominantly revisionist impulse in adapting the folk and fairy tale, as this study explores, differs in focus from many explicitly feminist adaptations, and also generally dispenses with the plot of the fortunate rise in social status; that said, the comic book series' portrayal of a continuum of masculine and feminine performances, as well as the social dynamics of a complex polis, is often framed within the emphasis typical to the folk and fairy tale on reward versus punishment, and on the desire for a "happy ending."

However much *Fables* is an example of contemporary fairy tale adaptation, it is also a fusion of various generic traditions historically associated with comic books, including fantasy or sword-and-sorcery, funny animal, horror, detective, war, romance, and even superhero stories (see Kukkonen 2013). At various points in this book, the analysis of plot patterns springs from a discussion of the primary features of a genre—especially of fantasy and of romance—or a discussion of the way the very idea of genre is linked to the production history of comic books (see Wright 2001); in these analyses, I make use of the work of genre critics such as Brian Attebery (1992) and Brian Stableford (2005) on fantasy, Barbara Fuchs (2004) on romance, and Rita Copeland and Peter T. Struck (2010) on allegory, as well as of comic book critics such as Matthew Pustz (1999), Bradford W. Wright (2001), and Randy Duncan, Matthew J. Smith, and Paul Levitz (2015), whose assessments of literary genre or genre in comics often show the links between typical generic features and the construction of a marketplace of readers. In *Fables*, the play with traits from various genres takes up the issue of readerly expectation and the marketplace, often in highly metafictional ways, whereby the inhabitants of Fabletown understand that their "lives" circulate among non–Fables (or "the Mundy") as stories. The focus in *A Tour of Fabletown* on the way plot patterns are used, disrupted, and—most importantly—recognized by readers draws attention to how the series portrays the act of reading as an act of community building: an act that binds a community while at the same time laying bare that community's hopes, fears, and expectations.

The issue of a "community's hopes, fears, and expectations" is also broached in this study's attention to the way contemporary social roles, world events, and political and economic relations are alluded to in *Fables*. As scholars Mark C. Hill and Wilson Koh have noted, the portrayal of war in *Fables*—especially the war with the Adversary, as depicted in the first eleven volumes of the series—operates in part as a fictional response to the United States' war with Iraq, which began in 2003 with a U.S.–led invasion of Iraq and, indeed, at many points in this study, the function of *Fables* as cultural commentary is highlighted. Also, following Hill, Rebecca-Anne C. Do Rozario, and Karin Kukkonen, *A Tour of Fabletown* considers the representation of gender in *Fables*, taking into account how comic books (as well as traditional fairy tales) are often associated with formulaic portrayals of hyper-masculine men and excessively sexualized and vulnerable woman (see Robinson 2004, Robbins 2010, Phillips and Strobl 2013, and Scully and Moorman 2014). As this study argues, *Fables* reacts to changing notions of gender in its representation of both femininity and masculinity as a continuum of expression, exploring the performance of self-sufficiency, vulnerability, aggression, and shame. Also of interest is how the history of the funny animal comic (not to mention the animal tale) is taken up in *Fables* with reference to the rise of posthumanist studies, as well as how the portrayal of racial categories—particularly the representation of the Arabian Fables and Geppetto's Wooden Soldiers— reflects contemporary discussions about cultural accommodation and national character. Another important cultural context that *A Tour of Fabletown* draws attention to is the context of globalization, whereby the representation of the movement across borders, of the circulation of knowledge, and of the flow of power exposes current anxieties about security and identity.

As noted above, I refer in this study to the work of scholars who have previously written on *Fables*, including Rebecca-Anne C. Do Rozario (a fairy tale and children's literature scholar), Mark C. Hill (a popular culture and film studies scholar), Wilson Koh (a popular culture and media studies scholar), Karin Kukkonen (a comic books and cognitive studies scholar), Laurie Taylor (a digital humanities scholar), and Adam Zolkover (a folklorist); of that work, Kukkonen's is the most sustained, as she includes a long chapter on *Fables* and genre in her monograph *Contemporary Comics Storytelling* (2013). I make particular note of the research areas of these scholars to draw attention to the increasingly interdisciplinary field of comic books studies in general, and, in particular, the way a series such as *Fables* might attract a wide range of scholarly approaches (and my own research expertise is contemporary Canadian literature, though my teaching often focuses on notions of literary genre). While it is no longer necessary, as it may have been in past decades, and certainly prior to the publication in 1986 of Art Spiegelman's *Maus* and Alan Moore's *The Watchmen*, to make a case for the legitimacy of comics as an object of scholarly attention, the recent explosion of the field has produced its own set of complications, as the methods associated with other fields are simply grafted onto the analysis of a new object (see Fischer 2010). In my capacity (and with my limitations) as a literary scholar, I have examined *Fables* primarily in terms of the way it can be *read*, i.e., in terms of the way it operates as a narrative that includes features such as plots, characters, settings, themes, images, and narrators, as well as the way *Fables* works as an example of literary production that self-consciously explores the act of reading; while I do at times read *Fables* as a visual as well as literary text, I do not explore the comic as a visual system. Also, perhaps because I am one, I have been sensitive to the ways in which *Fables* sometimes demonstrates a certain hostility to the work of literary scholars, poking fun at the stereotype of the jargon-obsessed academic. As Craig Fischer notes in "Worlds within Worlds: Audiences, Jargon, and North American Comics," the relationships among three communities that respond to comic books in writing, which he identifies as the fan community, the community of comic book reviewers, and the interdisciplinary community of scholars, is often characterized by polite discounting or outright derision. In attending to this conundrum, I have tried as much as possible to dispense with jargon (though lapses are inevitable, immersed as I am in a particular field of study), and also made of a point of considering how *Fables* exists within the particular history of and marketplace for comics, and how it reaches out to its own highly dedicated and highly literate fan community.

In *Fables*, the act of reading comic books is represented as a leisure activity: it is during their moments of boyish recreation that Pinocchio, Boy Blue, and Flycatcher load up on candy from Edward Bear's Candy Shop and a pile of comics. That said, the act of careful reading in more general terms is championed throughout the series as a necessary activity for cutting through lies, for understanding the flow of political power, and for a community's self-fashioning of its history and character. *A Tour of Fabletown* is also—ideally—a careful act of reading. It is the first book-length work to focus solely on *Fables*, as well as the first scholarly work to consider the main series in its entirety, now that Issue #150 is in the books; along with discussion of the main series, the book includes a survey of various *Fables'* spin-offs, from *Peter & Max: A Fables Novel*, to the *Jack of Fables* series, to *Fairest*, and so on. That said, trying to keep up with the extended *Fables* universe has proved impossible: the popularity of *The Wolf Among Us*, an episodic video game developed by Telltale Games, has provided impetus for—at the very least—an adaptation of the game's narrative into a comic book, which is being released in both digital and print form; also, an adaptation of the comic book series for film remains in the works. However, as a broad introduction to the main comic book series, the aim of *A Tour of Fabletown* is to open up possible lines of critical inquiry, ideally producing the kind of "spin-off" examinations that parallel the proliferating impetus of comics. The book is organized as a series of "introductions" on linked, but discrete subjects; though certain arguments—for example about the anxious representation of occluded power, or about the constraints of cultural scripts, or about the comforts of community—recur and develop as the book goes on. *A Tour of Fabletown*—unlike a comic book—need not be read serially. Though the book does presume familiarity with *Fables* (and is, by definition, one big "spoiler"), the analyses are meant to be exploratory, introducing a number of different frames for reading, engaging in the close analysis of text, and offering some provisional arguments about the way *Fables* responds to its cultural milieu.

Introduction:
In Praise of Muddlecock:
The Thematization of
Reading in Fables

In the *Fables* volume *Homelands*, which chiefly traces the adventures of Boy Blue's quest to kill the Adversary and rescue Red Riding Hood, writer and artist team Bill Willingham and Mark Buckingham depict a conversation between Ogren and Throk, two goblin soldiers of the 4th Horde who work in service of the Emperor. After Throk confesses to being both taken in and terrified by circulating rumors of a deadly Black Knight who hunts poor goblin menials, Ogren—clearly the more sophisticated of the two—scoffs at the tale, telling Throk: "only a bunch of poncy, college-educated aristo officers could ever believe such nonsense" (6.59). As it turns out, a knight does appear—though he is a Blue Knight, not Black—and Ogren's failure to take the tale seriously costs him and his compatriot their lives. Later in the same volume, a low level Empire bureaucrat named Muddlecock makes an urgent report to a higher level sorcerer—Senior Undersecretary Mudsnipe—in which he connects events occurring in various worlds to the work of a lone killer. Mudsnipe, knocked off balance by this intellectual feat, asks: "How did you put it all together, Muddlecock, from dozens of unrelated reports and documents?" Muddlecock replies, "I can't help but see the patterns in things. It's what makes me a good administrative comptroller" (6.92). The combination of these two minor incidents from the vast, complex, ambitious set of overlapping narratives that comprise *Fables*—a comic book series that ran from July 2002 to July 2015—reveals two important ideas illuminating these stories: first, both Throk and Muddlecock show themselves to be astute and perceptive readers who understand the importance of remaining sensitive to the meaning

7

and power of narrative patterns as they come to reflect cultural "realities." Second, the representation of Ogren's flippancy and Mudsnipe's initial hesitation shows that we should be wary of any attempt to dismiss popular tales as "nonsense," even when the words of folk tellers like Throk are taken up by poncy, college-educated types. In large part, the aim of *A Tour of Fabletown: Patterns and Plots in Bill Willingham's Fables* is to take seriously the way recurring narrative patterns in Willingham's text reflect contemporary cultural anxieties about gender, about power, about pain, anger, and hope, and—indeed—about the flow of knowledge.

Later in the narrative, the text provides another important juxtaposition: during the mostly one-sided war the Fables take up against the Adversary, as depicted in *War and Pieces* (Vol. 11), Sinbad—leader of the Arabian Fables, fast friend of Prince Charming's, and partner with him in their military success—is invited by Charming to spend an evening watching movie Westerns, "the Classics" (11.131). This gracious invitation is immediately juxtaposed with a scene depicting an Empire commander setting up what will be the first successful attack on the flying warship The Glory of Baghdad; as the commander explains to his unit, "the hardest thing for any military commander to do is alter his patterns in the face of one easy victory after another" (11.133). Again, this juxtaposition shows a complex thematization of the idea of reading for patterns: like many postmodern adaptations of the folk and fairy tale, *Fables* attempts to alter so-called "classic" narrative patterns so as to better sink some of our most comfortable assumptions about what it is that keeps us afloat as a culture. In his study *Why Fairy Tales Stick: The Evolution and Relevance of a Genre*, renowned fairy tale scholar Jack Zipes asserts "the fairy tale creates disorder to create order and, at the same time, to give voice to utopian wishes and to ponder instinctual drives and gender, ethnic, family, and social conflicts. In doing so, it reflects upon and questions social codes." Zipes further argues that—like other cultural memes—fairy tales are highly adaptable and that, "Conditioned by fairy tales, we insist that the fairy tale act out [current conflicts] through conventionalized language and codes that stimulate a play with ideas" (2006, 15). Crucial here is the notion that it is the familiarity of certain codes that constitute an awareness of a wish for order, but that also allows for a "safe" space to interrogate disorder, anxiety, and conflict. Thus, the success of *Fables* depends on readers instinctively comprehending what to expect from narratives populated by various archetypal folk and fairy tale figures: beautiful maidens, predatory men, animal helpers, adventurous young people, tyrannical rulers, and ambivalent sorcerers; without the bulwark created by expectation, the play with ideas produces chaos rather than meaning.

This is the first academic study to survey the completed run of *Fables*, thus building on the important foundation of work done by such scholars as Adam Zolkover, Mark Hill, Laurie Taylor, Rebecca-Anne Do Rozario, Wilson Koh, and—most significantly—Karin Kukkonen, a Finnish scholar of cognitive approaches to narrative, whose monograph *Contemporary Comics Storytelling* includes a long chapter on *Fables* and genre. In that work, Kukkonen also works with the notion that I have called "the bulwark created by expectation," asserting that the figures in *Fables* are part of our "Cultural memory [which] can be seen as organizing the macrolevel of comprehension. It is the shared symbolic reservoir members of a community tap into when making sense of cultural artifacts; it is their cultural 'public domain'" (58). In a 2010 interview with Geoff Boucher, published on the website *Hero Complex*, Willingham himself considers the activity of scholarship:

> I've almost grown to love the word "research." It's such an important, scholarly word. And I feel a bit of a fraud since what I do is just, well, read stories. I've always loved to read. I've been reading this stuff since childhood. Now I guess I can sort of justify it. But it still goes no deeper than just reading and rereading the stories I've loved for so long. As far as "research," I jot down notes if there's something interesting in them that I can use. And that's the extent of it. And yet lately, over the last few years, I've been referred to—and this even by, you know, pointy headed academic types—as a folklore scholar. And, well, gosh, that's kind of nice. If I'd known that that's all it took to become one of those, I'd have become a scholarly type *long ago* [Boucher, "'Fables' writer"].

The reference to "pointy headed academic types" is not encouraging. Also worrisome is the fact that—in a later narrative arc—poor Muddlecock is killed after he serves as scribe during a meeting of the most evil figures in the Empire (9.94). Such portrayals of the academic type notwithstanding, the practice of careful reading not only forms the context for Willingham's writing of *Fables*, but also becomes a matter of textual interrogation, as shown by the frequent references to the activities of spying, of doing detective work, of gaining intel, as well as in the first appearances of Kevin Thorn, an expert reader who sees himself as a character in some sort of Illuminati thriller. Keeping tabs on the Fables in a written journal, he writes, "If you are reading this, I'm most likely dead" (5.94). Later, in *The Great Fables Crossover* (Vol. 13), Kevin is depicted in the context of his underlying identity as a Literal, as the embodiment of storytelling and ostensible creator of the Fables universe (13.59), reflecting a familiar post-modern uroboros: the reader becomes author searching for the beginning of the story.

As many scholars have pointed out—following the seminal work of William Spanos and Michael Holquist—the figure of the amateur detective/expert reader is ubiquitous in postmodern literature, from William of Baskerville in Umberto Eco's *The Name of the Rose*, to You, the Reader, in Italo Calvino's *if on a winter's night a traveler*, to the various detective figures in Paul Auster's *New York Trilogy*. As Michael Holquist notes, the postmodern detective story undermines the rational movement toward solution, offering instead "strangeness, a strangeness which more often than not is the result of jumbling the well-known patterns of classical detective stories. Instead of reassuring, they disturb. They are not an escape, but an attack" (155). In combining conventions of the fairy tale— a genre appealing to our desire for wish-fulfillment and for the social and personal utopia—with conventions of the postmodern detective story— a genre marking contemporary interrogations into the stability of knowledge, especially self-knowledge—*Fables* confronts a distinctly post–9/11 anxiety about the circulation of competing narratives of certitude, which often operate in violent opposition to one another. In such a cultural space, how is it possible to know what story to wish for? What does a happy ending look like anymore? And—in deference to the fact that the genre conventions *Fables* is most deeply indebted to are those associated with comic books—what is justice? As Nickie D. Phillips and Staci Strobl note in *Comic Book Crime: Truth, Justice, and the American Way*, "across the various types of comics, themes of crime and justice abound, acting as a connecting thread throughout the medium" (13). In the *Fables* universe, however, crime and justice don't always emerge within the context of tales of vigilantism or even extra-systemic super heroics, despite the abilities of Bigby Wolf, the comic's detective figure. More importantly, there is a thematic connection made between the idea of justice and that of judgment: as Ambrose Wolf—another writer figure—laments, it is his destiny to grow old and "judge the rest, in my histories" (19.164). As much as the characters in *Fables* engage in the activity of desiring and questing, "detecting" and striving, they are also quite often forced to confront an age-old warning: be careful what you wish for.

In his foreword to the *Vertigo Encyclopedia*, Neil Gaiman explains that the imprint emerged in 1993 during the boom-and-bust time of collectible comics (Irvine, 7). As Julia Round notes, the combination of specialty stores and "speculative promotions ... led to the market crash in the mid–1990s" (19), as legions of speculating buyers of comics quickly came to terms with the poor returns of the market. Vertigo titles, however, were not caught up in the crash, because they had attracted, not collectors, but readers. The Vertigo imprint first began publishing titles emerging from DC's back catalogue: *Sandman, John Constantine: Hellblazer, Shade, The Changing Man, Doom Patrol, Animal Man,* and *Swamp Thing*; all were marked as age-restricted, a status that allowed writers and artists to explore mature subject matter. Round asserts that the "core titles were reconceived in the 1980s, not simply as 'more realistic' super heroics, but instead as mythological, surreal, religious, and metafictional commentaries upon the comics medium and industry" (16). Further, as the imprint's first executive editor Karen Berger notes in the introduction to the *Vertigo Encyclopedia*, the line specialized in creator-driven projects and the building of complete, complex, yet self-contained realities (Irvine, 8). Thus, *Fables* emerged in a time and space when both the audience for and the critical perception of comics was undergoing a radical shift, creating a necessary framework for its ambitious creative scope.

Berger lists *Fables*—among *Sandman, The Invisibles*, and *Preacher*—as one of Vertigo's "longest-running, popular monthly series" (Irvine, 9). The first issue of *Fables*—entitled "Chapter One: Old Tales Revisited"—was published July 1, 2002, and was written by Bill Willingham and penciled by Lan Medina (*Fables'* principal artist Mark Buckingham started working on the series at issue #6). In the years that have followed, *Fables* has established itself as a Vertigo "best-seller," though all Vertigo titles represent a kind of niche in a market still dominated by superhero titles. In "'Put Not Your Trust in Princes': *Fables* and the Problemitisation of Everyday Life," Wilson Koh states that "sales of the typical issue of *Fables* are limited to around 25,000 US $2.50 units across the board" (150), though as Marc-Oliver Frisch notes on his blog *Comiks Debris*, "as of April 2010, even sales [of] stalwart *Fables* permanently dipped below 20,000 units, apart from issue #100 in December 2010" (Frisch, "Vertigo and Wildstorm"). However, Frisch also notes that the market success of *Fables* is heavily predicated on the sales of the collected volumes: "As periodicals, [both *Fables* and *Y: The Last Man*] have been hovering around the 25K mark for years, outselling everything else Vertigo have been attempting by a league" (Frisch, "Collection Business"). The series—like other Vertigo titles—has also achieved significant "critical" success, winning several Eisner Awards in various categories, including "Best New Series" in 2003 and "Best Writer," which was awarded to Willingham in 2009. In an article published on the website *PopMatters*, interviewer shathley Q comments on the writer's ambivalent response to the status of the series:

> He speaks about how he is sensitive to the idea that *Fables* has been successful both as literary work (received well by critics and reviewers), and as popular fiction (time and again hitting bestseller lists and ringing true for fans). Willingham tells me that interactions with fans at the Cons do convince him of this success. As do the well-received reviews and reports of sales figures. But, it's with a kind of psychic resilience that only true artists can master, that Willingham offers a turn on exactly that thinking. It doesn't feel real, or lasting, or stable, Willingham admits. It doesn't feel as if it couldn't end at any minute [shathley Q: "The Long Game"].

Setting aside Willingham's comments about success, the fact remains that the series is at the point of taking on a new life, one that has less to do with "sales figures" and more to do with cultural circulation: in the coming years, *Fables* will become subject to historicization and critique, perhaps especially among pointy-headed academic types, but also—no doubt— among fresh readers of a now relatively closed fictional universe.

The subject of "popularity" and market circulation is embedded as a central conceit of *Fables*. Toward the end of *Animal Farm* (Vol. 2), Snow White—still recovering from being shot in the head by Goldilocks during a failed revolution at The Farm—is assailed by Rose Red, who tearfully recalls her own minimal status in the cultural imaginary as compared with her much more famous sister: "The Mundys adore you by the millions. By the hundreds of millions! ... But who remembers me?" (2.108–109). A critical effect of their difference in popularity is that—according to Fables metaphysics—Snow is practically invincible, while Red Rose is vulnerable; as she remarks, "If it had been me who'd taken a bullet, I'd be dead as a doornail" (2.109). This scheme, whereby Fables can acquire tangible strength and the capacity for healing in relation to the degree to which their stories have been circulated, playfully takes up the issue of the classical canon of tales as discussed among folk and fairy tale scholars, for example with respect to how that canon evolved from oral to literary forms, how tale variants emerge, or why certain tales "stick" (Zipes, 2006). In one of the earliest essays on *Fables*, Adam Zolkover criticizes the reluctance of folklorists to take seriously the way comic books adapt tales due to a disciplinary convention that discounts work not engaged in "prov[ing] the orality and traditionality of folklore items" (39). As Zolkover contends, a text such as *Fables* "cannot be usefully studied via the itemistic approach that has historically characterized scholarship on folklore in literature"

(40), because there is no attention paid to the fidelity to source material. As Willingham asserts in an early interview with Tim O'Shea "The sole determining factors on whether or not something will be used are: 1) is the character or story free for use—meaning in the public domain? and, 2) do I want to use it? That's it. No other considerations apply" (O'Shea, "'This is a wonderful job'"). Indeed, some of the figures in *Fables* are strictly speaking literary characters, for example those taken from Frank L. Baum's Oz books or Rudyard Kipling's *The Jungle Book*. Willingham's interest in circulation, thus, far exceeds the interests of traditional folklorists, as he is concerned not only with how variants of tales are produced, or with their didactic function, but also with how tales become part of contemporary popular culture. This concern is most comprehensively explored in Jack Horner's Hollywood adventures, collected in *Homelands* (Vol. 6). As Jack explains to one of the flunkies at Nimble Productions, the point isn't just making the "Jack Tales" films, it's "the merchandising, too. The toys. The action figures. The official adaptations, novels, and comic books" (6.40). As much as it is about anything, *Fables* is about the way stories become part of our lives, not just as moral signposts or sources of entertainment, but also as marketable objects, as part of our material and cultural economy.

Zolkover's important argument notwithstanding, traditional folklorists might be forgiven for some frustration with the title of the comic book series, which is hopelessly imprecise: in D.L. Ashliman's *Folk and Fairy Tales: A Handbook*, he defines and discusses a number of folk and fairy tale types, from myths to magic tales to legends to fables, and a quick scan of these classifications reveals Willingham's use of the term "fables" as confusing. A fable, Ashliman notes, is defined by "its didactic function," as well as "its brevity" (35); as a genre, the fable "has a propensity to function as an allegory" and "although [the characters—often animals or plants—in fables] exhibit human behavior only in a world of make-believe, in fables their words and deeds are still very much of this world" (36–37). In other words, the point of a fable is to communicate a pithy lesson about the human condition, usually via an exemplary tale involving non-humans, characters who are not required, or even expected, to belong in a social context: the man who cuts open the goose who lays golden eggs, hoping to find more gold inside, is not supposed to have to explain his foolish greed to an angry spouse, nor is it important to know for what purpose he would have used the extra gold. Though Willingham's *Fables* is clearly concerned with the human condition, the text is neither pithy, nor is it straightforwardly didactic: the "lessons" to be learned are complex and often self-contradicting or layered among other thematic matters. For example, the volume *Arabian Nights (and Days)* (Vol. 7) includes a scene in which Boy Blue scolds Prince Charming, who has been complaining about his new job as Fabletown's mayor: "You're entirely defined by what you covet. And now you expect me to feel sorry for you? Not a chance. My compassion's reserved for those you screw over in the process of getting what you want" (7.63). While this scene—arguably—endorses a similar didactic lesson to the fable of the goose that lays golden eggs, it is also situated within a much more complicated set of narratives about secretly gaining military intel, about the difficulties of cross-cultural exchange, and about the divergent ways these two men perform their service to the state, as well as their masculinity. Both structurally and thematically, the story arcs in *Fables* have much more in common with myths and magic tales, being concerned, in the first place, with what Ashliman refers to as "our relationships with supernatural powers ... origins and purposes, good and evil, life and death" (33), and, in the second place, with narratives that reflect fears and desires related to human social relationships, and which explore the fantasy of magical transformations that reward the good and punish the wicked.

This study takes as a starting point the way folk and fairy tale plots have been adapted in *Fables*, as well as the way those adaptations undermine or reinforce specific cultural narratives, for example about how loyalty is performed, how redemption is earned, or how leadership should be exercised. A pressing concern in *Fables* is the subject of "character," and whether character can be debased or—more importantly—reformed. Consequently, one of the most common plots depicted in *Fables* is some version of the quest, whereby the thematic focus is an inquiry into the potential for moral awakening and/or self-knowledge. Also crucial is the exploration of the very act of telling tales. Since tales are represented in their function of allowing humans to make sense of social and political realities, it is unsurprising that Willingham often uses the device of the embedded tale. Not only do major figures such as Bigby, Snow White, Geppetto, Boy Blue, and Rose Red have their backstories explored via this device, storytelling is continually shown to be a mechanism for teaching, for healing, and for the revelation of character, even when the tale refers to relatively peripheral figures. Toward the end of *Storybook Love* (Vol. 3), Bigby says to Flycatcher, "Plant yourself ... and I'll tell you a tale" (3.172), thus introducing the embedded narrative about the Barleycorn Women, which helps to make sense of both the social conditions and the collective mythology of Smalltown, particularly in terms of the quality of gender relations and cultural mechanisms for coming-of-age. Bigby tells Fly-catcher that when male Lilliputians—all soldiers in the war against the Adversary—finally made their way to the new world, they realized that the future of Smalltown was at risk of never being able to reproduce itself. A man named John Bullhorn (later Barleycorn) took it upon himself to travel back to the Homelands in search of the same magical barleycorn seeds that produced the pint-sized Thumbelina. As an adaptation, Will-ingham's version of John Barleycorn has very little to do with the source material, except perhaps metaphorically. In the *Fables Encyclopedia*, Jess Nevins comments that, in English and Scottish myth, Barleycorn comes to personify "liquor, [as] his death allows the cultivation of barley" (24). Here, the story, like hops, is fermented and comes to define the commu-nity's celebration of itself, through weddings and quests. In more allegor-ical terms, the trials of the refugee Lilliputians draw attention to the twinned thematics of the cost of war and the way groups rebuild them-selves. The embedded narrative also highlights the importance of telling within communities, as reflected in the framing of this tale: Bigby "teaches" Flycatcher about the importance of the rite of passage for the forging of character, a lesson that forms a context for Flycatcher's own developmental journey. Finally, through the device, Bigby reveals something of his own character, foreshadowing his function as father-figure and mentor within the community.

As much as *Fables* interrogates the cultural function of storytelling and of adapting folk and fairy tales, the series also provides commentary on contemporary cultural events or issues, for example America's military role during the invasion of Iraq in 2003; the way gender roles are being redefined in Western culture; or the idea that national identity may come into conflict with the impetus to accommodate cultural difference. This thematic introduction to *Fables* thus also makes use of what might be termed a "casual" cultural studies approach. I use the term "casual" here because for the most part the textual objects under scrutiny are the trade paperback collections rather than the individual comic book issues. Fur-ther, the aim is to consider all the collected volumes as a holistic piece, as one text in many parts. Consequently, this study only occasionally closely considers the interplay between any one story arc or issue and the cultural milieu in which it was created and published, though such an analysis would no doubt reveal fascinating intersections. For example, in *Camelot* (Vol. 20), Snow White tells her daughter Therese about being a sexual prisoner to the dwarves for six years, thus continuing the rich, persistent examination in *Fables* of Snow White's character: her stubborn individuality, her maternal identity, her complex relationship to sex and men. How different might an analysis of this conversation be if one considers that issue #133—which contains this scene—came out in September 2013, only months after the story of Ariel Castro and his sexual enslavement of three women was all over the news. Snow White's pronouncements about "endurance" and "survival," together with the text's focus on her triumphant execution of her clearly inhuman tormentors, bring into relief cultural anxieties about confronting criminality in the community, about the safety of women, and about the failure of systemic forms of justice.

What is important to note here is that, while *Fables* might certainly be read against other post–9/11 American allegorical responses to the changing culture, the decade-plus run of the series produces a text that shifts. This instability at the allegorical level of interpretation is reflected, for example, in the status of the Fables community, who are sometimes figured as refugees, sometimes as occupiers; they are both a colony of immigrants and a nation under threat. Another central conceit in *Fables* is that stories about Fables exist in the Mundy world because, after the arrival of the Fables in seventeenth-century New Amsterdam as exiles from their Homelands, the Mundys began to "absorb" their stories. What is clear from an examination of the text, however, is that Willingham's Fables have absorbed us.

Chapter One—"Plots: Adaptation, Genre and Allegory"—focuses on the most prevalent narrative patterns in the series, from redemption stories to quests. The first section on fairy tales and adaptation examines how *Fables* departs from a primarily feminist tradition of contemporary adaptation, how the notion of a community-oriented fairy tale is explored, and how the convention of "happily ever after" is dealt with. Next, the section on plot collisions examines the use of various comic book genres in *Fables*. The section on the quest plot focuses on the narratives of Boy Blue and of Flycatcher, showing how these arcs elevate the category of the humble everyman as a new version of the sacrificing hero. Finally, the section on self-knowledge and allegory compares the representations of Prince Charming and Prince Brandish (both former husbands of Snow White, both members of the noble class, and both very adept with a sword).

Chapter Two—"The Social World"—will consider how *Fables* represents characters in relation to one another, thinking through the portrayal of competing subjectivities. Section one provides an overview of the way animals are represented in *Fables*, looking at how the portrayals of Stinky/

Brock Blueheart and Reynard the Fox draw attention to philosophical discussions about a posthuman ethics. Next, the section on Father and Sons examines the wide-ranging and complex portrayals of this relationship, focusing on the North Wind and Bigby, Geppetto and Pinocchio, and the status of Bigby, Beast, and Rodney as "modern" fathers. The section on Snow White explores the complex, inherently contradictory femininity of this character, which transcends the source tale's emphasis on the character's beauty and passivity. The last section in this chapter focuses on Rose Red, looking at the portrayal of her sexuality, especially as it is problematically associated with public shaming and her status as "the bad sister."

Chapter Three—"Politics: History, Power and Leadership"—draws attention to the way *Fables* locates its social narratives within a universe caught up in the tensions produced by the dynamics of political power. Section one focuses on the character of Bigby as he functions as an emblem for America, whereby Bigby's dual status as predator and protector reflects a concern with America's complex history as an imperial power and place of refuge. The next section explores the various styles of leadership portrayed, whereby Geppetto represents the autocrat, Flycatcher the idealized absolute monarch, and Rose Red the flawed democratic leader, whose interest in social justice produces unrest. The section on "Mundane" matters of politics examines the representation of geography, history, and the economy, focusing in particular on how the series makes use of conventions associated with fantasy, and on King Cole's attention to money matters. Finally, the last section examines the basic Eurocentrism of *Fables* in relation to the portrayal of "foreign" bodies, for example the Arabian Fables and the non-human Fables, as well as in relation to the text's critique of notions of racial purity.

In Chapter Four—"Magic, Metaphysics and Metafiction"—the mechanisms for being in the world are explored, especially in terms of the central conceit in *Fables* that characters from folk and fairy tale are "real." The first section focuses on the complex representation of the system of magic in *Fables*, examining how the details of that system reflect current anxieties about the flow of power. In the next section, magic is explored in opposition to representations in the series of technology, religion, and language, focusing on the representation of scholarship as a means of power in the narrative arcs concerning Bufkin and Ozma. The section on fate versus fortune considers the way these concepts strain against the valorization of freedom in the series, while the last section in this chapter explores the metafictionality of *Fables*, looking at the rise of Ambrose

Wolf as a central authorial and metafictional figure and considering the way the series deals with the idea of a literate readerly community.

The concluding chapter of this thematic introduction to *Fables* surveys the reach of this universe beyond the central comic book series, briefly describing *Peter & Max*, Willingham's *Fables* novel, the spin-off series *Jack of Fables*, the *Fairest* series, the Cinderella volumes, the crossover with *The Unwritten*, another Vertigo title, and the video game/digital comic book series *The Wolf Among Us*. Importantly, what these spin-offs increasingly show is that Willingham's creation is itself now subject to the procedure of adaptation, as the myriad creators of these texts begin to play with the now canonical characters from *Fables*.

1

Plots: Adaptation, Genre and Allegory

Stories about stories: late in the comic series, little Ambrose Wolf plaintively asks his mother, "Aren't we the people in stories?" (19.165). Indeed, *Fables* is an ongoing narrative about "stories" insofar as the characters that populate its pages emerge from the old tales told at a child's bedside, tales that are as familiar to us as our own lives. But *Fables* works to make these familiar figures unfamiliar, new, and strange, asking the reader to reconsider why we're so eager for stories set "once upon a time," which make such outlandish promises about "happily ever after." *Fables* is not only about the characters in stories, but about the role of stories in our culture: what we tell, how we tell, and why we tell the stories we do. *Fables* recognizes that the enchanting simplicity and moral perfection promised by old stories jars against the complexities of the contemporary moment, a moment filled with the chaos of competing narratives. The series asks: Who tells? Who controls the narrative in a world filled with power struggle and threat, in a world in which heroics have been replaced by politics?

In this chapter, the issues of plots, genre, and telling are the focus. In considering the way *Fables* engages in the process of adaptation, in the deployment of competing genres, and in the plotting of redemption narratives, this chapter will consider the way old stories are renewed, with a difference, and what that tells us about our own hopes and fears.

Fairy Tales and Adaptation

Though the collected volume *The Great Fables Crossover* (Vol. 13) focuses primarily on the joint struggle among Fables and Literals to stop Kevin Thorn from rewriting the entire universe, the first short narrative in the volume consists of a quasi-religious vision presented by Stinky: in this vision, Boy Blue returns from the dead to vanquish all enemies, to establish a new age of peace and moral perfection, and to reward those who have remained faithful to what Stinky calls "the blue way" (13.15). Blue eventually sends a message via Bigby, telling Stinky—who has renamed himself Brock Blueheart—that he has no intention of coming back from the "Lands After Life," and furthermore that he detests the religion that has emerged in his name (20.114). Blue's sensibilities aside, the point of exploring Stinky's devotion to and promulgation of the myth of "the blue way" is to suggest the power of certain stories to be recirculated when the emotional and/or cultural need arises. Kevin Thorn's own distress that his stories have taken on a life of their own (13.134) is thus considered within a larger conceptual framework that posits *Fables* as a contemporary adaptation of folk and fairy tales. The self-reflexivity of *Fables* confirms its status as one of many postmodern adaptations of folk and fairy tales, genres for which both embedded conventions and literary history make adaptation a common practice. As a complex revision of prior tales, though, Willingham's narrative is distinctive in terms of the way it operates according to conventions of comic books, the way it differs in focus from contemporary feminist adaptions of folk and fairy tales, the way the text is linked to a particular historical moment, and the way the ideal of "happily ever after" is challenged. On the one hand, though many social institutions—for example, marriage, the military, the law, and the state—are shown to be flawed, the structures of those institutions are ultimately confirmed as necessary realities, as per more conservative adaptations of folk and fairy tales. On the other hand, the wishes and fears explored are distinct from those associated with folk and fairy tales, which—in general—tend to confront anxieties about poverty, about the process of courtship, about achieving sexual maturity, and about authoritarian power structures. In contrast, *Fables* is largely concerned with such issues as the problem of cultural belonging versus difference, the ideal of individual identity and purpose, the desire for safety in an inherently violent world, and the importance of controlling information.

As Claire L. Malarte-Feldman suggests in her entry on "Adaptation," included in *The Greenwood Encyclopedia of Folktales and Fairy Tales*, the practice of creating new versions of tales is as old as are the genres themselves, which have always lent themselves to retellings in both oral and written forms, across different cultural milieus, and across mediums (2). For traditional folklore researchers—from the Brothers Grimm onwards— the primary focus of scholarship consists of tracking down oral origins of written or literary tales, comparing and creating taxonomies of variants and motifs, establishing a canon of so-called "classical" (mostly Western European) tales, and producing anthropologies of tales from around the world. For later researchers, who have employed what D.L. Ashliman terms "Sociological" or "Aesthetic" approaches to the study of folk and fairy tales (2004, 146–150), the meaning of the tale in relation to its audience becomes paramount, leading to a different way of thinking through the function of adaptation. As Jack Zipes notes in *Fairy Tale as Myth / Myth as Fairy Tale*, "the fairy tale as a genre sets parameters for a discourse of the mores, values, gender, and power in the civilizing process ... only to be subverted in a process of *duplication* and *revision*" (8, emphasis mine). Zipes's thus distinguishes between retellings that merely duplicate and "[mimic] the original" (8) and those that revise and thus entail a "critical reexamination of the original work" (10). In their introduction to *Beyond Adaptation: Essays on Radical Transformations of Original Works*, Phyllis Frus and Christy Williams note that transformation or change is often central to the story of a folk or fairy tale (6): indeed, the basic plot of many such tales involves a transformation that occurs via magic and/or a transformation of a character's social status. The possibility of transformation also operates as a key question within the *Fables* universe, which explores the prospect that characters, as well as the worlds they inhabit, might be open to change. Thus, the representation of Stinky's religious vision is not merely a parody of other such narratives, but also an anguished challenge to the terrible idea of the world as static in its reproduction of violence, corruption, and chaos.

In his essay "Rewriting the Core: Transformations of the Fairy Tale in Contemporary Writing," Tom Shippey remarks that of the voluminous number of tales recorded and anthologized by folklorists, "one finds oneself dealing over the last three decades of the twentieth century with a small core-group of familiar stories," a group that—according to Shippey— includes "Bluebeard," "Snow White," "Cinderella," "Little Red Riding Hood," "Sleeping Beauty," "Rapunzel," "Beauty and the Beast," and "The Frog Prince" (261). While other lists of the "core-group" or canon of classical fairy tales may omit one or more of these tales, or may include one or more additional possibilities, Shippey's point is compelling, as is his subsequent argument that "the true linking factor [among the core-group of tales] is one of situation," whereby a "threatened" protagonist (usually female) is "always rescued, always triumphant" (261). Though Shippey's main concern is the use of this core-group of stories by contemporary authors who have produced feminist revisions (a subject I will return to below), also important with respect to *Fables* as an adaptation of folk and fairy tales is the convention of the single protagonist: the hero or heroine. As Ashliman notes in his discussion of fairy tale plots, the "separation" stage of such tales involves "the leading characters ... [finding] their new way by themselves, independent of traditional structures" (2004, 41). An important conceit in *Fables* is that these "leading characters" from various tale Homeworlds are now living together in Fabletown, or at The Farm. In the first place, the revision of the convention of the threatened single protagonist invites a more political reading, as not only are we dealing with a threatened community, but are also invited to consider how this community functions as a polis or political entity. The first story arc of *Fables* centers on the "story" of a murder, immediately positioning itself as yet another revisionist telling of the Grimms' "The Robber Bridegroom" or Perrault's "Bluebeard": in this case, the would-be bride of the murderous suitor fakes her own death rather than submitting to marriage. The primary action of *Legends in Exile* (Vol. 1), however, is less focused on the narrative of Bluebeard and Rose Red than it is on Bigby's investigation of the murder case, the way his methods come into conflict with the bureaucracy of Fabletown (1.60), and the way Snow White deals with the various contracts related to that case (between Prince Charming and Fabletown, and between Bluebeard and Rose Red), as well as with the political matter of punishing Rose and Jack (1.120–123).

The focus on community coheres with the status of *Fables* as a comic book series, a medium that has often explored the role of the superhero within the context of the super team. In "Jack Kirby and the Marvel Aesthetic," Charles Hatfield explores the way Kirby and Stan Lee created a distinctive superhero universe, one in which both the heroes and villains "had baggage" (139), and in which the idea of a "pantheonic approach to superheroes" (143) was central. Also, as Jason Tondro notes in *Superheroes of the Round Table*, the Arthurian symbol of the round table appears in various comic book stories: "DC's Justice League of America sits at a round table ... as does Marvel's Avengers," further cementing the convention of a team of superheroes "bound by ties of friendship" (13). While the lunchtime reunion of Snow White, Briar Rose, and Cinderella—depicted as a preamble to the story "Cinderella Libertine," collected in *The Mean Seasons* (Vol. 5)—is an instance when Willingham plays with the expectations of feminist retellings of folk and fairy tale (5.7–10), far more significant to the overall narrative is the way each of these figures takes on a strategic role in the final showdown against the Adversary, as shown in *War and Pieces* (Vol. 11). Cinderella (or Cindy) resumes her role as Fabletown's most capable secret agent in a long arc about her rescuing Pinocchio,

Briar Rose's sleeping enchantment is figured as a kind of superpower, helping the Fables to "take out the Empire's entire ruling city without firing a shot" (11.115–116), and Snow White acts as unofficial "commander-in-chief" of the entire operation (11.98). Reinforcing the idea that the individual Fables are part of a super team is the recurring use of the double page spread, which depicts multiple figures from the *Fables* universe, like the one featured at the conclusion of *War and Pieces* (11.176–177).

In addition to challenging the convention of the lone protagonist, *Fables* undermines such typical structural and thematic elements of the folk and fairy tale as the "coming-of-age" plot and the stage of "return," which Ashliman notes "is not a return to one's original home, but rather the integration into a new community, and nearly always in a much more powerful and prestigious role" (2004, 42). Revisions to the "coming-of-age" plot include the story of Boy Blue's quest to kill the Emperor and save Red Riding Hood (and it is significant that both Blue and Red are identified without reference to the adjective "Little," which forms part of both names in the source tales: while many of the lone protagonists in traditional folk and fairy tale begin their journeys when they are children, within the *Fables* universe, these figures are adults). As I discuss further in the "Quests" section of this chapter, Blue's quest narrative is a false plot, a cover story for a military mission: thus, his post-quest return is unsurprisingly unconventional, in that it leads to his (also false) imprisonment and a series of failures to win the girl. The story of Rodney and June, collected in *Arabian Nights (and Days)* (Vol. 7), includes a separation, a quest, and the very sort of transformation-as-reward stage common to magic tales (7.135): the standard coming-of-age plot, however, is undermined in two ways. First, the status of Rodney and June as agents for the Adversary complicates the typically simplistic moral binary of good and evil that frames most folktales, and draws attention to Willingham's revisionist interest in the topics of cultural difference and competing narratives. Second, after their transformation, Rodney and June experience episodes of anguish and fear, mostly related to their hopes for their unborn child (7.142–143), thus suggesting a cyclical rather than linear structuring principle and reinforcing the theme of the persisting desire for safety. Finally, even the child characters who do "come-of-age" in *Fables*, notably the cubs Winter, Therese, and Ambrose, are represented in adult guises that are not static, and do not necessarily represent a straightforwardly "more powerful and prestigious role." Winter more so than any of the other cubs seems to mimic the figure from folk and fairy tale of the disadvantaged child who, through the completion of tasks, emerges as a queen (or, as it happens, a king). She remains ambivalent about this role, however, as it necessitates her complete separation from "human" social institutions (18.13). Winter's "coming-of-age" represents not a transformation of standing, but a transformation of being.

The structural and thematic element of "return" is further complicated, simply because—in *Fables*—the concept of home is so multifaceted. Ashliman asserts that "the fairy-tale separation from familiar surroundings can be either voluntary or forced" (2004, 41), a convention that is certainly confirmed in the broad backstory to the founding of Fabletown, whereby "free" Fables choose to flee the Homelands rather than submit to the terrors caused by the regime change, though, presumably, most of the Fables live in places that are already ruled by authoritarian monarchs. The Adversary's invasion of the myriad territories is shown to be unwelcome because his soldiers are barbaric, because there is a resistance to the centralization of a totalitarian government, and because those who are aristocrats are threatened with a loss of power. The status of the Fables that arrive in New Amsterdam as refugees, who live in exile from home and are compelled to define the parameters of their new state, revises the conventional focus of the "return" phase, which in the folk or fairy tale often confirms a cultural aspiration for what Ashliman calls "upward mobility" (2004, 42). In *Fables*, the desire for home becomes a complex organizing principle for all social activity, though many in the Fabletown community have established rich lives in their new locale, a territory that itself is often under threat. Many of the images or matters of concern in the narrative confirm an interest in examining the uneasy relationship humans have to the concepts of nation, origin, and belonging, especially in an increasingly globalized world. There are frequent references to problematic borders, most notably with respect to The Farm, as well as to the issue of access between spaces: for example, a key element of "Operation Jack Ketch" is to destroy the Adversary's access to the gateways between worlds (7.95), thereby complicating any straightforward conception of return as wish-fulfillment. Further, a defining feature of Fabletown's political system is the Fabletown compact, which even Geppetto is allowed/made to sign (7.176–177); this symbol of the way state-making is arbitrary coheres with an abiding anxiety in *Fables* regarding how to define one's cultural identity. Finally, as explained by the narrator of "The Boys in the Band," a story arc included in *Camelot* (Vol. 20), "Fabletown was ultimately destroyed ... by the idea of why it was created in the first place" (20. 252). Despite offering a space of refuge for centuries, Fabletown is never truly identified as "home," even for second and third generation Fables, many of whom seem to want their own piece of the Homelands (14.115).

In her introduction to the critical volume of essays *Fairy Tales Reimagined*, Susan Redington Bobby notes that, not only is it the case that most "canonical contemporar[y writers] have focused primarily on feminist concerns," but most scholarship on revisionist fairy tale writing has also tended to "focus on a narrow portion of writers and theoretical approaches" (7–8). Indeed, in Shippey's discussion of revisionist approaches to the "core-group" of fairy tales, he argues that "the strong concern with sex- and gender-issues," together with an "attention to the self-reflexivity of the narrative," dominates contemporary rewritings of folk and fairy tales (270). While some scholars—notably Adam Zolkover and Rebecca-Anne Do Rozario—have explored the way Willingham's text challenges "the patriarchal prescriptions of Perrault, the Grimms and Disney" (Do Rozario, 198), Karin Kukkonen is less convinced. She argues that, while "one of the main ways in which postmodern fairy-tale retellings subvert the fairy-tale tradition is through their representation of women and girls" (61), Willingham's dependence on conventional depictions of femininity leave *Fables* "a far cry from feminist storytelling" (64). Though I will return to the issue of Willingham's constructions of femininity in Chapter 2, suffice it to say here that—in general—I concur with Kukkonen. *Fables* is not an "emancipatory" feminist text (Kukkonen 67). That said, what becomes interesting to consider is how the portrayal of a continuum of femininities, as well as of masculinities, reflects new anxieties about the performance of gender and sexuality. The character of Goldilocks, for example, whom Zolkover reads primarily in terms of the way her erotic "corporealization" relates to the "core sense of desire" found in the source material (47), may be examined as a feminine character, often defined by her sexuality; as a masculine character, who foments political unrest and favors big phallic guns; and as a queer character, whose inter-species relationship with Boo Bear makes her a cultural outsider. Further, as Mark Hill notes in his essay "Negotiating Wartime Masculinity in Bill Willingham's *Fables*," the series "serves as an important crossroads of genres … that map the incorporation, resistance, or continuation of hegemonic processes in American masculinity" (183). The continuum of masculine performance featured in *Fables*, from Bigby and Prince Charming through to Boy Blue and Flycatcher, is contiguous to feminist revisions of the fairy tale, as Willingham subverts the often predominantly male worlds represented in comic books. Ashliman notes that—normally—the activities associated with the "initiation" phase of the folk and fairy tale are heavily gendered: female protagonists perform domestic tasks or become "magically" isolated, for example in a glass coffin or behind a wall of thorns (2004, 41–42), while for male protagonists, "initiation usually requires strength, valor, and fortitude" (2004, 42). Despite Willingham's frequent play with almost hyperbolic femininity or masculinity, his representation of characters in action often troubles this binary.

Frus and Williams suggest that "when we think of fairy tales as a genre, we tend to think of their timeless quality," going on to argue that this "lack of [temporal] detail invites postmodern transformers to insert the context that is missing from the 'universal' tales" (6). As a revisionist adaptation, *Fables* is located squarely in a post–9/11 American milieu, so as to set so-called "timeless" wishes and fears in conversation with decidedly new anxieties, especially regarding the stability of social institutions that are proved to be less than transcendent. Interestingly, a stalwart from the folk and fairy tale world—that is, the institution of marriage—is upheld with confidence, despite Prince Charming's shenanigans in the Homelands, which lead to friendly exchanges among his three former wives. A central story element—perhaps *the* central story element—of the entire run of *Fables* is the relationship between Snow White and Bigby, which crucially extends beyond a somewhat unconventional courtship stage to consider the exigencies of married life. In what is arguably a conservative declaration about the sanctity of this institution, even after Bigby has reverted to behaving like a depraved, violent, predator, Snow White remains loyal, telling King Cole: "I'm gambling my husband won't try to kill me" (21.96). In contrast, the institution of the rule of law is scrutinized for its potential failures. On the one hand, the totalitarianism of Geppetto's empire represents a clear affront to social systems based on law, whether those systems are ostensible democracies, such as Fabletown, or whether they are monarchies, such as the one Flycatcher sets up in Haven. As I discuss further in Chapter Three, the absolutist government of Haven operates as a type of wish-fulfillment in *Fables*, whereby the benevolence of Flycatcher, the so-called "Good Prince," as well as the unqualified sense of "national" identity and loyalty among Haven's multiethnic citizenry, counters the messy interactions of Fabletown's inhabitants. On the other hand, Willingham suggests that the rule of law has the potential to be undermined or perverted—not via totalitarian overthrow—but via social justice projects. Goldilocks might, at heart, be simply spiteful and power-hungry, but her speech is steeped in Marxist, feminist, and anti-speciesist rhetoric, and the ostensible goal of the revolution at The Farm is to overthrow those who oppress. Even more problematic is Rose Red's social justice agenda, which informs both the creation of the new Round Table for knights of "second chances" (20.134) and her fateful decision to free

Brandish from being buried in cement, on the grounds that even he can be reformed (20.81, 20.86). Thus, while traditional folk and fairy tales tend to offer plots in which previously marginalized characters are rewarded with access to privilege within political and social systems that are themselves never questioned, Willingham's revisionist text locates itself in a time period when many of those systems are being challenged for their corruption or inefficacy.

In her essay "Snow White in the City: Teaching Fables, Nursery Rhymes, and Revisions in Graphic Novels," Laurie Taylor suggests that one avenue for teaching *Fables* would be to consider "the significance of revision and intertextuality [with respect to...] 'happily ever after' closure" (175). To be sure, the primary method by which *Fables* revises the folk and fairy tale is to explore what happens *after* the "ever after" (not to mention what happens *before* the "once upon a time"), as well as to overturn conventional conceptions of "happily." Taylor also refers to the seriality embedded into the form of the comic book (173), which works to reinforce the series' challenge to the idea of closure. Implicit in Taylor's essay and in other scholarship on the implications of the "happily ever after" ending in folk and fairy tales is that such an ending is limiting and oppressive. In her landmark study *Postmodern Fairy Tales: Gender and Narrative Strategies*, Cristina Bacchilega pursues a familiar argumentative course, whereby the scholar or postmodern writer "seek[s] to expose, make visible, the fairy tale's complicity with 'exhausted' narrative and gender ideologies" (50); in other words, a goal of postmodern revision is to demonstrate the way the common script of the folk or fairy tale promises so-called wish-fulfillment, but offers only a prescription for submission to repressive power structures. To my mind, what is especially interesting about *Fables* is the way Willingham explores as a common cultural script the *failure* of happiness to take hold, both "ever after" and at present. It is not only the case—in keeping with conventions of the comic book serial—that the vanquishing of one foe only makes way for a new enemy, as is the case when the destruction of Geppetto's empire makes inevitable the rise of Mr. Dark. More importantly, *Fables* considers the way both individuals and communities produce the conditions of their own unhappiness, whereby it is human agency and choice that generates cyclic patterns of strife. For example, in "The Last Story of Prince Charming," which is part of *Happily Ever After* (Vol. 21), Charming is depicted leading a motley guerrilla unit of Fables, who are fighting Sinbad's fleet of conquering flying warships. As Charming sardonically notes, his devotion to an old wartime ally is not sufficient justification for allowing "a new empire" to rise. Crucially,

Charming cites the fact that "good Fables died under my leadership, putting an end to the previous empire" as grounds for engaging in this new war (21.134). The text thus shows how enforcing a conservative rhetoric about the sanctity of war dead, one which posits war as a productive activity about "keeping faith," propels the destructive activity that causes human unhappiness.

To return to Stinky's religious vision that promises an absolute "happily ever after," in which "Blue will be the wise and loving Emperor ruling over us for all time" (13.14): while it is clear that the adaptation of folk and fairy tale in *Fables* tends toward revisionist critique of hackneyed formulae rather than mimicry, the objects of critique differ from the ones on which many scholars of postmodern adaptations have chosen to focus. *Fables* is concerned with exploring—not the individual's manner of rising in status within authoritarian social systems—but the way groups of individuals manage such systems. The text's play with the conventional idea of return reflects the anxieties of those living in a globalized world about the meaning of home and the function of borders. Also, the portrayal of gender—though not explicitly feminist—considers a continuum of feminine and masculine identities, all the while locating the performance of these identities within a situated time and space, so as to better offer critique of the perceived hollowness of social institutions. Finally, *Fables* considers the implications of the story convention "happily ever after": while folk and fairy tale scholars have argued that the element of transformation is central to these genres, Willingham's narratives are founded on the premise that transformations are not stable, and that the simple binary of reward and punishment is complicated by the way humans undermine the ideal of happiness.

Plot Collisions and the Control of Narrative

During his attempt to rewrite the universe, Kevin Thorn calls on a collection of figures referred to as The Genres, in hopes that any one of them might give him an idea of how to begin, though he ultimately rejects their suggestions as unhelpfully formulaic (13.62–67). A survey of these figures shows that the type of "genre" Willingham intends to satirize has little to do with notions of literary classification: while there is no Genre called Poetry or Drama, Allegory or Pastoral, or even Fable or Fairy Tale, there is one called Blockbuster, who is mostly concerned with how many explosions should figure into a given story. Priscilla Page—one of three sister Literals embodying the library sciences—mocks both The Genres and genre-fiction readers, who she calls "morons, semi-illiterates and penguin-stealing window lickers" (13.149). Also, the Genre called Literature is not like any of her companions in that she does not refer Kevin to conventional plot points: rather, she makes use of jargon associated with highly theoretical literary analysis. Literature's tendency to use phrases like "phallocentric, masculinist logocentrism" (13.66)—in other words, her tendency to talk like a literary critic rather than a piece of literature—makes her a similar object of ridicule to other "poncy, college-educated" types (6.59). As Craig Fischer points out in "Worlds within Worlds: Audiences, Jargon, and North American Comics Discourse," there exists an uneasy, sometimes hostile, relationship among the various communities—fans, essayists, academics—who write about comics, and a perceived dependence on jargon is only exacerbated when comic book scholars emerge from existing academic fields, such as the field of literary criticism (Fischer). That said, the collapsing of all the myriad works encompassed by the descriptor "literature," so as to be able to pinpoint common, easily consumable and repeatable plot points, is itself absurd, drawing further attention to Willingham's concern, not with how narrative forms are written, but with how narrative types are marketed. The play with genre in *Fables* thus acknowledges the production history of comic books, both in terms of older trends that connected genre diversification with market demands and the more contemporary situation, in which so-called mainstream comics are pitted against independent comics in the valuing of artistic merit. Further, Willingham's use of braided and proliferating narratives—which encompass his use of various genre conventions—is connected to his concern with exploring how the contemporary moment requires reading through various competing narratives about the world, as well as to the realization that most of these narratives are simply distractions, serving to hide the machinations of power.

In his introduction to *Comic Book Nation*, Bradford W. Wright delineates his interest in exploring the relationship between changing social milieux and what he refers to as comic book "formulas" (Wright xv), which is the term Wright uses as an alternative to genre. Paying attention to formula is important, Wright argues, because:

> The preeminent factor shaping comic books has been the commercial motive of publishers to craft a product that appeals to paying audiences.... This has prompted an incessant search for narrative formulas that can be easily duplicated with minimal variation and expense. Yet for formulas to succeed, they must also speak adequately to the concerns and expectations of their audience [xv].

As scholarly histories of the American comic book industry explain, the fall of superhero comics following the end of World War II coincided with the rise of many of the genres now associated with comics, including the western, horror, romance, science fiction, and crime (all of which are embodied as part of The Genre family, though "Crime" is named "Noir"). Quoting Stan Lee, Shirrel Rhoades records in his *A Complete History of American Comic Books*, "We and all the other publishers tried everything we could do to find a formula that would work in the postwar market. All anyone had to do was name a category and we slapped a few comics together in that department" (Lee, quoted in Rhoades, 47). Crucial here is the idea that Golden Age genre diversification was not driven by creative impulses, but rather by the desperation of publishers to shore up sales. Despite these ignominious beginnings—and despite Priscilla Page's damning assertion that there are "no new ideas" among The Genres (13.149)—the Golden Age genres have continued to be reinterpreted by contemporary writers and artists, as for example in Brian Azzarello and Eduardo Risso's acclaimed *100 Bullets* series, which fits into the crime genre, or Garth Ennis and Steve Dillon's *Preacher*, which is a western comic, or even in the reinterpretations of the romance genre by manga writers and artists.

Though such reinterpretations form part of the context for Willingham's self-reflexive interest in the function of formulas or genres, also important is the emergence of the creator-driven project and the peculiar space such titles occupy, both within the comic book market and within the framework of critical response. As Randy Duncan, Matthew J. Smith, and Paul Levitz discuss in *The Power of Comics: History, Form, and Culture*, the rise of "independent" publishers helped change the scholarly attitude toward comics by producing work that was not commercially successful, but "d[id] more to advance comics as an art form than anything put out by the mainstream publishers" (75). At times, however, the notion of critical acceptance is itself unhelpfully formulaic. In their introduction to *The Superhero Reader*, editors Charles Hatfield, Jeet Heer, and Kent Worcester point out that the ascendency of the graphic novel within scholarly circles has sometimes occurred at the expense of taking mainstream comics seriously, whereby—for example—studies of superhero comic books often focus on historical or political contexts for the form rather than the status of such texts as art (xiv). As a series, *Fables* explicitly plays with the idea of genre so as to trouble the too-easy distinction that can be made between mainstream, generically pure comics, which are often associated solely with market logic, and "alternative" comics, which apparently resist this logic by providing opportunity for the canny comprehension of the limiting scripts associated with genre formulae. Willingham's play with multiple genres, as well as with the structural features associated with braided and proliferating narratives, reinforce his thematic interest in the issue of competing narratives and their connection to the slippery relationship between means and outcomes.

In Karin Kukkonen's chapter on *Fables*, included in her 2013 study examining cognitive approaches to comic books, *Contemporary Comics Storytelling*, she discusses the way the series makes complex use of story-telling techniques associated with "generic decorum," which she defines as the fitting together of genre "schemata to a particular subject matter," so as to confirm readerly expectation (72). In her assessment of the points in which divergent genre schemata collide—for example, in the collision of schemata associated with war comics and horror comics in "War Stories," collected in *Mean Seasons* (Vol. 5)—Kukkonen ultimately declares that such collisions do not constitute "subversive modes of storytelling," as there is always enough information provided to make possible the "cognitive processing of storyworld construction" (80). In other words, Kukkonen argues that Willingham's play with genre decorum falls short of a postmodern assertion that readerly expectation is produced by the use of limiting, formulaic plot scripts (or vice versa: that overly formulaic instances of genre-comics are produced by the readerly expectations of "morons" and "semi-illiterates"). While Kukkonen examines examples of plot collisions (between fairy tale and fantasy, and between war and horror), as well as the way *Legends in Exile* (Vol. 1) merges schemata from different traditions of crime fiction (80), Duncan, Smith, and Levitz make note of two additional "modes of narrativity," both suggested by literary critic Marie Laure-Ryan, that are relevant to an analysis of Willingham's techniques: the braided narrative and the proliferating narrative (106–107). The braided narrative, which is defined by overlapping plots and subplots and a focus on the development of several characters over time, is especially useful as it draws attention to way the plot collisions in *Fables* often involve more than two genres. While Duncan, Smith, and Levitz connect the proliferating narrative with superhero comics—defined as it is by a focus on a series of adventures held together by only the thinnest plot connections, and dependent as it is on a certain stability of character—this mode is also gestured toward in *Fables* via the seriality of plots and via the failure of "happily ever after" to take hold. Thus, while I agree with Kukkonen that Willingham's play with various genres does little to undermine their comprehensibility, or their effectiveness as story-telling frameworks, I would suggest that showing how a multiplicity of stories can all be simultaneously comprehensible and powerful is the point.

Kukkonen's analysis of *Mean Seasons* is confined to the two issues that make up "War Stories," a narrative arc focusing on Bigby's exploits during World War II. In addition to the matter of genre decorum, this arc is also significant as a nod to the subject of industry history and the idea that the end of the war provided an impetus for the development of other comic genres; also available is an intertextual reading, whereby the arc explicitly references Mary Shelley's *Frankenstein* (5.50). Even more illuminating is to look beyond this arc at the entire collected volume of *Mean Seasons*, which shows not only an expanded roster of genres being used (culminating in more of a genre pile-up than a collision), but also—consequently—an important context for the return to the World War II setting. In the "War Stories" arc, Bigby is figured as a very specific type of American hero, despite the fact that—during his fight with Frankenstein's monster—he is drawn by Tony Akins as the iconic monster movie version of *The Wolfman*. In "Negotiating Wartime Masculinity in Bill Willingham's *Fables*," Mark C. Hill argues that this arc "invokes the cultural memory of the masculine hero-soldier in a war worth fighting," whereby "Never does Bigby or his 'Dog Company,' question the righteousness of the American cause" (186). Along with Bigby's military persona, which Hill examines in great detail, the framing of this tale reinforces the idea of the "righteous cause" implicit in the World War II setting. The frame of the narrative arc introduces Bigby's war buddy Duffy and culminates in the image of Frankenstein's monster's head in a cage in the Fabletown Business Office. While Duffy's gravestone describes him as a "brave and honorable friend" (5.73), exclusively marking his experiences in war and his relationship to his military company as the sum total of his life's meaning, the Nazi tattoo on Frankie's head ironically underlines the idea that, despite appearances, the notion of "monstrosity" is clear cut, as everyone knows who the bad guys were in World War II.

Hill admits to being "disquieted that during this current war [with Iraq]," the "War Stories" arc in *Fables* "perpetuat[es]" the notion of the "righteous" conflict (186). The moral simplicity produced by the World War II setting, however, is contextualized by the use of other genre formulae in the rest of *Mean Seasons*, all of which serve to underline the text's thematic concern with the way—simplistic fantasies about historical events notwithstanding—attitudes toward war and good and evil require us to maintain competing, often contradictory narratives. As a volume, *Mean Seasons* contains three primary narrative arcs: the first—"Cinderella

Libertine"—tells the story of how Cinderella entraps Ichabod Crane, proving him to be loyal to the Adversary; the second is "War Stories"; and the third—"The Mean Seasons"—is a four-part arc braiding together several stories, including the birth of Bigby and Snow White's cubs and Bigby's choice to leave Fabletown because he cannot live with Snow and the cubs at The Farm; the election of Prince Charming as the new mayor of Fabletown and the ensuing change in the political executive; the continued interrogation of Baba Yaga and the wooden heads; the arrival of the North Wind—Bigby's father—at The Farm; and the investigation into the mysterious asphyxiation deaths, which leads to the revelation of Bigby and Snow's seventh cub, Ghost. This unusually crowded arc ends with a pause in the plot, as various Fables enjoy the late spring weather, as the cubs celebrate their first birthday, and as the closing words of a quoted nursery rhyme refer to the way "spring replenished us all" (5.165–166). This pause is what one might call a moment of "happily, for now," occurring before a proliferation of new conflicts arises. The diffusion of genres made use of in the volume, which ran the gamut from spy thriller to romance to murder mystery, together with the way "happiness" is depicted as an in-between state, or even—with respect to the cubs—as a primary state that we tend to fall away from, helps to complicate the representation of Bigby and the way he stands for notions of the "righteous" pursuit of justice.

In "Cinderella Libertine," Bigby is the figure directing Cindy's activities, and his role as the "Boss" (5.23) not only includes flushing out the enemies of Fabletown, but eliminating them in callous fashion. His only explanation to Cindy as to why he kills Ichabod rather than arranging for a trial is that he wants to keep her status as an undercover agent a secret (5.28), though this particular killing may also be motivated by what Bigby refers to as Ichabod's notes outlining an "extended rape-fantasy about Snow" (5.25). The portrayal of Ichabod as not only a traitor to Fabletown, but also as a lecher and would-be rapist of Bigby's "girl," may help to frame Bigby's brutal act as less morally problematic, though the witty banter between Bigby and Cindy after the murder marks them both as cold, seasoned operatives. As the arc immediately preceding "War Stories," "Cinderella Libertine" works in ironic tension with the apparently more uncomplicated war story, as the tale of Bigby's bloody fight alongside "righteous" American soldiers and against the "monstrous" Nazis is set up by a tale about very different kinds of activities in a very different kind of war. In "The Mean Seasons" arc, Bigby's understanding of the new kind of war is further developed, as he and his confederates Cindy and Frau Totenkinder (and Beast, who is taking over as Fabletown's sheriff) engage in the interrogation of Baba Yaga (5.93) and the captured wooden heads (5.98–99). These scenes are surely a response to discussions about the United States's use of "enhanced interrogation techniques" following 9/11, though—in 2004 and 2005, during which time "The Mean Seasons" arc was published—many of the more abhorrent tactics that have since been publically condemned were not yet known. Indeed, the text's representation of the secret interrogation of state enemies seems approving, though Bigby himself realizes that such activity cannot hope to be widely accepted: as he instructs Beast, part of the job of being sheriff of Fabletown requires having "the strength and backbone to carry those burdens you have to carry alone" (5.105). Thus, while Hill argues that the depiction of masculinity in *Fables* coheres with the celebration of an explicit and specific military moment, an examination of Bigby's less obviously soldier-like new war activity suggests Willingham's interest in exploring the way the pursuit of justice, or even just the pursuit of a strategic military advantage, is never straightforwardly righteous.

"The Mean Seasons" arc introduces new elements of Bigby's character, traits that augment his function as a purveyor of wartime masculinity. In the first place, Bigby is immediately depicted as an interested and caring father: in a wonderful intratextual moment, the first series of panels of "The Mean Seasons" shows Bigby hurrying out of a cab, yelling "keep the change" (5.75), just as Jack is depicted in the first series of panels of *Legends in Exile* (1.11). However, whereas Jack actually owes the driver another quarter, Bigby's tip amounts to ninety-eight dollars, underlining Bigby's eagerness to be in the hospital during Snow White's labor, and contrasting him with the always scheming Jack. Bigby vows to love his cubs "without reservation" (5.89), warning Snow that he'd be willing to violate Fabletown and Farm law to see them, because "they're all that matters now" (5.109). Bigby's status as a proud and protective father is of a piece with the features of his traditional wartime masculinity, and Bigby's fatherly persona is unusually rich, especially in comparison to conventional folk and fairy tale fathers. Also, it is possible to connect Bigby's traditionalism with another element of his character, which marks him as a sort of middle-class hero. In Willingham's most explicit nod to the romance genre, Bigby and Snow's discussion of where the family might live devolves into an argument, during which Bigby accuses Snow of "cling[ing] to [her] fantasies of castles and princes" (5.109) when she refuses to take the cubs and go away with Bigby. Interestingly, the focus on domesticity does not destabilize the underlying focus on war that runs throughout *Mean Seasons* (and throughout most of the first half of the *Fables* series, up until *War and Pieces*, Vol. 11). As Wright argues, Golden Age romance comics thrived during the Cold War period, as narratives about "the virtues of domesticity and … [the importance of] securing the vital American home front" (110) harmonized with anti–Communist sentiment. Further, Bigby's contemptuous reference to the lures of "castles and princes" coheres with the way post-war romance comics tended to represent the "playboys of the upper class" as both "financially unstable [spendthrifts]" and "morally unstable too, in that they were portrayed as oversexed" (Gardner 124). Thus, Bigby's anger that Snow is unwilling to focus solely on the needs of their family, together with his status as a working man, is not meant to jar against his more ruthless actions: indeed, the panels showing Bigby and Snow's argument about proper attitudes toward domesticity follows almost directly on his conversation with Beast, in which he asserts that there is information the sheriff has that "you can never tell anyone—not even your wife" (5.105). Finally—with respect to his role as sheriff—Bigby is admired, not simply because he is, as Frau Totenkinder asserts, "a tough customer" (5.126), but because he understands the needs of his community. Toward the end of "The Mean Seasons," Rose Red scolds Beast for freeing Flycatcher, despite instructions from Bigby to "keep busting Fly for eating flies" (5.159). As Rose explains, Flycatcher's absurd "sentence" keeps him from trying to return to the Homelands to try and save his wife and children (5.159). Thus, unlike Stinky the Badger, who bases his beliefs on what he reads "in all the storybooks" (5.134), Bigby serves his community—during traditional wartime and in the new kind of wartime—by understanding how to control multiple narratives.

A later volume in the series—*Inherit the Wind* (Vol. 17)—provides another example of the way *Fables* combines genres in braided and proliferating narratives, to the purpose of exploring how humans negotiate multiple and competing stories. This volume is also organized into three arcs, though here the extended, crowded arc comes first: the four-part "Inherit the Wind" tells the story of the first forays back to normalcy after the defeat of Mr. Dark; of Bufkin's continuing adventures in Oz, where he leads a group of rebels who wish to defeat Roquat the Nome King, but is eventually captured and (apparently) executed; of Werian Holt's continued training of Leigh Duglas, as they anticipate the return of the Fables to Castle Dark, the new Fabletown; and of the activity surrounding the choosing of the new North Wind, which involves the testing of the cubs, the dealings with the three other Cardinal Winds, and Ambrose's revelation of the prophecy he heard from Ozma. Next, "All in a Single Night" tells the story of Rose Red's adventures on Christmas, as she is introduced to three other paladins of Hope. Finally, the arc entitled "In Those Days" includes four interlocking tales of wonder and magical transformation. If *Mean Seasons* might be said to be bolstered by an underlying concern with the narratives produced by new kinds of war, *Inherit the Wind* is focused on the desire for ordering principles that maintain notions of civilization: principles such as manners, custom, inheritance, and—indeed—various kinds of hope, which are all based in a belief in futurity. The preface page of "In Those Days" introduces a most formulaic ordering principle, whereby an improvisational comedian asks the audience for a character, an occupation, and funny phrase as the basis for his "artiface" (17.124), and the succeeding stories all explore how demand produces story: the king in "A Delicate Balance" demands that his adulterous wife learn humility and morality, so turns her into a turtle; in "The Way of the World," the laws of custom demand that the boy place his hand on the wall at the edge of the world before he can attain "all the rights of our people" (17.138); the sorceress in "Porky Pining" (who can be visually identified as Bellflower) demands that a rude porcupine learn some manners, so she curses him with the sexual desire for humans. Significantly, the spell cast in "A Magic Life" is so powerful that—for a while—the sorcerer, eventually known as Mr. Kadabra, escapes the demands of story, as the ordering principles of conquest and the desire for revenge are forgotten; it is only when he inadvertently becomes involved in someone else's story of revenge that he is killed. Along with being micro-instances of the braided and proliferating modes of narrativity, these tiny tales also show that "lessons" about the importance of loyalty, humility, and manners tend to be imparted by those who have authority, and often enormous magical power. This self-reflexive play with the conventions of folk and fairy tale, as well as of fable, indicates that the guises of civilization are simply trappings, and that the "morals" of stories are blind alleys, all disguising the true workings of power.

The issue of the way the guises of civilization mask ill intent is broached in "Inherit the Wind" in a number of ways. Werian and Leigh are represented as consistently preparing for a violent, underhanded showdown with the other Fables, and yet they both relish customs associated with formal dinners, with the skill of fencing, and with celebrating a "proper Christmas" (17.102). The Cardinal Winds—whose ultimate designs include killing "the wolf clan entire ... [and] all of their attendant winds as well" (17.63)—plan to use civilized customs to gain their advantage. The behavior of Werian, Leigh, and the Winds is juxtaposed in the volume with the behavior of Yoop, the unmannered giant of Oz who—before joining forces with the rebels—served the vicious Roquat, but has come to resent the "snooty pooty officers, who always make jokes and rude comments about [him]" (17.60). Together with this critique of notions of manners and civilization, *Inherit the Wind* offers a challenge to the notion of hope as a necessarily "moral" organizing principle. As Rose Red discovers during "All in a Single Night," the idea of hope is vague: Santa Claus informs her that she is required to "figure out what sort of hope you represent" (17.107), this after explaining to her his own role as a purveyor of the hope of justice, or at least nominal reward and punishment, as well as the hope "that things [will] turn out all right in the end" (17.105). Crucial here is both the imprecision and the paltriness of the sort of justice being served, which Santa Claus himself admits is merely "symbolic" (17.105). Also important is the degree to which the hope for justice is relegated to a future moment, whereby the corollary expectation is that one should simply put up with injustice in the present. A more blatant version of the problem of hope is represented by the Little Match Girl—a figure from the tale by Hans Christian Anderson—who is in *Fables* "the caretaker of hope deferred" (17.112): in his portrayal of this figure, Willingham is less concerned with critiquing society's treatment of the poor (though that idea is present), than with examining how the idea of hope is used to manipulate the desires and actions of those without power. Unlike Anderson's Little Match Girl, who is afraid of going home to an angry father who will beat her if she does not sell enough matches, Willingham's Little Match Girl is focused on selling matches so that she can save for the future: for the children she does not yet have, so that their lives may be better than hers. The contention that hope is a morally problematic organizing principle is finally reinforced in the representation of the "Avatar of the Hope of Revenge" (17.118). The character used is the wicked stepmother figure from the Grimms' "The Three Little Men in the Wood," who is punished for drowning her stepdaughter by being put in a barrel spiked with nails and then rolled into a river; as a paladin of Hope, her role is to nurse evil intentions and desires, even those that are couched in an appeal to "justice" (17.118).

Just as the genre collisions in *Mean Seasons* reflect the examination in *Fables* of problematic competing narratives, the use of braided and proliferating modes of narrativity in *Inherit the Wind* lays bare the relationship between narratives of custom, of hope, or of justice and the issue of who controls those narratives. Further, as a self-reflexive text, *Fables* connects such formal exploration with a more or less explicit commentary on the production and reception history of comics. While Kukkonen is right to assert that the narrative play in *Fables* does not subvert the notion of genre decorum, the text's insistence on making use of multiple genres suggests that the subject of marketing as it relates to genre diversification is a bit of a distraction, much like the principles of manners, customs, and hope. The efforts to convince readers (including academic readers) that the comic book genres are genuinely diverse, and therefore subject to critical stratification, is itself a game: genre makes no difference in terms of the outcome of the story; all that is being controlled is the means of telling.

Quests

As noted in the previous two sections, Karin Kukkonen's long chapter on *Fables* in *Contemporary Comics Storytelling*, examines a number of features in the series, including the way it differs from more explicitly feminist adaptations of fairy tales and the way the text makes use of different genre traditions. Aside from looking at genre schemata from war, horror, and crime comics, Kukkonen also considers the way *Fables* employs conventions associated with heroic fantasy, a sub-genre of fantasy, which is itself a sub-genre of the romance mode. In his entry on "Fantasy," contained in *The Encyclopedia of Comic Books and Graphic Novels*, Randy Duncan distinguishes between high fantasy, which "usually deals with archetypal themes such as a spiritual quest, death, and renewal and self-sacrifice" (202), and heroic fantasies, which "are generally simple tales of adventure in which the protagonist, often a roguish anti-hero, encounters a menace and kills said menace" (204). Further, Duncan notes that "Contemporary fantasy is often closely related to horror because it presents the unknown aspects of the world we think we know," and he specifically mentions *Fables*, as well as Neil Gaiman's *Sandman* series, as examples of contemporary fantasy (208). Kukkonen's main argument with regards to Willingham's version of heroic fantasy is that the quest stories involving Boy Blue and Flycatcher are remarkable because neither character conforms to the expectations readers have about romance heroes: Boy Blue is a "misfit in the community of heroes of 'The Last Castle'" (76), while Flycatcher's experiences in the Homelands are defined by his "helplessness" (76). With respect to the categories Duncan delineates, Boy Blue's quest story—featured in *Homelands* (Vol. 6)—is a heroic fantasy, while Flycatcher's quest story—portrayed in *The Good Prince* (Vol. 10)—has more in common with high fantasy, though both tales include various instances of magic. That said, the vulnerability of both Boy Blue and Flycatcher, together with the way their quest stories are juxtaposed with the political goings-on in Fabletown, make their narratives curious kinds of romances in that there is an elevation of the everyman figure and the representation of nostalgia for simplicity and sense.

Kukkonen's point about the unlikeliness of Boy Blue and Flycatcher as the protagonists of heroic or high fantasy tales harks back to foundational ideas about the mode of romance: as Barbara Fuchs notes is her study *Romance*, despite the myriad definitions of the term, the explanation developed by Northrup Frye, which considers romance as a type of narrative producing certain effects on its readers, is a good place to start. According to Frye, the romance "features a superior hero" (Fuchs 5) and—indeed—the development of the superhero so central to comic books owes much to the "mythos of romance [which] involves a series of adventures, collectively labeled a *quest*, that pits the hero against his antagonist in a simple dialectical structure" (Fuchs 6, emphasis in original). Additional Frygian elements of the romance that Fuchs mentions are the emphasis on "idealization and wish-fulfillment" and the "persistent nostalgia for some other time (or one might add, place) that undermines the social ideals of the here and now" (6). In other words, the intended effect of romance is to thrill readers with an adventure tale, often deliberately filled with various obstacles, featuring wonderful displays of the thwarting of ills, as well as the presentation of a world that is idealized as being somehow better—perhaps simpler, perhaps more given to noble activity, perhaps more just—than the world that exists. As Fuchs points out, these modal elements are present even in the contemporary romance novel, which are also defined by "delay and deferral," "the pleasure of the reader," "an emphasis on the marvelous over the quotidian," and "a nostalgia for other times and places" (130). What the contemporary female-centered romance novel does, though, is move the characteristic "fascination with female vulnerability" (130), also present in earlier romances, to the forefront.

The gendered nature of the romance is interesting to consider with respect to Willingham's play with heroic and high fantasy, as both Boy Blue and Flycatcher are often characterized by their own vulnerability. In his analysis of Bigby's outsize and "grown-up" masculinity, Mark C. Hill notes that "instead of building manhood in opposition to a femininity seen as weak, the men of *Fables* return to 19th century models of masculine identity that are formed in opposition to boyhood" (188). Together with Pinocchio—who has the physical appearance of a boy, if also the mouth of longshoreman—Boy Blue and Flycatcher are consistently portrayed as enjoying activities associated with boyhood: they read comic books, they enjoy trips to the candy shop, and they play with toys and games (4.129, 7.13, 12.54–55). Further, both Boy Blue and Flycatcher are presented as

sexually immature: aside from his sexual encounters with the copies of
Red Riding Hood—who seduce him in order gain military advantage—
Blue fails to form an adult relationship with a woman, not with the real
Red Riding Hood and not with Rose Red. The case of Flycatcher is even
more extreme: despite having had a wife and several children during his
time as a prince in the Homelands, the trauma of witnessing their violent
deaths, not to mention the rape of his wife and eldest daughter (*1001*, 68–
69), produces a forgetfulness which the Fables work to preserve, thus contributing to the maintenance of his childlike persona. It is only long after
he has completed his quest to create Haven that he is represented as sexually mature enough to invite the real Red Riding Hood to spend a night,
though she has long made clear her attraction to him (14.184). However,
in the text's exploration of tropes associated with heroic and high fantasy,
it is the vulnerability of the male heroes that makes them appropriate for
a thematic elevation of the everyman figure. While Kukkonen argues that
Boy Blue's status as the central figure of a heroic fantasy is comprehensible
because Willingham "adapt[s] the characters to this [generic] frame" (76),
I would posit that the characters of Boy Blue and Flycatcher remain stable:
it is the frame that is adapted so that Willingham can pursue an examination of cultural nostalgia for the ideal of common sense, as well as the
fantasy of the return to simple solutions for impossible problems.

The subversion of the generic frame of heroic fantasy in Boy Blue's
quest story does not end with the use of a vulnerable, sexually immature,
former office assistant as its protagonist: also important is that, despite
successfully "encountering" various "menaces" and triumphing over said
menaces, Boy Blue's fate is ultimately unheroic. After serving in the war
against the Adversary, not to mention attempting to save Bigby from being
hit with a magical arrow (11.145), Blue suffers an ignominious death, following a series of painful operations and surgical amputations: when he
finally dies he is literally only half a man. Soon after the funeral service
for Boy Blue, however, Pinocchio starts complaining about his friend's
general cultural standing, declaring, "Blue was a giant, swashbuckling
superhero! How did all of that escape the world of so-called writers?"
(12.138). Pinocchio's plan to force Mundy writers to create new "true
books" about Boy Blue's activities so that he'll be popular enough to return
from death (12.139) is similar to the plan Jack pursues during his time in
Hollywood, though—crucially—Blue himself is not party to this plan. Still,
Pinocchio is not alone in advocating for the recognition of Boy Blue as a
hero. Stinky/Brock Blueheart goes one further than even Jack by creating
a religion with the promise of Blue's return at its center. Importantly,

Stinky/Brock Blueheart designates Boy Blue—a human Fable—as the focus of his religious vision, this despite his frequent complaint that the human Fables treat the animal Fables with contempt (12.136). Also, after the accidental unbinding of the magical connection that connected the Business Office to the structures of Fabletown, Bufkin is trapped there with Frankenstein's monster's head and the Magic Mirror, not to mention Baba Yaga and the D'jinn of the lamp who are both on the loose. In trying to consider how to manage their dangerous situation, Bufkin suggests they try to imagine: "WWBD," or "What Would Bigby Do?"; Frankie counters, "Or you could go with WWBBD. What Would Boy Blue Do?" (14.51). When Bufkin warns Baba Yaga and the D'jinn, "Prepare to meet your doom at the hands of Bufkin the Brave" (14.72), he becomes another BB, and it is significant that—like Boy Blue—Bufkin seems an unlikely hero for a heroic fantasy, being not only a former office assistant, but also a monkey (albeit a wonderfully educated and scholarly monkey). The elevation of Boy Blue by the likes of Stinky, Bufkin, and Frankie, together with the concomitant devaluation of the heroic quest (a pursuit that is apparently available to almost anyone), suggests that *Fables* wants to challenge both the traditional function of the quest and the way the questing hero should be properly perceived. Despite an interest in the question of whether someone can change his or her character, Willingham's text frequently undermines the central convention that the heroic quest operates as an avenue for redemption or for the revelation of one's true nature. The fact is, neither Boy Blue nor Bufkin are in need of redemption. They are both civil servants of Fabletown and their seemingly heroic activity becomes part of their office job; ultimately, it is Boy Blue's very status as mere civil servant—not a leader—that makes him a palatable savior for Stinky.

A closer look at the framing of Boy Blue's heroic quest brings into further relief the thematic exploration of the importance of the quotidian and the way *Fables*—despite its portrayal of all manner of marvelous goings-on—often inverts a central feature of the romance mode, which, as Fuchs notes, privileges activity and experiences that are not ordinary (4). The story of Boy Blue's trip back to the Homelands is initiated by degrees in *Mean Seasons* (Vol. 5): the ostensible reason for his quest is that he wishes to rescue the real Red Riding Hood, an idea apparently floated by Bufkin, though only reported to the new mayor, Prince Charming, by Hobbes. While the rescue of a vulnerable maiden operates as a classic instigator of the heroic quest, the heavily mediated representation of this motive makes it potentially suspect. Further, the other references to Boy Blue in the volume—for example, Snow White's advice to Beauty that she continue to employ "both Blue and Bufkin," because "they know where everything is and everything that needs to be done" (5.101), and Prince Charming's irritation that Blue and Bufkin aren't around to hear his "first official pep talk" (5.112)—reinforce Boy Blue's status as an office assistant, which foreshadows the way his quest will ultimately be explained. Further, despite the various examples of generic schemata associated with heroic fantasy that Kukkonen identifies, including "progressing from duel to duel" (73) and the portrayal of "netherworlds and wastelands" (76), the status of Boy Blue as the protagonist of the quest depicted in *Homelands* is questionable not only because of the way he has previously been figured as too ordinary to be heroic, but because the quality of his character undermines the putative meaning of a quest. As Duncan notes, the heroic fantasy conventionally features the "adventures" of an "anti-hero," a frequent archetypal figure found in the genre of comic books, who is usually defined by a lack of a clear moral code. Boy Blue is not such an outsider figure, bent on pursuing justice on his own terms: he is an office clerk, who identifies profoundly with his job. As Doctor Swineheart attests, Blue does not want to be buried with the war dead who lost their lives battling the Adversary, because he "much preferred being a simple clerk and a musician" (12.127). (And, it is arguably as a jazz musician that Blue most explicitly behaves as a cultural outsider, though it is suggested that here too he misses the mark: Snow White recalls that the usual reaction in the clubs of Harlem to Boy Blue is "'you're too young, too white and too hayseed to play here, boy'" [4: 9].) Even with respect to the conventions of high fantasy, in which, as Duncan notes, the quest works as a context for "renewal and self-sacrifice," Blue's journey fails to be meaningful, mostly because, unlike many Fables, he is not in need of redemption, except to the extent that he survived the trip to the new world and many others did not. However, according to the rhetoric of the debt that is owed to the dead, which Boy Blue himself uses in "The Last Castle" (4.54), survival makes him not extraordinary, but even more ordinary.

Finally, as is revealed on the very last page of *Homelands*, Boy Blue's quest isn't really a quest at all, but rather a military operation designed to gain intel about the Adversary: the only people party to the details of the mission are Blue and Prince Charming (6.190). In fact, in keeping with the way this quest is first framed, whereby the commencement of Blue's journey is contextualized by references to his skills in the Business Office, the stories that are juxtaposed with the quest narrative—which include the charging and punishment of Trusty John for treason against Fabletown (6.136–137) and Prince Charming's deal-making with Mowgli—point to matters of politics, not heroics. Further, Prince Charming's nightm which he is accused by Trusty John of being the "prince of hypoc (6.140), indicates that Boy Blue's status as the protagonist in a hero high fantasy narrative is a trick: the real story of redemption at play ht concerns not the office assistant, but the new mayor. This juxtaposition of Boy Blue with Prince Charming continues in *War and Pieces* (Vol. 11), in which a panel depicting Prince Charming's image on a war memorial immediately precedes a panel showing the first of Blue's series of surgeries (11.171), as well as in *The Dark Ages* (Vol. 12), in which the double page spread showing Charming's well-attended state funeral is framed by images of Boy Blue in his hospital bed, now having lost his arm (12.66– 72). Also important in terms of the way Willingham represents the relationship between these two characters—indeed, between Boy Blue and a few Fables whose stories are associated with redemption, including Bigby and Rose Red—is Blue's willingness to scold others for what he perceives as their blind spots or moral failings. During the discussion about Boy Blue's sentence for "stealing" magical artifacts, those tools that were necessary for him to do the job he was assigned, Charming complains about the hardships of his own job as mayor. Far from being sympathetic, Blue repudiates his boss's character: "wisdom, judgment and delayed gratification are alien to you. You're entirely defined by what you covet" (7.63). The recurrent image of Boy Blue scolding other characters remains acceptable because he is not constituted as a hero; a coming-into-his-own self-knowledge is never the point of his journey. Blue remains self-consciously ordinary and thus becomes an important emblem for the way *Fables* champions the everyman, which includes an emphasis on—and a nostalgia for—the moral ease of common sense.

As noted above, Flycatcher is represented in similar terms to Boy Blue, especially with regards to his childlikeness, his sexual immaturity, and his class identity: in fact, Fly's social vulnerability is usually presented in more exaggerated terms than is Boy Blue's. While Blue works in the Business Office, Fly is a janitor, doing endless community service for a series of minor criminal infractions. While Blue is too shy to know how to respond to a quick kiss on the cheek from Rose Red (9.93), Fly's response to Red Riding Hood's new haircut is to revert into a frog (9.23). At the beginning of his quest narrative—in keeping with the conventions of high fantasy—Santa Claus, a quasi-religious figure, presents Flycatcher with a prophetic mission, letting him know that he will only be able to save his community if he is "willing to put away childish things and take up a man's burden again" (9.130). The subject of Flycatcher's manliness is also referred to by Red Riding Hood and Boy Blue, as both try to help him deal with the shock of his newly recovered memories. Visiting Flycatcher in the Business Office chapel room, where he sits all day refusing to eat, Red Riding Hood tries to shame Fly into recovery, repeating a number of times that "a real man" wouldn't simply give in to grief, but would find a way to act (10.13–14). When Flycatcher asks Boy Blue to help him learn how to use the Witching Cloak and Vorpal Sword, so that he can become "a destroyer of those foul things who destroyed me so long ago" (10.30), Blue tells him that he has "a child's view" of war and that "no magic is [so] all-encompassing" that it can defeat armies (10.32). Interestingly, both Ride and Blue are incorrect: in his guise as King Ambrose of Haven, Fly-catcher does possess a magic so "all-encompassing" that he is able to defeat Geppetto's Golden Horde of wooden soldiers (10.208–209). Even more significant, it turns out that Flycatcher's ability to act does not require him to be a "real man" at all, though—importantly—the characteristic at issue is not Flycatcher's masculinity, but his "realness." An examination of the way Flycatcher's quest narrative is braided among other stories that are told in *The Good Prince* (Vol. 10), indicates that Willingham wants to examine the phenomenon of cultural nostalgia, this time for the ideal of simplicity.

The depiction of Flycatcher's quest is much more conventional that that of Boy Blue's quest, cohering both with the idea that Fly is actually in need of spiritual renewal, due to his personal sense of guilt, as well as with his standing as a former prince and future king. The imagery and story stages the text makes use of in this high fantasy quest are almost all associated with the medieval version of the romance mode; they include: the chance for spiritual awakening or self-knowledge (10.52), the arming of the hero (10.68–70), the suffering of the hero in a wasteland (10.120), the duel with a monstrous figure (10.174), and so on. Also, the overlaying of Flycatcher's quest with Lancelot's tale (10.53) makes use of the still-powerful myth of Camelot, while instances of Christian imagery are frequent; for example: as in the biblical story of the Ark, birds are sent forward to scout for signs of life (10.131) and Flycatcher sacrifices himself in order to "defeat" the Sacred Grove army (10.205), an act that creates "new life" as the wooden soldiers turn back into trees (10.211). As Fuchs notes, unlike the use of the mode in the classical, renaissance, or contemporary periods, the medieval version of the romance is held in high regard by critics, even though—like all other versions of the romance—it was a highly popular form (38), and though—even more so than other versions of romance—the medieval romance idealizes the authoritarian power structure represented by feudalism and the court (40). That said, Fuchs argues, the narrative structure of the medieval romance undermines a straightforward idealization, as the narrator of the romance—often identified as a clerk—implicitly comments on and critiques the actions of the romance's protagonists. Willingham makes use of this conventional embedded irony most plainly in his use of a janitor as the protagonist of his high fantasy narrative. Unlike most medieval romances, this quest does not emanate from the court (or upper echelons of Fabletown) and therefore cannot be said to reflect the values of that estate. However, the figure of the janitor knight becomes emblematic, as Flycatcher's actions are almost totally informed by the character trait of humility. Thus, as his journey continues, it becomes clear that Flycatcher's character does not "develop" so much as become more embedded and exaggerated, making him seem more unreal.

As Flycatcher's quest becomes more and more conventional, the braiding of that narrative with other stories in *The Good Prince* (Vol. 10) serves as a self-reflexive admission of our cultural nostalgia for the simple solutions that goodness is supposed to promote (or, vice versa, for the good solutions that a return to simplicity will produce). From the opening panel of the volume—a close-up framing of one of the frog eyes on Flycatcher's baseball cap (10.9)—the recurring motif of eyes and such related ideas as looking, gaining knowledge, or surveilling is noticeable: while Cinderella works to get intel from her interrogation of Baba Yaga (10.16), Prince Charming and Hansel engage in insincere diplomacy, with each trying to gain military advantage (10.17–18); meanwhile, Beast and Charming discuss the difficulties in understanding the reports of the zephyrs, who are spies for Fabletown (10.19). Further, Kay and Frau Totenkinder engage in pointed discussion about his ability to magically see her more distasteful activities (10.25), which leads to Totenkinder's discussion with the Fabletown executive about her methods of surveilling in the Homelands (10.40–41), as well as Charming's idea to make use of a variation of this magic, so that the 13th floor witches can see through the zephyr's eyes and more effectively spy on Hansel and his operatives (10.65). Finally—and most importantly with regards to the issue of Flycatcher's unreality—there is the launch of "Fly TV." After completing his symbolic (and literal) cleansing, Fly asks the Magic Mirror to "keep an eye on [him], and let those back here see everything. It's important they know and understand what's about to happen" (10.64). The utter transparency of the vision supplied by the mirror—which allows those in Fabletown to see "everything"—is juxtaposed with the methods of espionage, which are based on the piling up of secrecy and deceit. However, this juxtaposition does not resolve in a critique of Frau Totenkinder and Prince Charming's methods, nor of the basic military plan, which is "to crush [the Adversary] ... to write an end to their filthy empire once and for all" (10.76). Such methods and goals are not only represented as warranted, but as somehow more comprehensible than Flycatcher's virtuous, clear-cut, and bloodless adventure.

Another narrative braided into the volume follows the preparations of the Fables for all-out war, whereby the ritualistic arming of Flycatcher (10.68–69) functions in stark contrast to the representation of Beast's glee-filled shopping spree for training facilities and military grade weapons (10.84–85). As these war preparations continue, however, more and more Fables become entranced by the adventures shown on "Fly TV," to the extent that the Wolf cubs fight over whose turn it is to "play" at being "King Flycatcher" (10.190). The purpose of these juxtapositions is to reinforce the idea that there is a gap between the stories we choose to consume and the way we act, which culminates in a gentle critique of the cultural attachment to stories of goodness. On the final page of *The Good Prince*, Willingham provides examples of the kind of irony Fuchs argues is embedded into the narrative structure of the medieval romance: while a long, narrow panel on the left-side of the page shows a snow man version of King Ambrose, the conquering knight, Flycatcher is shown back in Fabletown, engaging in his old janitorial duties. This image of the emblematically humble knight operates as a self-reflexive example of the nostalgic desire for the (artificial) power of simplicity and goodness, as is shown in Flycatcher's reference to his own desire to see "all three Jack films [which] are playing back-to-back," as well as in the narrator's ironically understated tone in the summative paratactic pronouncement: "And that about wraps up this story. A lowly janitor called Flycatcher endured many trials and saved many lost people and then became a powerful king and his kingdom was at peace. The End" (10.228).

The schemata associated with heroic and high fantasy are used in these story arcs not to alter the understanding of Boy Blue and Flycatcher's characters, which remain surprisingly stable despite the changes in their environs and the actions they perform: Blue remains resolutely ordinary and Fly resolutely good. What changes is the function of the quest or—perhaps—what is challenged is the supposed thematic function of portraying extra-systemic pursuits of justice or spiritual development. Such themes are revealed as modal tricks, whereby the true function of the romance—to provide thrilling amusement for a captive audience—is fulfilled. In the meantime, in the portrayal of the quotidian world of offices, meetings, negotiations, and the regular doling out of tasks and roles, *Fables* shows how the actual work of enacting power is accomplished.

Prince Charming versus Prince Brandish: An Allegorical Reading

At the end of the first section of *Animal Farm* (Vol. 2), Snow White and Rose Red look outside the window of their guest residence at The Farm and see the head of Colin Pig—one of the Three Little Pigs—which has been mounted on a stick; as Rose attests: "It's poor Colin. It also appears to be a literary reference. My guess is someone wanted to make sure we got a very specific message" (2.24). In the first place, the "literary reference" in question is to William Golding's 1954 novel *Lord of the Flies*, in which Jack Merridew places the head of a pig on a stick as a sacrifice to the island's reputed "Beast." Further, the title of the *Fables* volume, together with such story elements as Dun Pig's seditious speech to the non-human Fables and the thematic focus on revolution, marks George Orwell's 1945 novel *Animal Farm*—a critique of the events of the Russian revolution—as an additional intertext. Finally, Rose Red's comment about sending "a very specific message" calls to mind that both *Lord of the Flies* and Orwell's *Animal Farm* are exemplary contemporary allegories, a genre that is defined by the idea of communicating a specific message, albeit on a secondary level of meaning. Various writers and artists have used features central to the comic book form—in particular its dependence on emblematic characters and on visual signs and images—to construct allegories, the most notable of which is Art Spiegelman's Pulitzer Prize-winning *Maus*, published in 1986. In a recent article, "The Revolt of the Comic Books," Julian Sanchez discusses various contemporary superhero comics that act as allegorical commentary on The War on Terror, including DC's *Identity Crisis* (2004) and Marvel's "Civil War" arc (2006–2007). As I will explore here and further in Chapter 3, *Fables* often offers commentary on contemporary political issues, especially those that have become prominent in post–9/11 America. With respect to the use of allegory, though, Willingham's text differs from Golding's or Orwell's in that it does not present a stable political reading. Rather, many of the proliferating plots in *Fables* owe much to medieval conceptions of allegory, especially in terms of the focus on matters of character, morality, and interpretation. A comparison of ways of reading the representations of Prince Charming and Prince Brandish will explore how the redemption plot in *Fables* is tied to the idea that such plots are necessary to community building.

As Rita Copeland and Peter Struck explain in their introduction to *The Cambridge Introduction to Allegory*, the term "allegory" has always been complicated because, from its first usages in the classical period, the word referred to both "a manner of composing and a method of interpreting" (2). For writers of contemporary political allegory, including Golding, Orwell, and Spiegelman, allegory is primarily a means of composition that works very much like the composition of a traditional fable, a tale featuring characters—often non-human—whose actions within a simple plot are supposed to reveal a simple truth about the human condition; the extended length of works like Orwell's *Animal Farm* or *Maus* allows their authors to explore and comment on more complex human social systems and historical events. For medieval scholars, however, allegory was primarily a mode of interpretation, whereby the goal was to read scripture in such a way as to comprehend divine truths. Copeland and Struck write that "In the early fifth century, John Cassian ... outline[d] ... the four-fold system of scriptural interpretation: he spoke of a literal or historical sense, and of three spiritual senses, tropology (which concerns the soul), allegory (which concerns the revelation of mysteries prefigured in history), and anagogy (which concerns the divine secrets of heaven)" (4–5). Crucially, part of the point of treating allegory as a mode of interpretation was to confer authority on those who could "see" all the hidden layers of a particular text, thus reinforcing the power of Church leaders to frame moral lessons. As Deborah Madsen points out in *Allegory in America*, an American tradition of allegorical reading (and writing) began when Puritan settlers "read" their own experience as being prefigured in biblical texts: "Typology revealed to the orthodox congregationalists of New England that theirs was a divine mission to establish a perfectly reformed church which would stand as an example to all the nations of the world: their redeemer nation would be guided by God towards a glorious destiny" (9). At first, it appears to make more sense to consider how *Fables* might operate as a contemporary political allegory, along the lines that Sanchez proposes when he refers to Willingham's text as both an "openly conservative" and "brilliantly layered" comic (45). However, the status of *Fables* as highly self-reflexive, concerned not only with the subject of character but also with the subjects of reading and of the circulation and control of information, makes the four-fold medieval system oddly productive. The comparison of the portrayal of Prince Charming versus Prince Brandish shows how *Fables* prioritizes—at a very deep narrative level—the examination of whether or not the notion of "self" is static or capable of change, as well as what a notion of self has to do with the ability to inhabit or respond to cultural scripts.

The close relationship between fable and allegory rests on the way both genres often depend on the trope of personification, whereby characters do not possess complex histories or psychologies, but represent abstractions such as "greed," "vanity," "ruthless ambition," or "wisdom." In the *Fables* universe, the function of character is complicated: in keeping both with the comic book convention of the proliferating narrative and with folk and fairy tale sources, a character such as Prince Charming must remain recognizable and therefore stable, if not quite reducible to an abstraction. However, consistent with the text's exploration of the way humans manage social systems and with its destabilization of the idea of "happily ever after," the braided narratives in *Fables* are meant to test whether or not characters are at least capable of change and—perhaps more importantly—whether we can accept the idea that a change of character has occurred. Further, the self-reflexivity of *Fables* is in part communicated in the way characters are often aware of themselves as figures from story. The Fables will often insist on their own status as "real," as when Snow White tells Revise: "We're not stories, assuming we ever really were. We're people" (13.218). Yet, they also acknowledge their difference from—and relationship to—Mundy folk. This relationship is a source of magic, whereby the Mundys only know the Fables as stories and the Fables come to understand and depend on the power produced by this odd condition. As King Cole asserts to Bigby: "there's something special about this place that [gives] us our strength" (15.202). Further, with respect to the notion of allegory as an expedient interpretive practice, some Fables— and most certainly Prince Charming—make use of their emblematic status among the Mundys to help shape their own world. The Prince's first appearance in *Legends in Exile* (Vol. 1) shows him charming a waitress into picking up an expensive lunch tab he has no money to pay for (1.20– 21), and—later—while overseeing the raising of barricades prior to Fabletown's battle with the wooden soldiers, he is able to charm two police officers so entirely that they believe his story about a Bullfinch Street block party (4.167). Thus, it remains an open question for the Fables as to whether or not they should or would choose to rise above the very traits that give them power.

At the literal level, Prince Charming is often accused of having a static character: not only do his three former wives discuss his "chronic" inability to remain loyal (5.10), but—as noted in the previous section—Boy Blue baldly tells him: "You're defined entirely by what you covet" (7.63). Indeed, the accusations seem well-grounded. Despite his claim to Bluebeard that he has a "noble" reason for challenging him to a duel (3.127–128), within days of killing Bluebeard, Charming explains to Hobbes his ultimate goal: to control Fabletown and thus have access to all its wealth (3.165). During his election campaign, he actively stumps among the Fables, comparing their lives to those of "Mister Mundy [who] is cared for by his government" (4.83); he makes impossible promises of "government-sponsored trans-formations" for non-human Fables (4.87), and has Hobbes plaster Fable-town with election posters (4.112). Notwithstanding all this activity, Prince Charming assures Beauty and Beast that his victory is inevitable, explain-ing: "An election is just a romance writ large, with an entire community ... as the object of one's pursuit. And I always win the object of my pursuit" (4.136). Further, Charming's disenchantment with his mayoral role also appears inevitable. In explaining why he can't wake Briar Rose up after the Fables have dealt with Tommy Sharp in *Storybook Love* (Vol. 3), Charming notes "I'm only good for the chase" (3.63).

Thus, the slow-burning redemption story that transforms Prince Charming from a serial coveter into a war hero seems suspect, at least at the start, as his noble desire to attack the Adversary on behalf of Fabletown follows the same script as his noble wish to attack Bluebeard on behalf of Snow White. Once he learns from Frau Totenkinder of the Adversary's plans to invade the Mundy World (10.42), he abandons entirely the work of being mayor and starts "chasing" this new object. Soon after the king-dom of Haven proves secure, Charming replaces Beauty with King Cole as deputy mayor, only so that Cole can reenter his former role without an election after Charming resigns (11.40). Charming is then appointed as the "new Director of Homeland Recovery" (11.40) and is next depicted commanding the flying airship The Glory of Baghdad; once again—his goal is "to win" (11.81). Towards the end of his narrative, however, it appears that Prince Charming does change. When he first escapes the Homelands as Cinderella's husband, he is portrayed as not enough of a "real man" to stay, fight, and likely die (4.33). As is both explicitly shown towards the conclusion of *War and Pieces* (Vol. 11), and as is rehearsed by Sinbad (12.46) and then by Snow White at his funeral (12.70–71), Prince Charm-ing sacrifices himself in order to destroy the final gateway between worlds. The question remains, however: does this public recognition of Prince Charming's sacrificial act count as proof of redemption?

In her discussion of the history of allegory, Madsen distinguishes between allegorical interpretations that depend on personification and typological interpretations: "Personifications are essentially static, bound by the signifying limits of the concept that determines them. Characters which are typologically determined, in contrast, are involved in a dynamic historical process" (28). For the New England Puritans, a typological approach to reading allowed them to situate within the biblical narrative the trials and tribulations of their own settler community, as well as their own aim to colonize the land by whatever means, thus providing divine purpose for their experience and divine sanction for their actions. As a personification, Prince Charming represents the aristocracy: his social position is predicated on his title, and his objectionable actions flow from this particular worldview. It should not be surprising that, in *Fables*, the aristocratic worldview is critiqued, as the notion of American exceptionalism emerged in part as a rejection of such old world values. What is surprising, however, is that it is Prince Charming who upsets the formerly uncontested leadership triumvirate of King Cole, Snow White, and Bigby: the irony of an aristocrat insisting on democracy and republicanism is shown in *March of the Wooden Soldiers*, when a panel showing the Statue of Liberty is immediately followed by the image of the Fabletown executive discussing the problem of Charming's leadership bid (4.75). This irony is redoubled as Charming positions himself as the populist, left-leaning choice, the "Man for all Fables" (4.111). In typological terms, then, the ascendency of aristocratic values among the political class—left or right leaning—is the object of Willingham's critique, as he examines the way corruption undermines core republican values. While much of *The March of the Wooden Soldiers* (Vol. 4) and *The Mean Seasons* (Vol. 5) can be read as allegorical commentary on The War on Terror, the volumes also include pointed criticism of activity leading up to the presidential election of 2004. As the reality of Prince Charming's election bid begins to take hold, King Cole asks Bigby to "dig up some scandal on him, so he has to drop out early" (4.110), drawing attention to the way election cycles have devolved into a series of "gotcha" moments. Though the publication date of Issue #21 "Stop Me If You've Heard This One, But A Man Walks Into A Bar" predates the activities of the Swift Vets and POWS for Truth group, whose goal was to undermine the military record of John Kerry, the subject of Kerry's versus George W. Bush's respective military service—and the way their election campaigns connected such service to character—is criticized as undermining a rigorous democratic process. On the final page of *The March of the Wooden Soldiers*, Grimble and Hobbes refer to two competing—and almost identical—election posters, one portraying Charming and the other Cole, each claiming to be the "Hero of the Battle of Fabletown"

(4.231). Importantly, the value of civic service, crucial to the true political republic, which must be run by citizens rather than an aristocratic ruling class, is portrayed as debased, at least at the level of leadership. Thus, it is only within the context of active military service that a figure like Prince Charming might hope to find redemption, as the idea of war sacrifice is apparently still meaningful.

The tropological and anagogic levels of allegory, even more so than the typological level, are typically associated with interpretation that occurs within a religious framework, pointing as they do to the workings of the soul and to divine mysteries. Even for a secular text such as *Fables*, however, it is still possible to consider how such readings relate to a redemption story, as they offer a consideration of morality and of the power of art. With respect to his status as a personification, the moral tag that might be associated with Prince Charming has already been examined: he stands for entitlement and for the abuses of power that flow from that status. This examination, however, is too superficial to be tropological, as it is still connected to social rather than moral systems. Prince Charming is accused—by Trusty John and by Boy Blue, respectively—of hypocrisy and covetousness, and John in particular alludes to "the women" Charming has "wronged" (6.140). In her own narrative about Prince Charming, collected in *1001 Nights of Snowfall*, Snow White presents a competing tale of a wife's betrayal of her husband. In the story "The Fencing Lessons," the wife insists that her new husband—a young prince—teach her the art of fencing, a skill she uses to kill seven dwarves who kept her as a sexual slave for many years (or so the ambiguous narrative implies, and so the story Snow White tells to Therese years later seems to confirm [20.89]). The difficulties for the prince are twofold: first, the mysterious murder of the dwarves is leading to war between the human and dwarf kingdoms (*1001*, 48); second, he is tormented by the idea that his wife has kept the matter of her past from him and that he has been "played for a fool" (*1001*, 52). As Snow White explains to King Shahryar in the frame tale of *1001 Nights*, "her husband never quite trusted her again ... wiser listeners might conclude that the marriage really ended on the day she set out to be a destroyer" (*1001*, 55).

Though the meaning of all the tales told in *1001 Nights of Snowfall* is complicated by their purpose, whereby Snow White tells King Shahryar certain types of stories to rekindle his faith in women, the effect of this backstory is to transform Prince Charming's covetousness—his manic pursuit of "objects"—into an outgrowth of his intense need to be loved, whether by women or by the community, as well as his need to succeed, whether in politics or in war. Even more importantly, the layering of story that is offered might be considered in anagogic terms, as the effect of this other narrative of Prince Charming is to suggest the power of art to produce moral and social meaning. The public recognition Prince Charming receives at his funeral is framed within an explicit recognition of the intricacy of his character: Snow acknowledges that he is both a "rake" and an "honorable man" (12.70–71). The well-attended state funeral might be thought of as Prince Charming's definitive victory, as he finally wins the love of the entire community. However, at the anagogic level, the event also highlights the way Charming himself comes to transcend an entrenched stasis of character, as well as the way the Fables are moved to acknowledge the multiplicity and flexibility of cultural scripts. Both Charming and his community are shown to be receptive to the ideal that art can be read in transformative as opposed to typological terms, especially if acceptance of this ideal provides a means for mourning and for community healing.

A comparison of the portrayal of Prince Charming and Prince Brandish illuminates further the meaning of Charming's special relationship to his community, which allows for the mutual acceptance that character can be reimagined, reinterpreted, and thereby redeemed. Like Charming, Brandish is an aristocrat, a former husband of Snow White (or so he believes), and an accomplished swordsman—even his name evokes the verb "to brandish," or to display a sword ostentatiously. More so than Charming, however, Brandish is depicted as nakedly oriented towards accruing personal power rather than serving—or even being recognized by—a community. The issue of swordsmanship is relevant here: in *Storybook Love* (Vol. 3), Prince Charming proves himself to be a "master of blades" (3.81), so adept that he is able to lose convincingly to Bluebeard when they duel during a class at the Chateau d'If Fencing Academy. Later, of course, he handily defeats and kills Bluebeard, and it is significant that Charming insists they fight with swords: "isn't that how these things are traditionally done?" (3.126). The prince in "The Fencing Lessons" considers excellent swordsmanship to be a matter of both "philosophy," whereby the goal is to "destroy your enemy's ability to make war" (*1001*, 27), and extensive training and practice: the craft of swordsmanship thus requires both ability and a determined spirit. As his lessons for Ms. Spratt/Leigh Duglas show, Prince Brandish is also an accomplished swordsman, as the training regimen he insists upon is rigorous and highly technical. Further, like Charming, Brandish believes that the tradition of the duel must be respected: as he scolds Bigby, who—in his wolf guise—threatens to kill

Brandish, "a duel this important should have a modicum of ritual attached to its opening" (19.127). However, for real fighting, Brandish depends on "the Eastermark blade" (17.64), a magical weapon that "is actually a hundred magic weapons conquered and absorbed over the ages" (19.142). In other words, Brandish's capacity as a swordsman is not chiefly a matter of his own skill and character, as he is happy to take magical shortcuts if they will improve his position. When Brandish duels with Snow White, her superior training and innate attitude—which she verifies she learned about from Prince Charming—is the source of her victory (19.156–157).

While the literal representation of Prince Charming shows his character moving from stasis to redemptive change, the portrayal of Prince Brandish begins with a tale of transformation, as the nominal source for his character is the prince who has been turned into a bear from the Grimms' "Snow White and Rose Red." When Rose Red recalls this story as part of her healing process, she considers the transformation of the bear back into the prince as "the day I lost [Snow White to] ... the first of her string of handsome princes come to take her away" (15.53). In their mother's enlargement of the tale—which initiates Willingham's own revisionist adaptation of the source material—she explains that Prince Brandish's promise to marry Snow White as a "reward" for freeing him from an enchantment (15.52) stems from his self-interested wish to secure Snow's inherent magic by "attaching more power to [his] household" (15.58). And, if the story of the bear wasn't enough to make the issue of a Brandish's nature ambiguous, his next appearance is as Werian Holt, Esquire, engaged by Mr. Dark to become Leigh Duglas's fencing instructor (16.55), and also party to her plan to deceive the returning Fables by acting the part of prisoners of Mr. Dark (18.32). It is only after coming face to face again with Snow White that he reveals himself to be Prince Brandish, referring to himself as her "first and one true husband" (19.81). Brandish insists on this status because they "betrothed [them]selves to each other long ago" (19.87), although it is important to note that the text never depicts Snow making such a vow, even as a child, even to the bear. It is Brandish who keeps insisting on "the promise" he has made (15.52, 15.55). Even after this revelation, the text shows yet another instance of Prince Brandish's seeming transformation: not only is he killed by Snow White (19.163), but, during an autopsy on his body performed by Dr. Swineheart and Leigh Duglas, he comes back to life (20.49).

At the allegorical or typological level, however, all these literal transformations are shown to be a ruse, an outward show that—like his swordsmanship—is disconnected from the innate. As is revealed in *Camelot* (Vol.

20), even as a child Prince Brandish personifies all that is vile about an intractably patriarchal world view, murdering his mother because she has shown herself to be a sexual being; as young Brandish declares: "The Queen should be pure and chaste. Above reproach. My mother shouldn't act like an animal" (20.65). During his discussion with Snow White, after he has locked her in his rooms in Castle Dark, he makes it clear that his quest for personal power is simply a manifestation of his misogyny. Though Brandish tells his father that he wants to secure Snow White's magical energy in order to "give it to [his] sons" (19.88), he reproaches Snow for her marriage to Bigby, focusing mostly on such matters as her "unnatural lusts" and her "corrupted womb" (19.95). In specifically typological terms, the critique of Prince Brandish's misogyny is clarified by the way he depends on the law to support his cruelty: as he points out to King Cole and others, locking up Snow White against her will simply confirms "the sanctity of traditional marriage" (19.108). In 2012 and 2013, when the "Snow White" arc was published, cultural discussion about the repeal of Section 3 of the Defense of Marriage Act (DOMA) had reached a fever pitch, with any number of advocacy groups and individuals vociferating loudly about the need to "protect" traditional marriage (and though the conversation in 2012–2013 largely focused on opposition—or support—for same-sex marriage, organizations advocating for "traditional marriage" are also generally in favor of "a form of marriage where the ability to leave unhappy marriages is taken away or severely limited, adulterous acts are criminalized, men and women are required to adhere to traditional gender roles, and meaningful choice regarding procreation is limited" [Fineberg 305]). Arguably, Willingham's portrayal of Snow White's situation in this arc represents a radical feminist critique, as the Fables community becomes complicit in Brandish's insistence on adhering to a deeply patriarchal worldview; members of the community refuse to rescue Snow White from the locked room as such an action might compromise "various applicable laws" (19.115).

Thus, at the tropological level—an interpretive level that transcends the specific site of history and culture—Prince Brandish's consistent emphasis on magical oaths and traditional laws represents his intense need for fixed positions, for the kind of power that is achieved through stasis, and for the fear of change. This interpretation is reinforced by the image of Brandish's heart "locked away in a mighty fortress" (20.63), a scenario that effectively makes him immortal. Unlike Geppetto, who uses magical protections in order to serve his thirst for wide-ranging political power and to enforce loyalty, Prince Brandish exercises his immortality in solely personal, almost petty, ways: in sum, he wants a life without "visible scars" (20.49). At the anagogic level, the representation of Prince Brandish reflects a thorough condemnation of intractability. In the opening pages of *Cubs in Toyland* (Vol. 18), Bigby explains to Winter, who has been having nightmares about her own capacity for cruelty as the new North Wind, that even the idea of destiny isn't meant to be absolute; rather, the future is "sort of a menu ... and you're free to take what you want and leave everything you don't" (18.14). Further—with respect to both Brandish's attitude toward the concept of marriage and the inadequate response of the Fable community to his abusive behavior—Willingham shows his contempt for a lousy readership: with the sort of reader who tries to control (or ignore) evidence rather than learn from it. Even Rose Red's offer of a frame for Brandish's redemption is insincere. Though it first appears that Rose will provide Prince Brandish with the opportunity to serve the community, and thereby offer the community an occasion to reinterpret his character, her desire to give Brandish a "second chance" is almost exclusively an outgrowth of a self-interested wish to prove her own "purpose in life" (20.85). Moreover, unlike Prince Charming's military sacrifice, Brandish's service is unwelcome servitude, which he eventually defies (21.64).

In her conclusion to *Allegory in America*, Madsen argues that allegory persists in the American literary tradition because of the genre's inherent flexibility: "Allegorical interpretation, by exploiting the referential gap opened up between the literal story and the potential for significance, can supply dimensions of meaning that sustain the relevance and authority of the sacred book for the entire culture." Further—with respect to the way to the way allegory operates in a postmodern age—"The desire for absolute knowledge is served by the arbitrary attribution of meaning which is at the heart of allegorism" (168–169). In other words, even for secular writers and readers, who might scoff at the idea of the "sacred book," the quest for meaning remains a legitimate concern, most especially because the very idea of "meaning" has been called into question—what is left over is the *desire* for meaning. Examining the depiction of Prince Charming versus Prince Brandish using a medieval system of interpretation is—obviously—an arbitrary, perhaps "poncy, college-educated" choice; however, it is one that reveals the text's deep interest in the way redemption narratives actually work. What *Fables* suggests is that redemption requires acts of reimagination and reinterpretation, whereby one's actions in the past must be generally accepted as stages along a journey. Though this formula is perhaps hackneyed—and certainly there is something artificial about Prince Charming's state-funeral—the character arcs in *Fables* intimate that the formula is a necessary feature for building community identity. Communities not only create, but must believe their own stories; the cultural space that is made for notions of redemption is thus a highly tenuous construct, requiring mutual acts of imagination, flexibility, and forgiveness.

The fairy tale, the fable, the romance, and the allegory: the exploration of genre and adaptation in this chapter ultimately hones in on how stories operate as an avenue for control, but also for hope; in acknowledging the cynicism that pervades contemporary Western culture, *Fables* explores the enduring appeal of stories that champion simplicity and redemption, even while admitting that behind every compelling story is someone's attempt to gain or affirm power. This comic book series imagines the hero and heroine, no longer pursuing just his or her own adventure but caught up in a complex community, one with shifting notions of identity and social roles. In the next chapter, the matters of species, family, and gender in *Fables* are examined, as these figures from stories try to inhabit a grounded, cooperative reality.

2

The Social World

In the first pages of *Fables*, Bigby tries to insist on his right to work on the case of Rose Red's murder alone, only to be informed by Snow White that she will be accompanying him. In this world, no one really gets to work alone, despite each character's former role as the hero, heroine, or villain in his or her own story. *Fables* considers how these figures interact, how community is defined, and who remains inside or outside certain boundaries. A key issue in the social world inhabited by the Fables is the tension between freedom and confinement, whether the tension emerges because of law, because of threat, or because of the basic interrelations among ones' most intimate companions. In their social interactions, these figures show a consistent desire for freedom, though they are sometimes held fast to others by bonds such as love, duty, family, and history. And yet, as much as the community produces conflict, it also comes to define safety and is a venue for the individual to become more than just a mere hero or villain.

This chapter examines acts of sacrifice and self-determination, as well as acts that undermine subjectivity and choice. The focus is representations of the human-animal divide, of families, and of the femininities of Snow White and Rose Red; throughout, the crucial problem examined is the difficulty of defining oneself in relation to others and the burden of being defined. The social world explored is in no way fantastical, but rather acts as a magic mirror for current conversations about what it means to exist in community.

Posthuman Interrogations

From the opening volume of *Fables*, the complex issue of so-called human versus non-human Fables is raised, as Snow White reminds Beauty and Beast of a "most vital [Fabletown] law," which requires that Fables are able to pass as regular Mundy humans (1.15). Those that cannot pass for human must live at The Farm. As Lisa Brown argues in "The Speaking Animal: Nonhuman Voices in Comics," the locale of The Farm is a point of contention, as "the animal Fables realize that … [it] is as much a prison as it is a form of protection." Further, as my own reference to the notion of "passing" should emphasize, the lack of freedom accorded to certain members of the community, solely based on their appearance, "resonates as a metaphor for America's history with racial segregation" (Brown, 75). The thematic function of the animal Fables, however, is not entirely solved via this metaphor for the simple reasons that even Fables who appear to be human are not human, while the Fable animals are not mundane. Later in *Legends in Exile* (Vol. 1), Bigby has a conversation with Colin Pig, during which they go over their fraught history, with Colin arguing that he is "a living symbol of your lasting redemption" (1.35). Though Bigby—who now has a human appearance—shares his apartment and his smokes with Colin, he also offends him by offering his guest a breakfast consisting of "ham 'n' eggs" (1.35). The representation of animals in *Fables* thus engages the history of funny animal comics, as well as the rise of the field of critical animal studies. In its depictions of complex relations between human and non-human figures, as well as in its exploration of culturally sophisticated and persecuted non-human animal communities, the text takes up some of the inherent hypocrisy of human claims to being a superior species. However, although *Fables* acknowledges both the literary history and emerging theoretical context of animal and posthumanist studies, the text ultimately denigrates animals as a lesser status of being.

In his entry on "Funny Animal Comics," collected in *The Encyclopedia of Comic Books and Graphic Novels*, Leonard Rifas notes that "Above all other genres, funny animal comics have represented comics' role as light-weight children's entertainment" (234). Though they are among the oldest form of comics—with George Herriman's comic strip "Krazy Kat" earning early popularity and critical praise (Rifas, 235)—and though they prevailed mid–20th century, both during the post-war period when superhero comics went out of fashion and during the years when the Comics Code destroyed the market for horror and crime comics, Rifas notes that in the current American comic books market, the funny animal comic is almost entirely absent (241). That said, the representation of animals in comic books extends beyond those titles that were specifically promoted to young readers: both the underground comix movement of the 1960s to 1970s and the rise of the graphic novel in the 1980s provided new venues for such animal characters as Robert Crumb's iconic Fritz the Kat and the figures in Art Spiegelman's *Maus*. And, Rifas' point about the general decline of funny animal comics notwithstanding, it is important to note that the third best-selling comic of 2014 was Marvel's "Rocket Raccoon #1" ("Diamond announces") and that IDW's *My Little Pony* series has come to dominate the new growing market for comics for young readers (O'Leary). *Fables* makes gestures to all of these histories. In *The Dark Ages* (Vol. 12), Stinky discusses with Frau Totenkinder and Ozma the issue of Fable metaphysics, piquing Frau's interest with his notion of a "master storyteller"; when she commends him on his insight, however, Stinky assumes (wrongly) that he is being mocked: "Of course I can't be right because I'm just a funny little woodland creature!" (12.136). The oblique reference to Stinky's prescience recalls Walt Kelly's funny animal comic strip series *Pogo*, which ran for over 20 years; in the strip, Pogo the Possum and his Okefenokee Swamp mates made subversive and often self-reflexive references to cultural issues, including to McCarthyism and various political administrations (Goldstein, 86). The *Fables* figure of Porky Pine— who first shows up in *Sons of Empire* (Vol. 9)—references both *Pogo*, which featured a character of the same name, and the underground comix tradition, as the furry woodland creature admits his "perverse attraction to human women" (9.52). Finally, as noted late in Chapter One, a volume such as *Animal Farm* (Vol. 2) explores the allegorical tradition in comic books typified by *Maus*.

The representation of animals is also significant in the history of folk and fairy tale, with the conventional "animal tale" featuring entertaining, often comical figures who are more or less anthropomorphic (Ó hÓgáin, 42). *Fables* makes use of various characters from classic animal tales, for example those from the English fairy tales "The Three Little Pigs" and "The Three Bears." In rendering these characters, Willingham plays with their stereotypical features; for example, the pigs' customary loyalty to one another is subverted when Colin is interrogated by Dun and Posey, and then murdered (2.21–22), while the meaning of the cozy family compact exemplified by The Three Bears is complicated, not only by Goldilocks' sexual relationship with Boo Bear (2.31), but by Boo's death (4.201). Hilda Ellis Davidson points out that, even in stories that do not fit into the category of the "animal tale," animals often take up the role of "helper," sometimes responding to "generosity on the part of the central character" (99) and sometimes "giv[ing] wise advice and magical gifts" (100). Examples of complex helper animals in *Fables* are the toy animals in Toyland, such as Mr. Ives and Mr. Wellstuffed, who serve Therese, and Lord Mountbatten, the mechanical tiger who aids Darian in his quest to save his sister

(*Cubs in Toyland*, Vol. 18). Crucial even here is the subordinate status of the animal figure, whose role it is to "test" the protagonist for whatever character traits are to be affirmed, whether obedience or bravery or compassion. Davidson also makes note of animal helpers who are actually "a human being seeking freedom from enchantment" (102). Such enchanted figures often feature in tales using the motif of the animal bride or bridegroom; as Carole G. Silver notes, "while animal grooms are usually revealed as handsome princes, brides, masked in human beauty are sometimes exposed as monsters" (41). In *Fables*, the two characters who most closely resemble the figure of the animal bride are Baba Yaga, in her guise of Red Riding Hood, and Leigh Duglas, whose beauty masks her monstrous nature, though in both cases the "monster" is a witch, not an animal. More familiar are Prince Brandish, who was once a bear, and Flycatcher, the Frog Prince, though—in *Fables*—both of these figures strain against conventional notions of the handsome prince. Even when the animal in folk or fairy tale is itself the protagonist and/or antagonist—as in many definitive fables—such figures lack any sort of complex psychology, though this lack is not all that notable, given that many human characters in folk and fairy tale are also flat and static.

After briefly noting the way the representation of animals in *Fables* might be read as an allegory for race relations in America, Lisa Brown goes on to suggest that the interactions between the human and non-human Fables also draw attention to "the constraints of the human-animal divide" (75). As Michael Chaney points out in "Animal Subjects of the Graphic Novel," the centrality of animal representation to the history of comics allows for a reading of the form through the "dawning theoretical light of concepts known variously as animality, becoming-animal, or animetaphor" (130). With respect to the more subversive possibilities afforded by the representation of animals in comics, Chaney makes note, first, of "the way comics routinely problematize the human by blurring the ontological boundary between humans and animals according to the same logic that both fuses and separates words and pictures" (133), and, second, of the genre's association with young readers, which "leaves open the possibility that these certainties [about the human-animal divide] have not yet crystallized" (133). Chaney's point about the way comics trouble the "ontological boundary between humans and animals"—in other words, the way the apparent distinction and ensuing power relationship between the two categories of being is questioned—is relevant to an examination of *Fables*, as there are many moments in the text when the "superiority" of humans is challenged, or when the issue of humans consuming animals is broached. For example, in *Wolves* (Vol. 8), Mowgli's encounter with a pack of Mundy wolves who live in Chukotka, Russia not only suggests that the wolf pack possesses its own complex leadership system, language, and honor code, but also that the wolves have a more clear-cut sense of honor than humans: when Mowgli is injured after battling the pack leader for supremacy, he is left to heal by the rest of pack and acknowledges that "any cub could have finished me, but that isn't the way of the free *people*" (8.27, emphasis added).

Mowgli's references to the Mundy wolves as "the free people," a term meant to emphasize their fully formed political culture, operates as a blurring of the boundaries between species, though one might argue that the already highly mythologized figure of the wolf is afforded an even more specialized status in *Fables* because of the narrative centrality of Bigby Wolf. Even more unsettling, then, are the reminders throughout the text that—despite the presence of talking non-human Fables in their lives— human Fables routinely consume Mundy animals. In *War and Pieces* (Vol. 11), the ever-alarmist Chicken Little imagines that a special meeting called for the animal Fables will "inform us that they've decided Fable chickens and pigs and cows are now approved food items for all the new human Fables!" (11.14). Later, in *The Great Fables Crossover* (Vol. 13), Chicken Little returns to this theme, telling Beast, Beauty, and King Cole that "in the new world order [established by Boy Blue] there will be no more sick practices of hume Fables dining on the poultry unborn!" (13.163). Chicken Little's proclamations link up to posthumanist arguments regarding the tenuousness of the way the human-animal divide has been constructed. In the first place, the species divide—and hierarchy—is shown to be arbitrary as opposed to natural; when Chicken Little warns about new rules regarding the consumption of animals, the prevailing rationalizations for humans consuming other species are called into question, or at least shown to be subjective and informed entirely by human desire. Further, Chicken Little's use of the phrase "poultry unborn" echoes the rhetoric used by anti-choice activists, thus highlighting the hypocrisy of humanist avowals about the sanctity of "life." That said, the effect of these subversive ideas is diminished by the status of Chicken Little as a) a notorious and discredited doomsayer, and b) a very minor figure in *Fables*. Her words cannot hope to resonate as strongly as Rose Red's who—even as she experiences a prelapsarian communion with lion and lamb—reminds her cricket guide that "I'm all about the steak" (21.149). Thus, though the very presence of so many intelligent animals suggests the potential for a radical destabilization of the boundary Chaney refers to, there is also a persistent tendency in *Fables* to undermine such destabilizations through thematic and structural belittling of the "animal cause."

From a traditional humanist perspective, children are understood as more "primitive" than adult humans, which accounts for the way they can—as Chaney puts it—be seen as "as occupying a more proximate position to the animal" (133). Willingham's representation of Snow White and Bigby's cubs versus Bibgy's six brothers is an example of the way *Fables* emphasizes conceptions of primitivism, as well as of cultural superiority, by making use of comic book conventions that link children and animals. In the two-part arc "Father and Son," collected in *Sons of Empire* (Vol. 9), the Wolf family goes to visit Bigby's father, the North Wind, at his castle; during the trip, Ambrose Wolf has a terrifying encounter with six monsters, who are later revealed to be Bigby's six elder brothers (9.173). Michael Allred illustrates the brothers as monsters, drawn to resemble the monsters from Maurice Sendak's seminal children's story "Where the Wild Things Are," as is made clear from the tag in the bottom right hand corner of the splash page, which reads "Next: Wild Things!" (9.154). This intertextual reference, together with such story elements as Ambrose's narration, in which he sets up the tale as an explanation of how "I learned to trust that Dad would always look out for us" (9.135), as well as the depiction of Ambrose as a naked little boy under attack and the monsters' tendency to speak in rhyme (9.154, 9.158–159), frame the arc as a "growing up" story. Thus, it is Ambrose's status as a child that allows him to explore the psychic territory of uncivilized "wild things." Complicating this frame, of course, is the fact that Ambrose, the rest of his siblings, and Bigby all have the ability to shapeshift into wolves, but the arc contains this complication in its final panels, in which the very human-looking Wolf family regard a small fish tank now filled with the transformed monsters (9.178). Further, the brothers remain animals, even when Winter recruits them to her side in preparation for the show-down between Snow White and Rose Red (21.34), thus retaining the hierarchy whereby animals, like children, are not fully developed humans. Importantly, in their own adult guises, Ambrose, Winter, and Therese always appear human, while Bigby's degeneration and increasing lack of autonomy in *Happily Ever After* (Vol. 21) is depicted within the context of him becoming more beast-like.

Chaney also argues that the genre of the funny animal comic often shows its indebtedness to folktale fables, in which the anthropomorphic animal is just "Other" enough to make clear the object of critiquing human action. In this scenario, however, the animal is never really animal, but rather functions as "the vanishing point of the human ... [doing] so time and again in order to finally celebrate and naturalize the superiority of the human (as defined by the Enlightenment) as well as the insuperable difference separating the human from the non-human" (Chaney, 132). In other words, even the revolutionary animals at The Farm—in particular Dun and Posey Pig—retain their anthropomorphic and allegorical function only provisionally, so that the critique of their treatment is not sustained. When Snow White and Rose Red first arrive at The Farm, Rose marvels at "all the cozy little piggy things, just like in a real person's house," to which Posey retorts, "We are real persons, Miss Red" (2.17). In this scene, and in later scenes in which Dun explains to Snow White the error of appointing Weyland Smith, a human Fable, as overseer of the non-human Fables (2.27), the figures of the pigs embody a critique of the human propensity to insist on hierarchies among classes of beings (and, as Brown points out, it is possible to "read" the animals as racialized Americans, an idea that inheres with a long, fairly problematic history in comics of figuring the racialized other as animal [Soper 126]). However, this line of critique is soon muddied, first, by the introduction of Goldilocks, a human Fable whose hyperbolic, jargon-heavy speeches about thwarting the oppressor undercuts the possibility of taking the animals' grievances seriously (2.30) and, second, in the representation of many of the Kipling animals, who show themselves to be vicious, given to petty infighting, and easily tricked by Reynard the Fox, an animal who scoffs at the very idea of revolution (2.44). By the time Rose Red takes over as yet another human overseer of The Farm, the notion that pigs are also "real persons" has disappeared, as evidenced by Rose's cheerful explanation that the giants have been transformed into the "new" Three Little Pigs; as Rose explains, "Not one of [the Mundys] would know or care that they're different piggies, with different names" (2.112). As with the representation of children who grow up to have power over animals, the allegorical animals in *Fables* are only afforded an active political voice when they can be "read" as human; as animals, they have no individuality, and therefore are not regarded as an equal category of being.

The emphasis on the natural superiority of the human, and on the absolute difference between the human and the non-human, is apparent in the representation of language use, which—even in the depiction of Mowgli's interactions with the wolf pack—is deemed the only "rational" form of communication. The relationship between language use and power is significant in terms of the way the representation of animals in *Fables* reveals, as Chaney puts it, "the vanishing point of the human," or the way human culture is demarcated as normative. The presence of talking animals in the *Fables* universe coheres with the presence of such figures in folk and fairy tale, as well as in those canonical works of children's literature Willingham has made use of: thus, when Snow White and Rose Red intrude on Dun's speech to the other inhabitants of The Farm, the reader is encouraged to identify such figures as Puss in Boots, the Three Blind Mice, the Cow Who Jumped Over the Moon, the Tortoise and the Hare, the White Rabbit from *Alice in Wonderland*, and so on (2.13). Like the Fables who can pass as human, these figures are gleaned from literary sources, thus confirming a central conceit of the text, which is that the Fables have "escaped" their Homelands, and that their presence in the Mundy world has somehow translated into the production of Mundy stories. However, some of the animal characters featured in *Fables* are not associated with any particular folk or fairy tale source, for example Porky Pine and Stinky Badger. To be sure, there are also several human-looking Fables that Willingham creates, including Dunster Happ, Rodney and June, the Wolf cubs, and—of course—the various second- and third-generation Fables who exist mostly as background characters. Still, the new talking animal characters are distinct from the new human Fables in that their primary function is to be a talking animal, as opposed to a fully developed character or even an important plot device (an exception to this scheme is Bufkin, who is not specifically a character in Frank L. Baum's Oz novels; that said, Bufkin's status as a flying monkey does, to some extent, ground him within a particular literary history).

Thus, when Stinky/Brock Blueheart is represented, he is primarily figured as a mouthpiece for those talking animals who dream of a more equitable future. His "voice"—like Dun's—is mostly conceived in allegorical terms, and is not sustained beyond this context. When Stinky is assigned to be Bigby's driver during the failed attempt to locate Therese and Darian, the badger makes clear that he would like to use the opportunity to communicate with Bigby, going out of his way to "make the first deposit in the trust bank by admitting something you can never repeat" (19.67). Bigby's sole response to Stinky's various attempts at conversation, though, is the request that he stop talking (19.67). Further, Stinky's desire for a "sacred quest" (19.77) is undermined when Bigby returns to Fabletown to challenge Brandish (19.123), after which Stinky simply disappears from the main narrative. The representation of Stinky's incessant, mostly inane chatter during the road trip reinforces the sense that—notwithstanding the moment of metacritical insight that catches the attention of Frau Totenkinder—he really is "a funny little woodland creature" (12.136), whose vision of a new world is not to be taken seriously. After the events described in *Animal Farm* (Vol. 2), many of the portrayals of the animal Fables focus on their basic foolishness; for example, after Rose Red and Boy Blue inform them that they can choose to move to Haven, the discussion among the Tortoise, a cat, and the Three Blind Mice (as well as The Dish and The Spoon) centers on whether or not they will be able to give up TV and the Internet (11.22). In contrast, the residents of Smalltown discuss more complex notions of how "home" is constituted (11.23). The foolishness of many of the non-human characters in *Fables* thus undermines whatever status might have been afforded to them on the grounds that they can speak.

The clearest exception to the increasingly dominant depiction of The Farm animals as "comic relief" is the figure of Reynard the Fox, an animal who is given the opportunity to be human, but who chooses in the main narrative to exist as an animal (Reynard's human adventures are recounted in *Fairest: Clamour for the Glamour*). The figure of Reynard has a long, complex literary history: as Sanne Parlevliet notes in "Hunting Reynard," in the first recorded version of the character, Reynard the Fox is a criminal who manages to outwit various figures from King Noble the Lion's court, thus escaping punishment for his crimes. As per the conventions of the satiric animal tale, Reynard's ability to best a strong bear, a greedy cat, and the ambitious Noble himself reinforces the tale's critique of various human failings (108–109). Parlevliet goes on to explore how this 13th century narrative is adapted over the years, so as to make Reynard's character more appropriate for a children's story, in the first case, by emphasizing only his cleverness and eliminating references to violent and criminal behavior (113) and, second, by altering the basic plot of a villain triumphing over the authorities (113). In *Fables*, Reynard retains his reputation for cleverness: in *Animal Farm* (Vol. 2), Reynard is not only able to parse Goldilocks' high-minded rhetoric, but is also able to escape the clutches of Shere Khan and Baghera by turning the two arrogant animals against one another (2.44). However, unlike Reynard from folk and fairy tale, who continually acts more or less outside the law, in *Fables* Reynard is from the beginning allied with the political elite of Fabletown and The Farm. He personally saves Snow White from Shere Khan's attack (2.57) and aids her as she works to retake The Farm from the rebels (2.51, 2.79); Reynard is then officially acknowledged for his service by Prince Charming (2.97). When Ozma transforms Reynard into a man, she refers to him as "Prince of loyal friends" (14.132), thus signaling her desire to retain him as a political ally. Finally, Rose Red includes him as one of the first six knights serving the new Camelot (20.182). In this fundamental adaptation of the source material, Willingham complicates reading Reynard as either a depiction of exalted animality or as yet another example of the denigration of the animal.

As he is helping her to escape the rebels, Reynard lets Snow White know that he finds her sexually attractive, further suggesting that her relationship with Bigby proves she is amenable to a cross-species liaison (2.54). The subversiveness of this desire, however, is mitigated by an implicit suggestion that Reynard wishes to be human. After making note of Reynard's service to Fabletown, Prince Charming says to him "I hope you'll forgive us for putting off any formal recognition of your inspirational acts of heroism for another occasion" (2.97). Though Charming never articulates what might constitute "formal recognition," Reynard connects the ideas of reward and transformation in his rebuke to the new mayor of Fabletown: "You didn't keep your promise to provide all the animal Farm Fables with permanent transformations.... If you had, I could have become a man" (8.96). When Ozma refers to Reynard's "loyalty" after transforming him, she reinforces the idea that to be human is a reward, a fulfillment of the animal Fable's dearest wish. This apparent deprecation of the value of the animal, however, is challenged in two ways. First, Ozma's act is not really a reward, but rather—as Geppetto points out—it is "a stunt" to advance her own political desires (14.139). Further, as Reynard sets out to test his new situation, he shows that his true desire is not to simply be human, but to have the ability to escape the confines of The Farm (15.28). As the narrative progresses, it becomes clear that Reynard still enjoys his animal guise, so that by the time he is chosen as one of Rose Red's six knights, she refers to him as "Sir Reynard, the fox knight" (20.182). Thus, it seems, the depiction of Reynard offers a challenge to the notion that humans are the superior species. When Geppetto scolds Reynard for daring to appear before him in animal form, Reynard—much like his predecessor from the original folktale—draws attention to Geppetto's own human failings, his "overabundance of self-esteem in the face of a ridiculous amount of self-inflicted calamity" (19.96).

Even in this most complex representation of the human-animal divide, however, it is difficult to see a real challenge to the humanist paradigm, perhaps because—in *Fables*—Reynard the Fox is not nearly as controversial a figure as he is in the source tales. Willingham's version of Reynard is "foxy" only insofar as he is like other clever Fables. The Reynard of the medieval period—though clearly a character in a beast fable—at least acts in ways associated with foxes: he steals things, he is sometimes violent, and he escapes capture time and time again. Thus, like many of the other

representations of animals in the comic book series, the potentially destabilizing effects of Reynard's animality are contained. Further, like Stinky,
Reynard fades from the main narrative once the focus shifts to the final
showdown between Snow White and Rose Red. For all the ways *Fables*
introduces the subject of borders and revolution, perhaps to invite questions about the arbitrariness of the hierarchical divisions humans have
devised, the representation of animals in the comic book series is ultimately contained and controlled, much like the non-human Fables on The
Farm.

Fathers and Sons

Toward the end of the crisis in *The Great Fables Crossover* (Vol. 13),
when the Fables have stopped Kevin Thorn from rewriting the universe,
Bigby and Snow White offer thanks to Jack Frost whose act of freezing
the air within Kevin's protective cube has stopped him from writing his
fateful words (13.212). Jack Frost is almost apologetic about having gone
forward with his heroic feat, due to his status as a mere "novice hero"
(13.213); he had been sent on the quest to find Thorn at the behest of his
father, the ever wily Jack Horner, who—in trying to avoid his son's questions—misdirects him by leaning on story conventions: "You can't just
walk up to your long-lost father, who you've been pining for for centuries,
and then simply start barking questions. That makes for a dull story. You've
got to first complete some sort of heroic quest, to prove that you're worthy
of getting the answers" (13.175). Despite her own frequent misgivings about
the various schemes of Jack Horner, Snow White stops Bigby short of
insulting him in front of Jack Frost, charging, "Don't tear down a man's
father right in front of him" (13.213). The portrayal of the relationship
between the two Jacks, father and son, is—in the first place—a satire of
the various profound quests undertaken throughout the *Fables* series, as
Jack Horner's exploitation of this narrative to get rid of his son undermines
the idea of the quest as avenue for spiritual awakening or the proving of
character. Importantly, Jack Frost is just as successful in defeating an adversary as, say, Boy Blue or Flycatcher, despite the dubious impetus for his
adventure. In the second place, this narrative arc brings into further relief
the multiple Father-Son relationships the text presents, including the relationship between the North Wind and Bigby, between Geppetto and
Pinocchio, and between Bigby and his own cubs, especially Darian and
Ambrose.

The multiplicity and narrative complexity of Father-Son plots in *Fables* strains against the fairly limited way fathers are portrayed in fairy tales, where their function is often reduced to: absence, subservience to a dominant female, cruelty, or task setting. As D.L. Ashliman notes in his entry on the "Father" in *The Greenwood Encyclopedia of Folktales and Fairy Tales*, while there are "[c]ountless stories [that] feature children abused by stepmothers ... the fathers typically are negligent ... or they are absent altogether" (334). Further, if one focuses solely on the role of fathers in relation to sons in fairy tales, the "cruelty" or "task setting" functions are given even more emphasis. Finally, unlike malign or benevolent mother figures, who are consistently active characters throughout a fairy tale, for the most part fairy tale fathers fulfill their function only to initiate a plot, though they may very well reemerge at the end of a tale to offer rewards or be punished. As Ashliman further remarks, however, while "[f]olktale mothers and stepmothers who mistreat their children typically are spared no punishment..., unlike their female counterparts, [cruel fathers] are seldom punished" (2008, 335). In a very basic sense, the *Fables* series eschews classic fairy tale functions of fathers simply because these plots have already been activated and are being explored *in medias res*, or—even more often—post-dénouement, though sometimes the back stories of important Father-Son relationships are revisited, as in the case of Geppetto and Pinocchio (6.157–162) and North and Bigby (*1001*, 72–84). Still, with respect to making use of fairy tale conventions, the clearest duplication of a classic fairy tale Father-Son plot is in the portrayal of Prince Brandish's relationship with his father, the King of the Golden Realm and House of Descry.

Like other kings from fairy tales, Brandish's father takes an active role in trying to manage his son's marital inclinations: he forbids his son from "marrying any peasant girl" (15.57). This use of the motif of the "cruel father" adapts to some extent the type of story where a king disowns his son, though the King of the Golden Realm most resembles folk and fairy tale fathers who are cruel to their daughters, as in, for example, the Grimms' "The Maid Maleen," a tale about a father who locks his daughter underground because he does not like her suitor, or even "The Robber Bridegroom," in which a father is so happy to get his daughter married that he gives her to a rich suitor, who also happens to be a murderer. In Prince Brandish's story, the King of the Golden Realm is both willful and cruel, plotting that the girl his son wants to marry be killed, so as to break the engagement vow (15.62). That said, what is most significant about this adaptation of the fairy tale motif of the cruel father is that the king's sons do not offer a moral corrective to their father's attitude: the second son,

Holben—whom Brandish has "promised" to young Rose Red—is presented as lazy, eager to be granted the throne, and mostly interested in having a wife so that he can bed her, no matter how young she is (15.57–58); Brandish is even more morally bankrupt, as is clear from the rest of his narrative. Even in this early scene, however, he does not counter his father's decree on the grounds of being in love; as he asserts: "I'm not addled by love, father. Far from it. I'm interested in attaching more power to our household" (15.58). Thus, this version of a father's cruelty initiating a plot does not resolve itself in a son achieving "happiness" or even with a sense of settling conflict, which suggests that Willingham is disinterested in rehearsing these types of plots.

Perhaps more so that any type of fairy tale, Freudian psychoanalysis seems to be a powerful guiding mythology for the explorations of fathers and sons. In a narrative arc entitled "The Destiny Game," collected in *Cubs in Toyland* (Vol. 18), the Big Bad Wolf encounters a turtle with a teacup on its back, but is too depressed to rouse himself and attack. The turtle inquires as to the source of the great Beast's melancholy and learns that the Wolf is upset that he will die "before any of my lofty goals were accomplished," his goals being "Standard stuff, really. Hunt and kill my father" (18.167). As Freud asserts in *The Interpretation of Dreams*, "*Oedipus the King* is what we call a tragedy of fate," a story as bound up with the strange permutations of destiny as any story in *Fables*. However, Freud goes on to note that "If *Oedipus the King* is able to move modern man ... [it is because his fate] could have been our own.... King Oedipus, who killed his father Laius and married his mother Jocasta, is only the fulfillment of our childhood wish" (202). In an almost textbook mapping of Freud's notion of the oedipal complex onto Bigby's story, we learn that Bigby was born the runt of a litter of seven cubs—much as Oedipus himself was born with a lame foot—and was treated with especial love by his mother, a wolf "as white and glistening as the snows" (*1001*, 73). The young wolf soon learns to hate his father, North, whom he blames for his mother's death (which is figured as her own lack, the emptiness she feels when North abandons her). The young wolf vows to conquer his castration/runt complex (*1001*, 77) and eventually become strong enough to kill his father (*1001*, 82). Though Bigby fails to kill North in their first meeting, the vow endures (*1001*, 84). Later, in fulfilling the second feature of the oedipal destiny, Bigby marries a woman whose name "Snow White" draws attention to her skin, which is "as white as snow." Willingham's playful adaptation—not only of the Grimms' tale "The Wolf and the Seven Young Kids," but also of Freud's famous oedipal analysis of Sergei Pankejeff, a patient

referred to as "The Wolf Man"—is not meant to reiterate Freud's theories
of childhood psychosexual development, but rather to draw attention to
the cultural importance of Father-Son tales, tales that have informed so
many human mythologies, social-scientific, spiritual, and storied.

Though *Fables* does not interrogate the quasi-incestuous relationship
between Bigby and Snow White, the ongoing conflict between Bigby and
his father emerges as a major subplot, one that explores, in the first place,
the qualities of identity as it is associated with "nature" and family and,
in the second place, the relationship among one's sense of guilt, of duty,
and of the impetus toward sacrifice. During Bigby and Boy Blue's philosophical discussion in the transitional space leading to the so-called
"Lands After Life," Blue suggests to his friend that a major source of his
power emerges from self-knowledge, chastising him: "After all this time,
you still don't know who you are, do you?" (20.109). Significantly, even in
this scene in which Bigby is visually represented as a majestic wolf, Blue's
instruction focuses on his status as "The Seventh Son of the North Wind,"
indicating that Bigby can neither ignore nor destroy his father's role in
the formation of his identity. The issue of familial identity has already
been raised via the introduction of Bigby and Snow White's cubs, who not
only enjoy the status of "royalty" because they are "grandchildren of the
North Wind" (15.139), but have been encouraged—both by North and
then by Snow—to fully explore their wind identity. North tells Snow that,
if the cubs are going to be able to hide the fact that they are "inhuman,"
they must be taught "to shapeshift ... if you wait too long, they won't be
able to learn it" (5.148). North's advice here suggests that it is important
that these children of a mixed-species union be taught to "pass," though
he also acknowledges the complexities of raising children born of two
"cultures," noting of his own son: "Bigby refused to be anything but a wolf,
since he never cared for me, and took more to his mother" (5.148).

In the final showdown between father and son, however, Bigby suggests that, when it came to his relationship with Winter, Bigby's mother,
North was unwilling to take seriously the inherent difficulties of such a
union if it meant he had to compromise a very self-serving definition of
identity: "I think claiming you have no control over your moods and core
beliefs is something you've made up to excuse your bad deeds" (16.98).
Here—as elsewhere—Bigby argues in favor of honoring the mongrel identity, the collision of natures, as attempts at purity tend to beget a type of
tyranny; this idea is most fully explored in Bigby's contemptuous response
to the incestuous, pure-blood community of werewolves that have settled
and interbred in Story City, Iowa (*Werewolves*). Purity of nature and its

relationship to identity becomes a direct source of conflict between Bigby and North, as North has threatened to kill Bigby's son Ghost, a so-called "Wild Zephyr," referred to by North as "a corrupted version of my kind. Something of an extreme birth defect" (5.151). North even suggests that it is because Snow White is "tainted" that she "produced a monster" (15.145). The portrayal of the North Wind's attitude toward what might be thought of as someone with a disability, or someone differently abled, reflects the text's clear contempt for purity-based eugenics: what is important in terms of identity formation is not purity of blood, but rather purity of character. Bigby ultimately accuses North of using the same excuse of "every other common villain" who, in order to enact power, retreats into morally suspect notions about identity as "nature" (15.98); the son thus forces his father to consider his responsibilities—not as the North Wind— but as a parent.

In the aftermath of this conversation, North participates in the most compelling version of the sacrificial narrative explored in *Fables*. In the rising action of *Super Team* (Vol. 16), in which Pinocchio and Ozma prepare for an imminent showdown with Mr. Dark, Pinocchio explains to Ozma, "A super team always beats the bad guy. It's like a giant unbreakable rule" (16.39). The battle with Mr. Dark, however, does not quite live up to this rule, as the bad guy is defeated, not by a super team, or even by the worthy opponent Bellflower, but by the sacrifice of North, who realizes that he loves his grandchildren so much that he wants them to have a father, one who is not absent (16.105). What the North Wind comes to realize in making his decision to trap Mr. Dark and himself within his casket of primordial winds is that parental duty is sacrosanct. The structuring of the Bigby and North plot prepares the reader for understanding the context for North's act which—to a great extent—seems out of character, and which otherwise undermines the story conventions that so galvanize Pinocchio and Ozma. Earlier, Snow White has magnificently guilted Bigby into attempting a reconciliation with the man he's vowed to destroy, arguing that "Mr. North is our children's grandfather and they adore him.... We're parents now, which means the kids absolutely come first, no matter what uncomfortable positions that puts us in" (9.112). Later, Bigby gamely returns the favor by using a similar argument against Snow when she resists leaving Haven before the battle with Mr. Dark: "Grow up and agree to do what you know is right. Your duty as a parent supersedes any responsibility you have to stay here and die bravely with me" (16.86). After North has sacrificed himself—and thereby proved the purity of his character— Bigby finds that he can no longer hate his father (16.128), thus suggesting that North's sacrifice is as much a part of his son's redemption story as his own. When the Fables were still preparing to battle Mr. Dark, Ozma expresses concern that both Bigby and Beast are weakened by their love for their family (16.56–57). However, the symbolic value of North's love for his grandchildren—and through them his son—suggests the importance of a different kind of strength.

Another intricately developed Father-Son relationship explored in *Fables* is between Geppetto and Pinocchio, as the text considers such notions as monstrous parenting and loyalty. In the opening scene of *The Dark Ages* (Vol. 12), a brief showdown occurs between the newly amnestied Geppetto and former Fabletown deputy mayor, Snow White: when Geppetto insults both Snow White's relationship with Bigby and her inability to comprehend the political consequences of undermining his empire, Snow counters with an assertion of zealous maternal self-righteousness: "You threatened my children. Do you think I'd hesitate to throw a thousand worlds into chaos to protect my cubs?" (12.15–16). What is interesting here is that—although *Fables* consistently represents Geppetto as a political father-figure, as a man whose love for his wooden "children" is crucial to his identity—his idea of parenting is shown to be totally illegitimate, especially in comparison to the claims of "Mama Bear" Snow White (12.17). Whereas Snow White's maternal role is metaphorically linked to an animal known for its "natural" protectiveness, Geppetto is most often linked with the literary figure of Dr. Victor Frankenstein, the man who creates new life through science. In *March of the Wooden Soldiers* (Vol. 4), Pinocchio explains to Boy Blue his attachment to his wooden soldier collection: "they're the only things I have to still remember my dad, who for all I know may be dead—or even worse—enslaved all these years" (4.79). The panel that includes this speech shows Pinocchio holding a copy of the novel *Frankenstein*, which he has been reading. Much later in the narrative, well after Flycatcher has transformed the army of wooden soldiers back into trees, Geppetto sends one of Pinocchio's former toys—named Woldred—on a quest into the newly located sacred grove, which Geppetto is banned from entering. When the toy soldier reaches the trees, they refer to their former "father" disparagingly as a "tyrant" bent on "remaking us into his own creatures," referring to Woldred himself as a "little construct—[a] little Frankenstein" (20.201). One clear consequence of Geppetto's unnatural approach to fatherhood is the failure of his first son to fully mature; although Pinocchio blames the Blue Fairy for his predicament, mostly with regards to the way his boyish appearance affects his sex life (15.10–11), Geppetto's failure to engage with Pinocchio as an equal—in the way that North engages Bigby—ensures that his son stays caught within a continuous plot of service, never emerging as the hero of his own life. One of the most startling intratextual cross-references in *Fables* links James Jean's cover image for Issue #76, "Around the Town" (12.9)—a narrative focusing on Pinocchio's first attempt to introduce his father to Fabletown—to a splash page in Issue #99 drawn by Inaki Miranda (15.142), in which identical Mundy figures are represented, now as Mr. Dark's witherlings. This cross-reference not only indicates the malign effects of Mr. Dark's presence in New York, but also reinforces the status of Pinocchio as mere servant to his father.

Comparing the relationships between Bigby and North and between Pinocchio and Geppetto thus reveals an inquiry into appropriate manifestations of loyalty in Father-Son relationships. In Bigby's view, parents are honor-bound to provide moral instruction to their children; as he asserts to North, "Any half-decent father can—and does. You support the good over the bad and thus teach the good" (9.174). Conversely, the intense loyalty Pinocchio feels for his father is shown to be, in the first place, ironic, and, later, perverse. In *March of the Wooden Soldiers* (Vol. 4), Pinocchio asserts at several points his belief that the existence of the wooden soldiers planning to attack Fabletown "prove my dad's alive" and that he is "the Adversary's slave" (4.164). Further, during the attack on Fabletown, Pinocchio runs into the battlezone to try and "stop [the] fighting" (4.204), showing that his loyalty to Fabletown is of a piece with that held for his father. Once it becomes clear that Geppetto is not a slave to the Adversary, but is "the power behind the throne—hundreds of thrones in fact" (6.149), Pinocchio's loyalty is retrospectively destabilized. Significantly, however, the text does not follow up this revelation with the son's rejection and/or usurpation of the cruel father, as might be conventional in a fairy tale plot. Rather, in representing the resurrected Pinocchio, whose loyalty to Geppetto is no longer "natural" but enforced through magic, the text allows for a more complex investigation of that quality as it might define character. In *War and Pieces* (Vol. 11), Pinocchio explains to Rodney and June that loyalty to his/their father means trying to help Geppetto to relinquish his despotic tendencies: "Out of our loyalty to him, we have to get him free of all that crap" (11.75). When Pinocchio emerges as one of the leaders of the F-Men, it is significant that he adopts a role similar to Dr. Charles Xavier, benevolent father-figure and mentor to the X-Men, or to Dr. Niles Caulder, leader of the Doom Patrol. Pinocchio here displays the maturation of his "natural" sense of loyalty, whereby the magical connection to his father does not inhibit his sense of right and wrong. During an argument with Ozma about the time he is spending interviewing volunteers for the F-Men who are clearly inappropriate, he argues that it is crucial "to honor [everyone's] willingness to sacrifice" (16.67). Thus, Willingham further undermines the relevance of an oedipal or a fairy tale model for exploring Father-Son relationships, as Pinocchio is able to "grow up" without destroying his father, and even without managing to save him.

As a foil to its examinations of relationships between adult sons and their fathers, the text also depicts Bigby parenting his cubs, especially Ambrose and Darian. On the surface, it appears that Bigby's approach to parenting is simply a continuation of his outlaw hypermasculinity, whereby he asserts his fatherly responsibilities via attacking and threatening hostile forces: when his six elder brothers—now monsters, living in the woods outside their father's castle—attack Ambrose, Bigby battles with them and then turns them into goldfish (9.178); when the three other Cardinal Winds suggest splitting up the cubs to see which one will emerge as the new North Wind, Bigby responds with predictable bravado: "No one is putting a hand on my cubs without my permission. And where each of you is concerned, permission is permanently denied" (17.56). However, in his interactions with the cubs, Bigby is arguably portrayed as the more emotionally responsive parent. After North dies, Ambrose admits to his father how much he misses his grandfather, lamenting, "I'm such a big baby. Not like you" (17.27). Bigby's response to his son is intimate and caring, and he is visually portrayed holding his son in a tactile expression of fatherly concern (17.27–28). Even more striking: when Ambrose relays the prophecy about the cubs, Snow White's expression of maternal care—her cry, "One of my babies is going to die?"—appears oddly irresponsive to Ambrose's clear distress in comparison to the attention Bigby has shown (17.32). Another remarkable portrayal of Bigby's standing as a loving father occurs when he meets Darian in the transitional space leading to the "Lands After Life": when he sees Darian emerge from the distance, Bigby transitions from the guise of predatory wolf, taking on human form so as to better hold his child (20.117). Crucially, the final discussion between Bigby and Darian, during which Dare proposes to tell his father—"man to man, wolf to wolf"–about the events in Toyland, does not produce a tale of competition, but of love. In terms of adapting the fairy or folktale, Darian's previous participation in a version of the Fisher King legend here recalls the Chrétien de Troyes variant, in which the Fisher King's narrative is associated with a story of finding the lost father (Kleiman, 969). However, unlike folk and fairy tales that culminate with the adult son taking the place of the father, the striking splash page showing Bigby and Darian walking into white space together portrays them not as man and man, but clearly as boy and father (20.118). Thus, the Father-Son relationship does not simply activate a plot, but is explored as emotionally complex and multifaceted in and of itself.

Finally, *Fables* depicts "modern" fathers who have daughters, not sons: Beast and Bliss, and Rodney and Junebug. Though many critics have read classic folk and fairy tales as containing cautionary and/or exemplary directives about the behavior of girls—for example, Perrault's "Little Red Riding Hood" or de Beaumont's "Beauty and the Beast"—the most powerful ur-narrative providing a context for both Beast's and Rodney's fatherly concerns is the backstory of Prince Ambrose/Flycatcher, as related in "A Frog's-Eye View" (*1001*, 64–71). In this tale, the Adversary's soldiers break into his home and, because of his surprise and fear, the prince reverts to a frog as per an old enchantment; he is then forced to watch helplessly as his younger children are killed, and as his wife and eldest daughter are raped (1001, 69). What is significant here is not the representation of sexual violence against women, which is, at least metaphorically, of a piece with many folk and fairy tales. The cautionary tale told here is not directed at potentially errant young girls who need to learn how to protect their chastity, but instead reflects a masculine anxiety about the importance of keeping one's daughters safe from sexual violation. Beast's fairy tale origins derive from a literary fairy tale—in particular de Beaumont's version—in which the father plays a prominent role, not only in terms of promising his daughter to her monstrous "suitor," but in terms of Beauty's willing sacrifice for her father. Inverting this narrative pattern, Beast's relationship to Bliss focuses on his desire for her safety, as well as his willingness to sacrifice himself for the community. In *Cubs in Toyland* (Vol. 18), Beast suggests to Beauty that their family stay in Haven, "away from the grind and danger of Fabletown" (18.33); Beast's suggestion constitutes the utopian dream about raising a daughter in what is basically a gated community. Later, however, in *Happily Ever After* (Vol. 20), Beast leaves Beauty and Bliss in Haven to go help the Fables fight Bigby, asserting to Beauty that his "duty to Fabletown," to the very community that offers the family sanctuary, comes even before his individual role as husband and father (21.68). When Bigby kills Beast, Beast's final words are for Beauty and Bliss (21.84). A similar modern father is Rodney, whose desire for Junebug is that she be safe: when Rodney, June, and Junebug move into Castle Dark, Rodney encourages Junebug to explore her new surroundings, explaining to a nervous June: "Kids go on adventures. She's on a great one now. And since there's nothing that can harm her here, let he have her grand, scary fun" (20.21).

Rodney's realization that Junebug's story of the giant rats may be true simply reinforces the idea that this former wooden soldier is now faced with
a real human fear about the safety of girls, even in seemingly sheltered
spaces.

Whereas many fairy tale fathers exit the story once the rising action
has been activated, most of the father figures in *Fables* are portrayed in
far more complex terms, at once challenging the conventional focus on
villainous or benign mothers and proposing that parent-child relations
need not resolve themselves via some sort of usurpation. The relative
complexity of these plots/relationships suggests a number of things,
including Willingham's interest in examining contexts for personal heroism that emerge irrespective of a family dynamic, as well as his concern
with depicting a wide range of masculine behavior. Unlike many folk and
fairy tales, the narratives in *Fables* represent the role of the father as something other than a cultural given; rather "fatherhood" is a status to be
proved or earned.

Snow White's Complex Femininity

In anticipation of an attack on Haven by Mr. Dark, Pinocchio and
Ozma work to assemble a "super team" of Fables who will do battle with
their new foe. While Ozma's primary focus is identifying those Fables who
show the least fear, thus undermining Mr. Dark's ability to feed on that
emotion (16.56), Pinocchio is more concerned with reproducing comic
book conventions, as he insists that the code of comic books necessitates
that "a super team always beats the bad guy. It's like a giant unbreakable
rule" (16.39). High on Pinocchio's list of priorities is the issue of costume,
a concern that calls to mind the way female superheroes are traditionally
depicted in comic books. While the issue of the costumed male superhero
has its own complexity, *Fables* calls attention to the objectification of
women in comic books in Rapunzel's retort to Pinocchio: "So basically,
you've been wasting my time with nine different costume fittings. Was all
this a dodge just to watch me undress so often?" (16.62). In her survey of
"Feminism," included in *The Encyclopedia of Comic Books and Graphic
Novels*, Trinna Robbins traces the often uneasy relationship between
women and comics, which are—for better or worse—"often thought of as
a thoroughly masculine realm" (212), and which "often [present] female
characters in a hypersexualized manner" (215). But the objectification of
women in a male-dominated genre is not the whole story, as Robbins—
herself an important force in underground comics—is quick to point out.

Lillian Robinson's *Wonder Women: Feminisms and Superheroes* considers such remarkably complex figures as Wonder Woman, Sue Storm/Invisible Woman, the Scarlet Witch, and She-Hulk examining the nexus of superhuman capability, desirability, professionalism, and traditionally "feminine" virtues, in particular the "temper[ing of] masculine violence" with "love" (19). In seeking out expressions of a feminist politics in comic books, Robinson welcomes a diversity of female characters and narrative situations, citing as a concern that comics will simply "reiterate[e] the now less than revolutionary notion that women can be powerful and that there is nothing left to prove or fight for" (134). In the construction of Snow White in *Fables*, the dealings with feminism and femininity are not straightforward; rather, various contradictory elements are left intact. Thus, even the more traditional elements of Snow White's femininity—for example, her attitude toward mothering or her outward appearance—are unsettled by her status as an active and self-sufficient woman.

In Vanessa Joosen's entry on "Snow White," included in *The Greenwood Encyclopedia of Folktales and Fairy Tales*, she notes that folklore scholars have "counted more than 400 variants" of the tale from most parts of the world. Alternatives to the figures of dwarves include "bears, monkeys, thieves, and old women, among others," while the apparent killing of the protagonist is accomplished in any number of different ways (885). In Joosen's summary of key features of the Grimms' 1857 version of "Snow White," the most well-known of all the variants, she enumerates the presence of a mother who wishes for a child and a queen who is jealous of the child's beauty (and in the Grimms' earliest collected version of "Snow White," the mother herself becomes jealous of her daughter—by 1819, however, the figure of the stepmother is added). Other important elements are the magic mirror, which confirms for the queen that the child is more lovely than she is; the deception of the queen by someone who convinces her that the child has been killed; the child's sojourn with the dwarves, whom she keeps house for; the poisoning of Snow White by the jealous queen; the presence of a prince who falls in love with the seemingly dead girl's beauty; her subsequent revival; and the punishing of the jealous queen (Joosen 2008, 884). Joosen's survey of various adaptations of the Grimms' version of the story—from duplications such as Disney's 1937 film to revisionist adaptations such as Robert Coover's 1973 story "The Dead Queen," Angela Carter's 1979 story "The Snow Child" and Tanith Lee's 2000 novel *White as Snow*—reflect a tendency to focus on and rethink the relationship between the queen and the child (2008, 885). That said, as Christine Shojaei Kawan points out in "A Brief Literary

History of Snow White," other contemporary writers—in particular Donald Barthelme and Günter Grass—have focused on the girl's relationship with her hosts, the dwarves (341). In considering variants of the tale that precede the Grimms' various versions of "Snow White," what Kawan observes is a "double theme of love and hatred," whereby "the heroine is persecuted by a jealous woman," and is also the love object of men, both those who are "personified [as] essentially dangerous things ... who would harm anybody else" and the one man whose deep mourning over a dead girl "is often on the verge [of] abnormality" (325–326). In considering how Willingham has rendered his version of the *tale* of Snow White— which is all the more complex in reconstructing, as it is developed over 150 comic book issues and many, many years—what is striking is the extent to which the representation of Snow's femininity in *Fables* depends on her exceeding the traditional and often adapted role of being "persecuted by" and "the love object of."

In a recent article entitled, "Wonder Woman Wears Pants: *Wonder Woman*, Feminism and the 1972 'Women's Lib' Issue," Ann Matsuuchi offers a fascinating analysis of the way Samuel R. Delany's infamous *Wonder Woman* #203 has been read, examining, for example, the disapproving response by Gloria Steinem to the choice to clothe Diana Prince, the Wonder Woman, in a white pantsuit (120). The anguished discussion among feminist readers of *Wonder Woman* as to the meaning of her customary costume, which has the potential to sexualize the female body but is also a marker of Wonder Woman's Amazonian power, is only relevant to the examination of Snow White in *Fables* because—until she receives her magical armor—Snow White, deputy mayor of Fabletown, almost never wears pants. Even during her duel with Prince Brandish, an uncommon instance when Snow is presented using a weapon rather than directing a battle, she is dressed in one of her customary shirt and skirt combinations, although she does take a moment to remove her heels before the duel (19.155). Though, as will be explored below, the traditional aspects of Snow White's femininity are often destabilized, it is also important to note the way she is sometimes constructed as one of the "weaker" sex. When Bigby returns from his mission to destroy Geppetto's Sacred Grove, now having been granted Wolf Valley, a space where both he and his cubs can live, he proposes to Snow White, using similar terms to those he used in *Mean Seasons* (Vol. 5), when he accused her of "cling[ing] to ... fantasies of castles and princes" (5.109). In fact, at no point in *Fables* does Snow White ever express any such desires; rather, when Rose Red balks at having to share a room with her sister at The Farm, it is Snow who reminds her sister that their hosts "can't afford to keep more than a single VIP guest room empty" (2.22). Still, in his proposal Bigby reminds her that he "can never offer you riches and palaces or any sort of luxury ... what I can offer you is a home in our valley, where we can raise our kids" (8.91). This scene reinforces the post-war romance comic convention that "The story ends happily when the woman marries an unexciting but nice man whom she had earlier rejected. The stability and security that he will provide is what matters most" (Wright 129). Though Bigby is clearly not a typical "unexciting but nice man," the union of Bigby and Snow White represents a celebration of her "self-denial for the sake of marriage" (Wright 130), as is reflected both in her response to Bigby's proposal, in which she concedes "you've defeated me" (8.92), and in the ensuing portrayals of Snow White in a domestic rather than professional space. Snow's standing as a traditionally feminine, self-denying wife and mother, however, is only one aspect of her character, and it is this ability to perform a number of traits that makes the portrayal of her feminine identity complex, dynamic, and potentially radical.

As Adam Zolkover notes in his article on *Fables*, "When we first meet the deputy mayor of Fabletown in the first issue of the series, even if we were to miss the nameplate prominently displayed on her desk, she would be almost immediately recognizable.... As she is illustrated, she evokes the famous description ... from the Grimms' *Kinder- und Hausmärchen*" (43). In Willingham's adaptation of the tale, however, Snow White's distinct physical features play only the slightest part in her tale, both in terms of structure and theme: Prince Brandish is attracted to her because of her "elegant energies" (15.58); her beauty does not stop the dwarves from harming her (15.69, 20.88); Prince Charming does not engage in any untoward adoration of Snow White in a glass coffin (15.71–72); and—as Bigby explains to Snow during their sojourn together in the woods—to him, she simply "smells right" (3.123). In the retelling of Snow White's tale that is part of Rose Red's recuperation, the figure of the jealous queen (the girls' aunt) is present, as is the magic mirror who pronounces on Snow White's loveliness (16.66); however, the reference to the jealous queen is so cursory as to be totally overwhelmed by another antagonist in this story: her sister, who blames Snow for her own unhappiness (15.74). Though Rose Red does claim to be jealous of her famous sister's relative popularity (2.108), the issue of Snow White's beauty isn't remotely the point. Thus, in this adaptation, the tale of Snow White isn't a cautionary lesson about vanity, nor does it explore the potent—even dangerous—motivating power of idealized beauty, which explains why the Magic Mirror in *Fables* becomes more closely associated with characters like Bufkin and Flycatcher. Interestingly, in a later scene in *Rose Red* (Vol. 15), Snow White herself broaches the issue of beauty, acknowledging to Nurse Spratt that "attractive people are always going to have advantages over those lacking physical beauty" (15.178). Snow's shaming of Nurse Spratt—not for her ugliness, but for her unkindness—does initiate a "Snow White"-like plot, in which Spratt wishes that "all those pretty ones [are ...] ugly" (15.207). However, Snow White's active role in initiating this plot differs from simply being beautiful, as per the source tale; as she explains to Beast, her reproach of Spratt is meant to "transfer her scorpion tongue away from you and onto me" (15.179). Further, Nurse Spratt's revenge plot is diffuse, as the object of her payback becomes Fabletown, not just Snow. Notwithstanding Zolkover's claim that Snow White in *Fables* looks the part, her tale is not advanced on the basis of the way anyone—female or male—responds to her physical beauty, making other aspects of her characterization more relevant in terms of the construction of her feminine identity.

Cristina Bacchilega's analysis of postmodern revisions to the "Snow White" tale explores the way various authors approach the idea of "the passively beautiful female character with very limited options" (29). In *Fables*, Snow White is anything but passive: in her first appearance in *Legends in Exile* (Vol. 1) as "Director of Operations," she explains to Beauty and Beast, "I do the real work of running our community" (1.17). Finding textual examples of Snow White's active role might even be overwhelming, though, in *Happily Ever After* (Vol. 21), Maddy the cat helpfully provides an overview. She cites key moments of Snow White's leadership, making note of The Farm Insurrection, and Snow's order to "burn the barn"; her overseeing of the Battle of Fabletown; and her role as Commander-in-Chief during the "invasion of Geppetto's empire" (21.25). Importantly, Snow White's activity is always reactive, by which I mean she retains her characteristic "goodness," working solely to protect herself, her family, or her community from harm. In this way, she resembles her mother, Lauda, whose response to the tradition of sibling "winnowing" is to try and find a way to "live out my life in peace—without murdering anyone" (21.167). Also like her mother, however, Snow White will respond with alacrity and enormous force if she or those she means to protect are threatened; soon after the scene depicting Lauda's offer to her sisters, the text depicts Snow White's dream that Bigby has killed the children; in response, she arms herself and flies to their rescue (21.171). Snow's reactiveness may thus be read as a bold revision of the source tale's representation of the way she keeps house for the dwarves, as she spends a lot of her energy in *Fables* "cleaning up" various messes made by others. However, in a moment of self-analysis, Snow White connects her mode of activity to self-sufficiency. When Snow reiterates her "tale" to Therese in *Camelot* (Vol. 20), the text provides a third version of her response to the dwarves' abuse, following the mediated account given in "The Fencing Lessons" (*1001*, 23–54) and her mother's account (15.66–72), which is somewhat suspect, due to its chief function as a healing story for Rose Red and due to the fact that the teller is really Hope (15.90). In her own telling, Snow White emphasizes to Therese that from a young age, she was on "her own" (20.87) and that she was determined to "survive" (20.88); her act of killing the dwarves is not an act of magic or even anger, but an act of "time," "practice," and "will."

The revisionist adaptation of Snow White's stay with the dwarves is also interesting to consider as it relates to representations in comic books of women undergoing violent treatment. Robbins notes that, "In 1999, a group of comic fans created a Web site titled 'Women in Refrigerators' ... to list and criticize the death and disempowerment of women in comic books," especially because such representations primarily served as plot devices to spur the male hero into action (216). At various points in *Fables*, the representation of the sexual violation of women operates within this sort of context. In *1001 Nights of Snowfall*, the tale "A Frog's Eye View" explains that being forced to watch helplessly as his children are murdered, and as his eldest daughter and wife are raped and then killed, addles the mind of the Frog Prince (*1001*, 69–70), and it is the later recollection of these acts that spur Flycatcher to "put away childish things and take up a man's burden again" (9.130). In *Rose Red* (Vol. 15), the depiction of Mr. Dark's damaging effect on the Mundy population returns again and again to the issue of controlling female sexuality: a Mundy police officer kills his partner and then himself after hearing about his wife's unfaithfulness (15.25); a Mundy construction worker is psychologically tortured by images of a former lover having sex with another man (15.127); and a Mundy police officer responds to the report of a violent sexual assault by telling the woman "it's no wonder, the way you're dressed" (15.135). Within Snow White's own sprawling narrative, there are three micro-versions of using the sexual violation of women as a plot device in a male character's narrative: in *Mean Seasons* (Vol. 5), Bigby suggests that his violent punishment of Ichabod has as much to do with Ichabod's "rape fantasies" about Snow as it does with Ichabod's disloyalty toward Fabletown (5.25), while, more complexly, the prince in "The Fencing Lessons" feels betrayed by his wife's refusal to share with him the violent experiences from her past (*1001*, 52–53). Finally, when Prince Brandish locks Snow White is his rooms, Bigby arrives to save her, bellowing "Where's my wife?" (19.123). This preoccupation with a very particular sort of female "disempowerment," however, occurs in contrast with the depiction of Snow White saving herself from her abuse— both from the dwarves and from Brandish—enacting revenge with clinical and terrible energy. Yet again, *Fables* presents an inherently conflicted vision of Snow White's feminine identity, whereby her identity always exceeds the source tale's focus on the way she is acted upon.

In contrast to her sister, Rose Red, whose sexuality will be explored in the next section, Snow White's relationship to sex is ambivalent, which is perhaps not surprising given the years of abuse she suffers. Despite their central status in *Fables* as an emblematic married couple, the sprawling text seldom broaches the issue of Snow White and Bigby's sex life, and the depiction is always somewhat troubled. After their night of conjugal sex in the Sacred Grove, following Bigby's long absence from Haven scouting potential sites for a new Fabletown, Snow White expresses embarrassment about having been "seen" by the trees (16.50); even more significant, she is clearly upset by Geppetto's reproach that she and Bigby "are allowed to carry on within [the Grove] like filthy animals" (16.51). In stark contrast to her customary facility for sharp retorts—such as the one she gives Geppetto when he questions her judgment about demolishing his empire (12.16)—in this moment, Snow White blushes deeply while Bigby soothes her (16.51). The disparaging description of Snow White and Bigby's sex life as bestial is also made by Prince Brandish, who talks about "pictur[ing] in my mind's eye you and that thing together" (19.93). Even Rose Red's response to her sister's demonstrative welcome of Bigby after the Battle of Fabletown refers to Snow as "suddenly so animal" (4.217). Though such comments about the nature of Snow White and Bigby's sexual relationship come from others, the text itself reinforces the idea that their sex is somewhat unseemly. *Storybook Love* (Vol. 3) opens with the graphically illustrated tale of Jack Horner and his lustful Southern Belle (3.22–23), and includes depictions of the violent deaths of several characters, including Tommy Sharp (3.74), Rex the mouse (3.93), Bluebeard (3.142), and Goldilocks, whose hyperbolically gruesome demise is depicted over seven pages (3.150–156). In this same volume, however, the sexual union of Snow White and Bigby is barely hinted at. Despite being on the run from the maniacal, homicidal Goldilocks, Snow White has the wherewithal to express concern that "there was only one tent and one sleeping bag" (3.120). Further, their sexual intercourse is only confirmed after the fact, when Snow White reports to Bigby that she is pregnant (3.167).

Thus, there is something about the representation of Snow's pregnancy that echoes a narrative of immaculate conception, recalling the Christian myth of Mary that Robinson marks as one of the foundational myths for a figure like Wonder Woman (15). Somehow, despite being the first pregnant Fable the community has seen in years, Snow remains sexually pure. In contrast to her ambivalent relationship to sex, however, Snow White understands herself as a mother in essentialist terms: even before giving birth, she expresses her belief that motherhood is sacrosanct, rebuffing Doctor Swineheart's suggestion that she might get an abortion and asserting that, unlike the Mundys, she understands her "duty and responsibility" (3.68). Somewhat contrastingly—though emerging from the same system of belief—she accuses the zephyr Mistral of being "inhuman" when he remarks that simply waiting for the death of every cub but one might be a useful procedure for determining the new North Wind (17.81). The point here is to draw attention to Snow White's distinctiveness in caring for her offspring in a way that is uninterested in other "great forces" of societal need or destiny. Ultimately, however, even Snow White's maternal identity is associated, not with her capacity to engender or express love, but with her strength: Therese admires her mother's stories about her heart "made of stone" (20.90), while Winter—in her all-seeing capacity as the new North Wind—declares "no one in all the many worlds is stronger than Mommy" (20.168). Both with respect to her sexual identity and her maternal identity, then, Snow White's femininity is both traditional and radical, stable and unsettled; importantly, however, she is never a passive recipient of persecution or of admiration.

When Maddy provides her overview of Snow White's history of being "the one who wins wars" (21.25), her goal is to convince Snow that—while the previous course of being reactive and protecting herself and her loved ones from harm may have been sufficient—a new strategy might be necessary, as Rose Red "is gathering an army right under your nose" (21.23). The final narrative arc of *Fables* revolves around the battle between the two sisters, though Snow White initially believes the sudden appearance of her black armor is related to keeping her safe from Bigby (21.47). In exploring Snow White in the guise of a magical knight, the text departs entirely from the source tale as, astonishing beauty notwithstanding, the fairy tale Snow White is not magical; crucially, it is the figure of the cruel mother/stepmother who possesses the powers of the witch. In this final arc, Willingham adds further layers to Snow White's already complex feminine identity, showing her both as a woman warrior and as a sorceress, able to transform herself at will, and even fly (21.171). In his entry on the

"Woman Warrior," collected in *The Greenwood Encyclopedia of Folktales and Fairy Tales*, John Stephens notes that such figures tend to "challeng[e] assumptions about both what it means to be a woman and the idea of the heroic" (1035), going on to note that in comic books the figure of Wonder Woman, the iconic female warrior, "mingled strength and autonomy with physical beauty and susceptibility to the lures of femininity" (1036). Like Snow White, Wonder Woman has hair as black as ebony, lips as red as blood, and skin as white as snow, a physical resemblance recently made use of in *JLA* #47–49, in which the evil queen from the Grimms' version of the fairy tale mistakes an image of Wonder Woman for her stepdaughter and puts her into an enchanted, death-like sleep (Waid). Buckingham's illustrations of Snow White's and Rose Red's armor (21.42), together with the Nordic names used in the tale of their mother and aunts (21.157), also recalls the work of British illustrator Charles Keeping, especially his drawings of Norse warriors, including Brunhilde who is one of the Valkyries. The Scandinavian mythological context that is increasingly apparent in these final depictions of Snow White—where even her raven wings recall the *valravn*, a creature from Danish folklore—complicates the way Willingham's version of the character, though never passive, is always associated with goodness. Though Flycatcher, among others, point out to Snow that her black armor "looks a bit sinister" (21.61), Snow White rejects the idea that she is "the villain" (21.47). Indeed, what the Scandinavian context suggests is that moral binaries are difficult to establish among such increasingly godlike figures, and that Snow White's femininity cannot be read as simply antithetical from that of her "bad" sister.

In the last complex story arc in *Fables*, entitled "Farewell," the two "sides" to Snow White's femininity are retained. One the one hand, she is time and again referred to as an excellent and deeply moral military strategist: though Winter scolds her mother for not "doing enough to prepare" for the showdown with Rose Red (22.49), in his guise as the narrator, Ambrose Wolf points out that Snow White's initiative to ask Flycatcher for help is an example of her "leadership" (22.59), as the involvement of the undefeatable wooden army would have resulted in—as Snow puts it— "less blood all around" (22.65). On the other hand, Snow White's military leadership is presented as emerging out of her domestic, maternal identity: even with the impending, potentially world-shattering battle with her sister looming over her, she muses to her husband and children, "I suppose someone should make some lunch soon" (22.48). At the end of the "Farewell" arc, the matter of Snow White's dual identity is disregarded, as— according to Ambrose Wolf, the writer of the Fables' histories—the main conflict that defines the "Final Battle" of the Fables is the struggle within Rose Red's heart (22.78). Though some readers hoping for a more explicitly feminist figure may balk at the hyperbolic heteronormativity suggested by the notion of "the Patmat" (22.144), or at the way Snow White's warrior instinct is primarily related to her role as a mother, what is potentially radical about this adaptation of the source tale is that Snow White is never a pawn in her own story, needing to be sacrificed, or rescued, or simply admired.

The Shaming of Rose Red

As noted during the discussion of Snow White's femininity, the magical arming of Snow White and Rose Red, which seems to occur in response to the threat Bigby poses to the Mundy community, prompts at least some in Fabletown to presume that a moral binary has been established. Snow White rejects the idea that her black armor signals that she is "the villain in some fantasy duel with my sister" (21.47) and, indeed, Rose Red's status as a "golden knight" is presently called into question. After she kills Leigh Duglas and takes her magical ring, Rose Red's armor becomes blood red and—as Hope suggests—this transformation doesn't merely reverse the binary, but makes it irrelevant: "it's not about who is the hero and the villain anymore" (21.128). At the metaphysical level, Hope's assessment may well be true, as the nature of Snow White and Rose Red's conflict proves to be related to matters of destiny, inheritance, and the properties of magic. A survey of the entire text of *Fables*, however, undermines Hope's judgment, as Rose Red is presented from the beginning as "the bad sister"; further, Rose's "badness" is often associated with her feminine identity. Thus, though Rose Red is, on the surface, a less "traditional" woman than her sister, a closer examination of her spates of unkindness and childishness, and even of her sexuality, shows a surprisingly disapproving representation of her feminine identity, one which often culminates in the idea of shaming.

In exploring the figures of helpers and adversaries in fairy tales, Hilda Ellis Davidson notes that "siblings of the same sex are in general hostile figures in the tales" (113); further, Davidson asserts that while the "human characters who most frequently seek to destroy the hero are his two elder brothers" (114), the adversary of a female protagonist is most likely to be a stepmother (112), with stepsisters taking a "less active [role] in evil doing than their mothers, but marked out by their spitefulness, envy, and lack of sympathy for others" (111). A tremendously widespread version of sisterly sibling rivalry is the tale type "The Kind and Unkind Girls," which in broad strokes "pits a good, obedient, self-effacing, or kind girl against her opposite, showing how proper behavior will be rewarded and bad behavior punished" (Martin 533). As Laura Martin points out in her description of such tales, they "most frequently [dwell] on traditionally female tasks of cooking, cleaning, and caring for others, and on virtues traditionally held to be feminine, such as obedience and modesty" (534). Thus, when the kind girl—who has been mistreated by her stepmother and stepsister—is rewarded, the advantages of performing properly feminine tasks and qualities are reinforced. Interestingly, though even in *Legends in Exile* (Vol. 1), reliable Snow White is contrasted with "wild child" Rose Red (1.23), the source for Willingham's version of these figures is not an example of "The Kind and Unkind Girls" tale. The Grimms' "Snow White and Rose Red" is collected in the third edition of *Children's and Household Tales*, though their own source was German writer Caroline Stahl's "The Ungrateful Dwarf"; in Stahl's version, there is no distinction made between the sisters, who are only two of a "poor couple['s] … many, many children" (Stahl 772), and the focus of the story is how the helpful girls are rewarded and how the ill-mannered dwarf is punished. The Grimms added a marriage plot and magic to the story, as the first part of their version of "Snow White and Rose Red" describes the girls' kindness to a bear, who is eventually proved to be an enchanted prince. The Grimms also enlarged the characterization of the two sisters, describing Snow White as "more quiet and gentle than Rose Red, who preferred to run around in the meadows and fields, look for flowers and catch butterflies" (Grimm 774). It is this nominal distinction between the girls, together with their childhood promise to "never leave each other" (Grimm 774), that forms the basis of the revisionist adaptation in *Fables*.

On the one hand, the "wild child" version of Rose Red in *Fables* recalls the playful girl who delights in nature from the Grimms' tale. Though the reason she presents to Snow White about her desire to run The Farm is that "at long last we're back to being equals again" (2.110), she is much beloved as a leader and seems to have genuine affection for the non-human Fable community. In the period leading up to her final showdown with Snow White, a cricket offers her the chance to be a "queen of [a] new Eden" (21.145), suggesting that—if not for other influences—Rose Red once had the potential to retreat entirely from the human social sphere. Willingham also enlarges the source tale's emphasis on Rose Red's playfulness in two important ways: first, her "wildness" is revised as a kind of bravado, whereby the young Rose Red claims "if anything tried to hurt me, I'd chop it up with a sword" (15.33), and, second, her love of nature is revised as a type of reckless kindheartedness, whereby—as the narrator of "Diaspora," a story contained in *1001 Nights of Snowfall*, attests—her willingness to aid a dangerous witch emerges from the same impulse as her tendency to "adop[t] injured animals and broken-winged birds" (*1001*, 112). All of Rose Red's generosity and liveliness, however, is set in tension with other aspects of her character that are reminiscent of the archetypal "Unkind Girl." Especially when it comes to dealing with her sister, she is sometimes driven by spite and envy; for example, her desire to seduce Prince Charming is entirely a product of her wish to "punish" Snow White (15.87). More significantly, Rose Red is often portrayed as engaging in bad behavior, of the very sort that in the tale type would mark her as unfeminine and undeserving of any sort of reward. While the contradictions of Snow White's identity destabilize the attempt to mark her more traditional activities as proof of a retrograde vision of femininity, Rose Red's bad behavior, which is visible in her redemption narrative, in her function as a paladin of Hope, and in her status as sexually active woman, offers a much narrower vision of appropriately feminine conduct.

To suggest that the depiction of Rose Red in *Fables* represents a more conservative conception of proper femininity than the depiction of Snow White seems, at first glance, to be absurd. For every skirt and shirt combination Snow appears to have in her wardrobe, Rose Red has a pair of pants and a t-shirt; while Snow White blushes in response to Geppetto's disparaging reference to her sexual life, Rose Red—from *Legends in Exile* (Vol. 1) forward—is shown to be comfortable with her own desiring body; while her sister, after giving birth, leaves her professional position, gets married, and takes up the traditional role of the housewife and mother, consistently putting forward the position that "the kids absolutely come first" (9.112), Rose Red transitions from party girl, to administrator of The Farm, to magical agent of Hope, to the second coming of King Arthur, dedicated primarily to her own ambitions. Further, her early association with bad behavior (as opposed to evil or great power) makes her a good candidate for a redemption narrative, a plot structure that, in *Fables*, is primarily associated with male characters and their negotiation of (admittedly complex) forms of masculinity. Like Flycatcher, Rose Red emerges from a lengthy funk after having been given a charge: to "fight for the people you love" (15.89). Also like Flycatcher, Rose completes various important tasks associated with the redemptive quest: she bathes and arms herself (15.92–97); she gains wisdom through a trial, which in Rose Red's case is not a journey through a wasteland but rather a day spent listening to the complaints of numerous Fables (15.113–115); she triumphs over those who would undermine her leadership, forcing the removal of Geppetto's bodyguards, Alder and Aspen, from The Farm (15.119) and allying herself with Brock Blueheart's religious vision (15.117). Toward the end of the day during which Rose Red reestablishes her role as rightful leader, she engages in a moment of spiritual renewal and proper humility, asking forgiveness of her sister (15.122). However, unlike Flycatcher who ultimately proves his worthiness through suffering, battle, and self-sacrifice, Rose Red doesn't actually get the chance to "fight for the people [she] love[s]." At the crucial moment when Rose Red has put together an advisory council and declared the framework for their preparations to fight Mr. Dark, Frau Totenkinder—now in her younger guise of Bellflower—shows up to announce her intention to "slay the Dark Man in a formal duel—single combat" (15.120). Further, when Mr. Dark escapes his gold "prison" and apparently destroys Bellflower, Rose Red calls for a retreat to Haven (15.199). While these moments serve as a striking plot twists, and are perfectly in keeping with the proliferating narratives of *Fables*, both Bellflower's pronouncement and Rose Red's call for "abandoning The Farm today" (15.199) underlines an important feature of her narrative, which is the absence of the depiction of real suffering.

At one point during Rose Red's day of attending to community grievances, Bigby shows up—not to complain, but to let his sister-in-law know that "Snow and I have your back, kid. Always" (15.115). While Bigby's gesture, along with hearing the tale of Snow White's torment at the hands of the dwarves, provides context for Rose Red's plea for her sister's forgiveness, the use of the label "kid" is also crucial, as it is the consistent representation of Rose Red as immature that undermines her role within a legitimate narrative of redemption. While the boyishness of Boy Blue and Flycatcher connects to their standing as everyman figures, elevated as heroic purveyors of nostalgia for common sense and simplicity, Rose Red's immaturity marks her only as a "brat." It is sometimes the case that Rose self-consciously makes use of her "bad girl" reputation to fool others, as is the case during the revolution at The Farm when—according to Bigby— "Rose convinced the revolutionaries that her sympathies were with them" (2.102), in order to buy time and prevent the immediate execution of Snow White. This highly mediated evidence of Rose Red's prudence, however, is not enough to counter the prevailing idea that most of her schemes derive from both her playfulness and spitefulness, which is in keeping with the adaptation of the source material. Not only does the text show Rose Red dressing up as a pirate to play revolutionary (2.48–49), but after the failed revolution and Snow White's recovery from being shot, the legitimacy of Rose Red's anger at her sister is called into question. On the one hand, Rose Red is brought to tears by thoughts of her own unpopularity, complaining "no sister needed or desired, thank you so very much!" (2.109). In contrast, the final panel of the volume shows Snow White grieving in private for the sufferings of those at The Farm, for the thought of her once-lost sister, and—most significantly—for the death of Colin Pig (2.112). This uneven juxtaposition, which highlights the relative paucity of Rose Red's notion of suffering, is repeated later in *Fables*. As Boy Blue lays dying, Rose refuses to take part in the vigil for him, telling her new husband, Sinbad, "No one needs me for nothing. Don't you get it? I'm the bad sister" (12.115). Later, in contrast to the portrayal of Snow White's horrific history, the representation of Red Rose's ungrateful response to the news that her sister is alive underlines Rose's self-centeredness (15.74), recalling not the playful figure from the Grimms' version of "Snow White and Rose Red," but rather the ever-aggrieved dwarf from Stahl's story. Even her anguished response to hearing the tale of the Little Match Girl culminates in Rose Red's demand that her cricket guide take her away on the grounds that the scene is upsetting (17.113). The representation of Rose Red's tendency to sulk, especially in comparison to portrayals of more serious pain and suffering, undercuts the idea that she is a fully developed adult woman, despite all external evidence to the contrary.

Bigby's assertion that Rose Red is an "insufferable little brat" (12.119), an accusation he levels when Rose Red selfishly refuses to visit Boy Blue on his death bed, is thus a fairly accurate assessment of the way her character is often portrayed. The volume *Camelot* (Vol. 20), which includes the narrative of Rose Red's attempt to recreate the kingdom of King Arthur, opens with the story "Junebug," in which Rodney and June's daughter is sent off to explore Castle Dark and "have an adventure" (20.16). What Junebug discovers is a hall full of giant rats, though when she tries to report this to her parents, they assume she's making up a story (20.28–29); only when Rodney and June see the scratches on their daughter's back do they consider that she might be telling the truth (20.30). This prefatory tale that pits a child's real terrifying ordeal against adult assumptions about the child's propensity to merely play at adventure operates in ironic tension with the representation of Rose Red's scheme to recreate the iconic Round Table. Other representations of children in *Camelot*—for example, of Winter, of Darian, and of the now grown Therese—reinforce this irony, as in comparison with the serious mindsets and/or sufferings of these figures, Rose Red seems childish. As Rose is watching the series of challenges between her would-be knights, Winter, the new North Wind, spends her time monitoring her realm and visiting such figures as Santa Claus and Lumi, making sure of their allegiance to her and to Snow White (20.175, 20.180); as Lumi observes, Winter is both a "little girl in aspect" and "weighed down by the heavy wisdom of centuries" (20.179). Darian is shown only briefly, as he talks to his father in the space leading to the "Lands after Life": though Darian is a child both in aspect and in psyche, he has suffered and sacrificed in ways that give profound weight to his question for his father, "Did I do okay?" (20.118). Like Darian, Therese has also suffered greatly, and it is during her explanation to her family of the awful experiences she and Darian had in Toyland that Rose Red barges in, demanding to see her niece and nephew (20.41). The depiction of Rose Red's interruption of the family scene works to increase the sense that her Camelot plan is ill-considered, this even before the Lady of the Lake warns her about "drag[ging] all of it up again" (20.150). The first tier of the page depicting Rose's arrival shows the image of Ambrose's toy knights circled around a miniature round table (20.41) and, when Rose Red steps back in surprise after being told that the woman she doesn't recognize is Therese, she breaks this table (20.42). Further, her questioning of Therese about the events that occurred in Toyland does not produce empathy or sorrow or horror, but simply gives Rose Red the idea that she too can play knights; the text emphasizes the inherent and problematic playfulness of Rose's idea, first in the way she refers to Therese's experience as a kind of game, calling the subjects of Toyland "toys" (20.50), and second in the final full-tier panel of the scene, which shows a close-up image of the broken table (20.52).

Even after she has initiated her plan of collecting a cadre of Knights of Second Chances, Rose Red's method of negotiating with others—for example, with King Cole, who is worried about community expenditures, or with Snow White, who is furious at Rose for releasing Brandish—relies heavily on childish forms of manipulation: as she remarks to Cole, "you and I both know I'm going to get my way in the end. So why not save time and surrender now?" (20.125). While the concept of the "second chance" connects with Rose Red's tendency to advocate for social justice projects, a feature of her leadership style that I discuss more in Chapter Three, the project also sheds light on the paradoxically narrow representation of Rose's femininity. When Rose Red first bursts into Dr. Swineheart's consulting room, gun blazing (20.70), her act of dealing forcefully with Prince Brandish seems refreshingly straightforward, especially in contrast to the previous equivocations of those in Fabletown and to Dr. Swineheart's

amoral stance. Later, however, this seeming attempt at extra-systemic justice—of the very sort that Snow White engages in when she takes on the
dwarves—is proved to be part of Rose Red's Camelot "game." As she
explains to her sister, "If Brandish can come back from all he's done …
then the concept of the second chance is proven" (20.81). The ensuing
argument between Snow White and Rose Red, however, makes clear that
Rose Red's primary agenda is not to provide a context for Brandish's moral
edification, but rather to pursue her own "absolute, until-the-end-of-my-
days purpose in life" (20.85). Such a statement about a life's purpose might
be read as evidence of Rose Red's maturity, as well as of her ability to articulate clear goals for leadership and community building. However, the
braiding of narratives in this section of Camelot (Vol. 20) undermines this
reading: juxtaposed with the conversation between the sisters are scenes
in which Ozma and Morgan Le Fay report to King Cole, and then to Snow
herself, that she is destined to die "from a sword thrust, straight through
the heart" (20.96), as well as Snow's recounting of her traumatic past to
Therese (20.87–89). Again, in contrast to these representations of Snow
White's costly sacrifice and real suffering, Rose Red's proclamations about
purpose seem both childish and narcissistic, whereby she resembles not
her resolute sister but the evil queen obsessed with her own appearance
in the magic mirror (20.87). Finally, despite her childish statement to Cole
that "Snow will forgive me eventually" (20.125), the text confirms that
Rose Red's act of freeing Brandish is both self-indulgent and irresponsible,
as proved when he murders Weyland Smith (21.65).

The cumulative effect of the focus in Fables on Rose Red's playfulness,
on her narcissism, and on her irresponsible choices is to deepen the sense
that—in fact—she is one of the "Unkind Girls," whereby her failure to display appropriately feminine traits warrant punishment. Importantly, the
text's most compelling depiction of the sort of punishment Rose Red
undergoes is also the text's most retrograde vision of her problematic femininity. Adam Zolkover argues that the consistent representation of Rose
Red's sensual and sexual self "serves as a manifesto for the subversiveness
of the series" (45), suggesting that such emphasis on the corporeal "exposes
the rigidness and prescriptive moral didacticism of fairy-tale patriarchs
like Perrault and the Brothers Grimm" (48). Though it is true that Rose
Red is presented as a desiring woman, the depictions of her sexuality
appear to culminate in a narrative about shaming, thus undermining the
idea that all moral didacticism is absent from the exploration in Fables of
the continuum of feminine identities. As Zolkover notes, "over and over
throughout the course of the first ten issues, [Rose Red] is depicted

consistently in flirtatious or amorous relations with the opposite sex" (45), a pattern that continues beyond the segment of the series Zolkover's early essay examines. In opposition to her sister, whose relationship with Bigby retains many of the traditional features of fairy tale notions of "true love," Rose Red has many lovers, though her relationship with most of these figures is in some way based on deception, insincerity, or misery. In *Legends in Exile* (Vol. 1), her relationship with Bluebeard is proved by Bigby to be part of an elaborate money-making scheme cooked up by her boyfriend, Jack, and—crucially—the revelation of this deception occurs in public. At the center of Bigby's beloved enactment of "the famous parlor room scene" (1.105) is the image of Rose Red, who is often shown in the midst of the other Fables in postures depicting her embarrassment (e.g., 1.105, 1.114, 1.116). Though the depiction of her (failed) relationships with Sinbad and Jack don't contain such public performances of being humiliated, the relationships themselves are presented as humiliating. Her short-lived, superficial marriage to Sinbad is dealt with only insofar as the text depicts how Rose Red finds Sinbad's tales of military heroics sexually arousing (12.44), and how she "divorces" Sinbad upon learning of Boy Blue's illness (12.115). During her also short-lived reunion with Jack at The Farm, she allows him to have sex with her despite having no desire for the activity, or for him. The implicit degradation of this act is reinforced, first, in the way Jack's metafictional reference to the voyeuristic position of "the Readers" makes the sex more "public" and, second, in the way Rose Red's inert posture is almost immediately juxtaposed with the image of Beauty laying on top of Beast in a moment of post-coital, conjugal happiness (13.88–89). Significantly, while the text implies that the sex between Beauty and Beast is procreative, a "magical" event that will produce Bliss (13.89), Rose Red's response to sex with Jack is to state "the fact that I let you back into my bed is the proof that I've hit rock bottom … you're the man I deserve" (13.102).

Finally, the representation of Rose Red's relationship to Boy Blue, which is ostensibly the impetus for her redemption narrative, emphasizes not her right to make her own choices in love or sex, but rather the appropriateness that a woman like her should feel shame. In the first narrative of *War and Pieces* (Vol. 11), the portrayal of the backroom political machinations preceding the attack on the Adversary are prefaced by Boy Blue's botched attempt to woo Rose Red. In this scene, it is Boy Blue's response to rejection that seems petty: when Blue accuses Rose of acting like all women in being incapable of seeing past their friendship, Rose points out the unfairness of his claim, stating "I don't represent all women. I have enough trouble just speaking for myself" (11.26). In the aftermath of the war, however, the text explores the twinned narratives of the rise of Mr. Dark and a renewed confrontation between Boy Blue and Rose Red. The juxtaposition of these stories is significant, as the text explores the idea of just and unjust punishment. As Frau Totenkinder explains to Snow White, Mr. Dark's interest in the Fables is not arbitrary: "I think it wants to redress some wrong we did it, but so help me, I can't pin down what that might possibly be" (12.114). As it happens, Mr. Dark himself explains the source of his anger, which is that the Fables have made use of his magical bag, having turned it into the Witching Cloak (12.56). However, the notion of a rational explanation for Mr. Dark's actions is undercut by his status as one of the Great Powers, as simply "the dark one just out of sight … as the scary thing lurking under every bed and hiding in every closet" (12.113). In other words, the idea that the Fables might indeed deserve the redress Mr. Dark insists on pursuing evaporates in the face of his symbolic function as the embodiment of darkness and fear; thus, the Fables remain on the "right" side of the contest and Mr. Dark's desire for punishment is marked as unjust and irrational. In contrast, Rose Red—whose marriage to Sinbad has already been proved to be a matter of her whim and possibly perverse fancy—apparently merits the rebuke she receives from Boy Blue when she suggests, in a moment of profound sadness at her friend's predicament, that they get married before he succumbs to his injuries. Blue, who self-righteously claims the privileges of a "dying man" (12.122), uses his last moments with Rose Red to itemize her character flaws, pointing out to her that every sexual and relationship choice she has made has been inappropriate. Boy Blue thus rehearses a complex, though increasingly typical misogynist response to the figure of the sexually empowered woman, which is that because of his own "goodness"—his self-professed "crav[ing] … to be dull and ordinary" (12.123)—he somehow deserves Rose Red's love. It is due to Rose's lack of feminine obedience to this narrative that she is justifiably punished, shamed, and summarily dismissed. Importantly, the text confirms the rightness of Boy Blue's judgment of Rose Red, as shown in her own commitment to the idea that it is now her task to "becom[e] worthy of him" (12.137).

In the final volume of *Fables*, the redemption of Rose Red is the core theme. After raising her army of "monsters, demons, and grumpkins" (22.54), as well as those soldiers who "died while holding out hope" (22.57), she takes time during the evening before battle to disguise herself and walk amongst her troops. During this walk—which alludes to Act IV, Scene i of Shakespeare's *Henry V*, when King Henry takes a similar walk on the eve before the Battle of Agincourt—she meets a cloaked figure who gently disputes with her the rights of "great personages" to send common folk into battle (22.71). This cloaked figure, who is drawn to resemble Boy Blue, reminds Rose Red that Snow White has borne sons (22.72), thus indicating to her that the prophecy that defines the sisters' family history is inconsistent and therefore subject to further revision. Whereas King Henry's lesson in humility forms the context for his rousing Saint Crispian's Day speech to his troops, during which he proclaims his commonality with the brotherhood of soldiers, Rose Red's new understanding occasions her total retreat. She leaves the Mundy world by herself, with an apology to her sister for the way she "drop[ped] the ball—a lot" (22.77). Thus, the redemptive "battle" that takes place in the "heart" of Rose Red culminates with the self-proclaimed "easy" (22.39), bad girl walking away, alone. The final image of Rose Red in the main series occurs in "The Last Snow and Bigby Story," when Rose Red is escorted to a massive family reunion hosted by her sister and brother-in-law. Here again, even after a thousand years of self-imposed exile, Rose Red is sidelined, tucked into the upper left-hand corner of a double barreled gatefold, looking at the extended Wolf clan (22.148). For all Rose Red's wit, sensuality, bravery, and personal vision, in the *Fables* universe, such a woman is necessarily marginal.

Family and community members, the powerful, the shamed, and the excluded: the examination of interpersonal relationships reflects a persistent concern in *Fables* with how we attain a secure subject position, especially in a world in which traditional roles are undergoing change and in which old privileges are under scrutiny. The community is represented as a site of comfort and belonging, but also of conflict and—sometimes—real cruelty. Though *Fables* is a comic book series peopled with archetypal figures from old tales, it explores the emotional toll of intimate, complex interrelations and power struggles and stratifications. In the next chapter, this community is explored as a polis, as an entity that must function in practical terms and that defines itself as a type of nation.

3

Politics: History, Power and Leadership

During a candid discussion with Cinderella, Rose Red acknowledges that becoming the administrator of The Farm likely means she'll "have to get [her] own hands dirty"; according to Cindy, Rose's ability to be honest about political dishonesty leaves her "miles ahead of just about every other bureaucrat in history" (8.116). Though *Fables* often reflects various histories, the world it most often grapples with is explicitly contemporary, and often overtly a post–9/11 American space. In this space, power struggles often require duplicitous behavior and often result in violence. Paradoxically, the representation of the "real" political milieu in *Fables* emerges via the pursuit of a number of fantasies—fantasies about manhood, about leadership, and about the nation. A key issue within these overlapping fantasies is the pursuit of justice and whether such a thing is possible, or whether we are left with nostalgia for a simpler time when stories about nation could be believed.

This chapter examines acts of leadership and administration, as well as acts that seem to complicate and challenge the role of citizenry. The focus is the way Bigby comes to represent the myth of America, the way governmental systems operate, and the way notions of cultural difference and of political expediency are intertwined. The examination of political dilemmas and machinations brings into relief the exploration in *Fables* of how we read systems, how we worry about security, and how we try to understand the mechanisms of power and politics.

Bigby as America

In chapter two of "March of the Wooden Soldiers" (collected in *March of the Wooden Soldiers* [Vol. 4]), the newly arrived Red Riding Hood balks when Mayor Cole informs her that—like all other recent emigrants from the Homelands—she will have to be interviewed by Bigby Wolf, the sheriff of Fabletown. In response, she exclaims, "you'll have me interrogated by the wolf who tried to kill me? This is a world of madness!" (4.98). Riding Hood's reaction is understandable, as the former status of Bigby as a monster and dedicated killer persists as a concern amongst many Fables, even those who depend on him to maintain order in the community. Earlier in the volume, Bigby questions Mayor Cole on his handling of the case of Prince Charming's murder of Bluebeard, suggesting that Cole's desire for Bluebeard's fortune has muddied the investigation. Even in this situation—when it is Bigby who argues that "working with the law takes time" (4.66)—the Mayor all but threatens to remove him from his job, and the pictorial image of a giant wolf towering over Manhattan indicates the instability of Bigby's social identity. By the end of the narrative arc, it is Bigby in monstrous wolf form that saves Fabletown from the wooden soldiers (4.208), and Red Riding Hood, now revealed to be Baba Yaga, who must be defeated (4.219). On the one hand, a tremendous ambiguity is built into Bigby's character, as he is at once animal and man, monster and god, predator and savior, outlaw and sheriff, loner and family man, killer and progenitor; on the other hand, the figure of Bigby is a steadfast anchor in the text, as crucial to the entire series as the fated, dueling sisters Snow White and Rose Red. In his commentary about Bigby Wolf, contained in Jess Nevins' *Fables Encyclopedia*, Willingham asserts, "He's my template for what America used to be, and should be still: the best guy to have as a friend, especially when you're in trouble, and someone you never want to have as an enemy. I suppose it's obvious I like the fellow" (30). And though it is the character of Ambrose Wolf who most fully stands in for the author-figure, it must be acknowledged that only Bigby Wolf shares the initials of Bill Willingham. In its complex depiction of Bigby, the text shows its nostalgic dependence on traditional notions of American masculinity, while also reflecting an increasing anxiety about the possibility of emasculation and the weakening of certain conceptions of nation.

As many comic book scholars have noted, the superhero genre in general—and the figure of vigilante hero in particular—is weighed down by moral uncertainty. In *The Power of Comics: History, Form, and Culture*, the authors note that a defining feature of the superhero comic is violence: "Superheroes do not just oppose evil, they *fight* it" (200, emphasis in original); further, the goal of defeating evil is almost always pursued through extra-systemic means, whereby "superheroes teach the lesson that justice is more important than law" (208). In "The Rise of Vigilantism in 1980s Comics: Reasons and Outcomes," Tyler Scully and Kenneth Moorman explore the cultural context for the contemporary emergence of increasingly violent, yet also self-reflexive titles featuring vigilante protagonists, arguing—first—that vigilantism in America has its roots in the 1800s, which was a frenzied period of settlement and fortune seeking: "In an environment lacking an organized system of crime control, an alternative emerged from the citizens themselves in the form of the vigilante mob" (636). Second, Scully and Moorman point out that, in the 1980s, crime rates in the United States were reported (sometimes in exaggerated terms) to be at historically high levels, leading to such trends as increased incarceration rates, increased gun ownership, and a decrease "in the typical citizen's faith in the traditional institutions of law and order" (638). It was in this cultural milieu that a new vigilante hero emerged, one who did not simply apprehend villains and turn them over to police, but who meted out "justice" in the form of more or less violent punishment (642). More recently, in the post–9/11 environment, the role of the vigilante hero has become even more complicated, as the state itself is often portrayed as operating "outside the law," and as fear is understood to be a manufactured way of controlling the citizenry. Nickie D. Phillips and Staci Strobel point out in *Comic Book Crime: Truth, Justice, and the American Way*, that "in the post–9/11 age, superheroes may be resonating with readers who are experiencing political frustration at the pervading world view of fear and of the perceived need to protect only oneself, at the expense of the collective" (50). In the case of Bigby, the tension between operating inside or outside the law, and between standing for state-imposed control versus community protection, is embodied in the dual persona of man/ wolf. In his guise as the chain-smoking, trench coat-wearing sheriff, Bigby functions as a no-nonsense minder of an eccentric and volatile population; as a wolf, he is an enforcer of justice that eschews due process. As a man, he is involved in all manner of state surveillance, secret interrogations, and strategic wartime maneuvering; as a wolf, he acts instinctively, not strategically, and is a devoted and powerful protector of his community, especially those he loves.

Willingham's description of Bigby as a "template" for "America" is a tantalizing assertion, suggesting that the ambiguity of his character—the veering between predator and protector—does not in any way undermine the essentially honorable function of enacting certain types of political power. Willingham's description also draws attention to Bigby being a certain kind of "guy," equal parts best buddy and dangerous enemy. The complex characterization of Bigby brings together conceptions of America, of vigilantism, power, and justice, and of being "that guy," reflecting the text's concern with the way the meaning of righteous power has become muddied, as well as the way that this muddiness can be linked to current discussions of the so-called "crisis in masculinity." As various scholars and theorists have discussed, the contemporary notion of a crisis in masculinity (a notion that has persisted at least since the 19th century, undermining to a large extent the definition of "crisis") refers to the way the previously privileged social, legal, and economic status of white, straight males in Western culture has been challenged, leading to a sense that—in Sally Robinson's words—white men have become "marked," in that their privileged status has become both visible and subject to contestation (2–3). Michael Kimmel's cultural history, *Manhood in America*, discusses both the historical and structural forces leading to the "general confusion and malaise about the meaning of manhood" (288), as well as the way such confusion leads to current reactions like "nostalgia" and "seething anger" (290). In *Comic Book Crime*, Phillips and Strobel examine, in the first place, the way hegemonic conceptions of masculinity are embedded in comic books and, in the second place, the way those conceptions are countered by the introduction of, for example, gay characters or female crime fighters (168). Yet, in their conclusion, the authors gesture to the notion of crisis or backlash commenting on their experience interviewing focus groups: "Readers may be attracted to comic books precisely for the conservative ideological content—from retribution to white hegemony.... Further, the assumption of whiteness or maleness may elicit a certain transgressive thrill in the contemporary globalized world, particularly when coupled with the kinds of American nostalgia the books often evoke" (225–226). In other words, because the discourse of masculinity in crisis situates white men as a group that is now under threat or marginalized, the representation in comic books of a re-centered white male American hero assuages to some extent feelings of confusion or anger in certain readers. In considering *Fables'* long-term exploration of Bigby's character, it is useful to consider how the portrayal of this complex figure evokes nostalgia, the desire to prove manhood, the fear of emasculation, and the way a certain kind of masculinity is metaphorically connected with the fortunes of the nation.

In his discussion of popular representations of masculinity between the wars, Michael Kimmel points to a growing preference for figures who would allow men to pursue escapist fantasies, as "For most men the Depression was emasculating both at work and at home" (144). One such figure, who emerged in Dashiell Hammett's 1920s work, was the "cynically crusty detective," a resolutely autonomous figure who functioned as "the urban pioneer, making the world safe for women and children," though without ever succumbing to the domestic sphere (154). The detective figure was also central to the rise of the comic book: *Detective Comics*—a title that featured the name of a newly formed company that would eventually become known as DC Comics—started out as a collection of hard-boiled crime stories before becoming famous for its introduction of the Bat-man. Later, Kimmel argues, in the post–World War II period, the figure of the suburban father became synonymous with appropriate masculine performance (164), as can also be seen in the romance comic book titles that became popular after the war (Wright 110). Thus, in many ways, the figure of Bigby Wolf—especially in his guise as the sheriff of Fabletown and paternal head of the Wolf clan—harks back to a number of histories, showing him to be a vessel for nostalgia for anachronistic forms of masculine identity. Importantly, these forms of masculine identity are doggedly traditional, even dull: as he notes to the crowd gathered to hear his solution to the mystery of Rose Red's fake murder, "the typical cop's life can best be described as unending hours of mind-numbing drudgery … all in all, I can't say I've had what could be described as an exciting career—or even a very interesting one" (1.104–105). His proposal to Snow White, too, is marked by Bigby's insistence on being "old-fashioned" (8.91). This paradoxical and somewhat overstated emphasis on Bigby's dullness and traditionalism operates as a projection, calling to mind the fantasy of a time when a man's role at work and at home was at least comprehensible. Further, even in his guise as the God of Wolves, Bigby evokes masculine traits associated with another time and space: freedom, aloofness, brute strength, and a symbiotic relationship with the land, all of which gesture toward the myth of the American pioneer and outlaw or—as Kimmel puts it—the "primitivist narratives of innate, instinctual manhood" (46). Thus, in the dualism of Bigby's character, a wide range of nostalgic masculine performance is somehow made coherent.

Kimmel argues that throughout American cultural history, the anxiety about a capacity to prove one's manhood—especially within the context of the expressly American figure of the "self-made man" (Kimmel, 14–19)—often results in attempts to demonstrate "self-control, exclusion, and escape" (238). In other words, any real or perceived threat to the ability of the American man to fulfill his destiny of becoming an anti-aristocratic man of "independence," "usefulness," and "economic autonomy" (Kimmel, 15–18) will result in particular sorts of cultural fantasies.

With respect to the fantasy of exclusion, Kimmel draws attention to various efforts by American men (especially white men) to bar women, people of color, and/or immigrants from fully participating in the public sphere. In *Fables*, the fantasy of exclusion is rarely pursued, except in terms of the way notions of "home" are idealized in the face of the unsettling forces of globalization. In fact, the representation of racial difference is often far more progressive than representations of racial purity. The masculine fantasies of escape and of self-control, however, are variously explored throughout the text whereby, for example, the many quests and wars operate as manly opportunities to escape the confines of Fabletown; whereby Prince Charming's fencing ability is connected to the question of his character; and whereby Flycatcher's curse is connected to his childlikeness and sexual immaturity. In the dual nature of Bigby, Willingham provides another instance of the idea that masculine qualities such as independence, usefulness, and autonomy might be harnessed in performances of escape and self-control. Bigby is the only Fable who acknowledges participating in the Mundy World Wars: as he explains to Snow White, he fought on the side of America because "A wolf grows up knowing he needs to protect his territory or risk losing it" (4.92). Thus, Bigby's service fulfills the idea that—in war—a man positions himself in relation *to*, but apart *from*, the domestic sphere, affirming that the role of protector can be fulfilled via what Bigby refers to as "extended leaves of absence" (4.91). When Snow turns down Bigby's request that she and the newly born cubs escape with Bigby into the "forests ... where no one will ever find us" (4.109), he leaves her, holing up in a cabin accompanied by booze and a new woman (8.43–44), while Snow White raises the children and maintains the illusion that they will one day "meet [their] father" (8.12). Even after the two are happily married, Bigby continues his routine of taking sporadic leaves of absence—to command Fort Bravo during the war against the Adversary, to find a possible site for a new Fabletown, to search for the lost cubs, and to terrorize the streets of Manhattan—though, as will be argued below, these forms of escape are increasingly related to emasculation.

Along with escape, Kimmel notes that self-control is central to the American ideal of the self-made man: "If social order, permanence, could no longer be taken for granted and a man could rise as high as he aspired, then his sense of himself as a man was in constant need of demonstration" (32). In the World War II tale included in *The Mean Seasons* (Vol. 5), Bigby temporarily inhabits the role of The Wolf Man, the iconic B-movie figure, and battles both Nazis and Frankenstein's monster (5.56–57). Despite references in this narrative arc to conventional werewolf mythology, including the threat of silver bullets (5.65) and a "lyncanthropic virus" (5.66), Bigby does not generally behave like a werewolf, in that he can control when and if he transforms from man to wolf or vice versa; like his father and children, Bigby is a shapeshifter, and a crucial aspect of his character is the way that, in either guise, Bigby is able to perform his mastery of various situations. Notwithstanding Mayor Cole's threatening references to his past identity as a monster, Bigby makes clear that he has, in human guise, endured the "general tedium of police work ... for more than two hundred years" (1.104). His transformations into a wolf, especially in the period before the war with the Adversary, are always strategic and effective: he thwarts Bluebeard's attempt to interrogate and/or kill Jack (1.71–72); he eliminates the threat of the burning wooden soldiers during the attack on Fabletown (4.208–209); he saves Ambrose from his own monstrous brothers (9.64–65), and so on. As his inclusion on Pinocchio's "Super Team" makes clear, Bigby's dual identity is not a curse so much as it is a superpower (16.75). It is only during his battle against Brandish that Bigby's ability to transform into a wolf is figured not as an outgrowth of his self-control and mastery, but of his rage (19.123); thus, it is not surprising that, in this instance, Brandish is able to embody the "civilized man ... [who triumphs] over the most brutish forces of nature" (19.139). Importantly, the nostalgic vision offered in *Fables* by Bigby's conglomerate of masculine roles also reveals anxiety about their tenuousness. As the series continues, the notion of a "crisis in masculinity" is reflected in Bigby's increasing failure to productively escape, and thereby perform a manly duty that confirms the integrity of the domestic sphere from a safe distance, or to project self-control.

The cover of the trade paperback *Snow White* (Vol. 19) echoes in color palette and imagery the cover of *Legends in Exile* (Vol. 1), a volume that shows Bigby not only in his identity as the "crusty detective," but also as the would-be wooer of Snow White (1.125) and the wolfish enforcer of justice (1.71). In the later volume, however, Bigby no longer commands the center of attention and no longer fits comfortably into an iconic version of American masculinity, even a version that goes on an adventure. As the search for Therese and Darian gets underway, Stinky persistently tries to frame the trip within particular plot conventions: first, he refers to their activity as a "road trip" (19.67), introducing a popular contemporary version of masculine escape; second, by referencing his desire to avoid a "Thelma and Louise ending" (19.70), Stinky calls to mind the "buddy movie," which involves risk and bonding, though of course the allusion to *Thelma and Louise* does undermine the masculine ideal; finally, Stinky suggests that they are on a "sacred quest" (19.77), intimating that—at the very least—their actions can be understood within a profound framework of masculine self-knowledge and heroism. Bigby, however, refuses to be drawn into any conventional narrative of escape, and continually insists that the trip is simply a "search" (19.67, 19.77); even more importantly, it is a search in which his detective sensibilities ultimately fail him. Though his tracking abilities allow him to catch Darian's scent in various worlds, Bigby cannot comprehend any design in his son's travels (19.110). Further, Bigby abandons the search altogether once he learns from Ghost that Snow White is being held captive by Brandish and, in an example of structural irony and pathos, the reader has learned about Darian's death and Therese's return in the previous volume. Bigby's failure here to act as a protecting agent for his children foreshadows his inability to protect his wife. As per the pattern Sally Robinson notes in various works of literature and film produced in the late-twentieth century, the figure of the "wounded" white male body operates as a metaphor for the way American white men feel themselves to be "under siege" (6). It is true that both the acts of turning Bigby into glass and shattering that glass are committed by another white man—Brandish—whose entire character is saturated in a retrograde misogyny that the text vociferously rejects. However, what the text also depicts is that somehow Bigby, once the most powerful of men and monsters, has been weakened, perhaps by his extended participation in the domestic sphere he seeks to protect. It is also significant that the emasculation of a wounded Bigby, reduced now to a fiend without self-control or language, is exacerbated because a piece of him is controlled first by Leigh Duglas and then by his sister-in-law Rose Red.

Both Kimmel and Robinson make connections between their assessment of shifting representations of masculinity in American culture and an abiding concern with the status of the nation: Kimmel argues that "Since the founding of the country, the electorate had always been assessing the manly strength and conviction of its leaders" (275), while Robinson notes that the increasingly ubiquitous figure of the wounded white male comes to represent "The American body politic ... in decline" (49). Willingham also points to this notion of the nation's deterioration when he suggests that Bigby is a "template for what America *used to be*, and *should be still*" (Nevins, 30, emphasis added). As a mouthpiece for political conviction, Bigby operates as a champion of defensiveness, strength, and libertarianism. Just before destroying Geppetto's sacred grove, Bigby explains his admiration for Israel, a country he says possesses the admirable (and traditionally masculine) qualities of "grit and iron" (8.76); after dealing with the problem of a power-hungry pack of werewolves in *Werewolves of the Heartland*, Bigby leaves the community to function within his own version of "freedom" (*Were*, 119), asserting that he will not intervene as long as they "behave [themselves]" (*Were*, 120). However, as the series progresses, Bigby shows himself to be in a kind of retreat, increasingly unable to enforce the "sloppy" freedom that he says is better than the "tyranny ... of those who insist on a perfect world" (*Were*, 119). In the battle of Fabletown, he is able to beat the wooden soldiers in his guise as the God of Wolves (4.208–209), while in the battle against the Wooden Emperor, he attacks in his human form, managing to knock the massive puppet off balance before Boy Blue finishes him off (11.167–169). Later, though he prepares to fight Mr. Dark as a member of the Super Team, Bigby's services are not required due to the actions of his own father (16.121) and his attempt to save Snow White from Brandish fails completely (19.143). Finally, in the lead up to the promised showdown between Snow White and Rose Red, Bigby's plan to sow terror among Rose Red's troops on the eve before the battle is thwarted because Rose still retains the controlling ring: as she tells him, "You're still leashed pal" (22.69).

In his function as an emblematic figure for the American body politic, Bigby's retreat and personal emasculation might be read thus: in the battle of Fabletown, Bigby's power recalls the might of the American forces in World War II—though he shows up to the battle a bit late, his massive presence provides a decisive framework for victory over the enemy. In the battle against the Wooden Emperor, Bigby is fighting a figurehead, a representative of a totalitarian dictatorship; thus, in keeping with American Cold War ideals, Bigby's choice to fight as a man alongside Boy Blue, using "a common tool found in any Mundy garage" is somehow more democratic, as is the image of the giant "wienie roast" enjoyed at Fort Bravo following the Emperor's defeat (11.168–169). In keeping with the text's increasing response to the exigencies of globalization, Mr. Dark may be thought of as an unstable, more inscrutable threat: the kind that can bring down buildings and infiltrate the mood and minds of regular citizens. Bigby as America—together with the Super Team of allies—tries to imagine conventional ways to fight this new enemy (and in Pinocchio's fantasy, it is Bigby the Wolf who manages to destroy Mr. Dark [16.75]). As Bigby himself admits to Snow White, however, conventional forms of warfare are likely to fail against the new enemy (16.84). In the end, Pinocchio's superheroic fiction is replaced by an equally fantastical and magical solution to an impossible problem, and it is significant that Bigby's personal failure in this theatre of war leads to a narrative about succession, as if to underline the notion of America's waning powers (16.128). Similarly, the new proliferation of such enemies as Nurse Spratt/Leigh Duglas and Werian Holt/Brandish Descry—enemies who originally appear as friends—represents an increasing anxiety about America's role on the world stage, as does the disappointment of Bigby's "search and rescue" mission. Even Bigby's act of leaving his community to pursue the trail of cubs can be scrutinized for the way the useless journey—on which mileage is measured in "blood" (19.63)—leaves the domestic sphere more vulnerable to threat, as the emergence of Brandish as the persecutor of Snow White occurs while Bigby is away. Finally, when Bigby returns to the Mundy world, he is an unstable predator and terrorizer, a role that suggests the role of America on the world stage has devolved into a broken caricature of what it once was.

In the final volume of *Fables*, Bigby is reduced to a secondary character, almost entirely associated with the domestic sphere, and operating most effectively as Snow White's better half in the Patmat (22.151). That said, the representation of the lesser Bigby at the end of the series coheres with what Kimmel sees as the best hope for what he refers to as "democratic manhood" (293): as he suggests, "After all these years of running away, pumping up, and excluding everyone else, American men have started to come home" (294). In the "Farewell" narrative arc, Bigby's most significant act is not one of protection or attack, but of allowing himself to be healed by his son, Connor. The threat of the shattered Bigby—wounded, manipulated, reduced to a peripheral position in the community he used to safeguard—is neutralized only when Connor suggests to his father than he has grown "better and stronger than you" (22.12). Even in his reduced cognitive state, Bigby makes the choice not to fight, but to once again embody a loving father figure, taking pride in his son's development. Further, when Rose Red presents her idea of retreat to Snow White, it is Bigby who convinces his wife to "give up" on Fabletown (22.76). In the dream for America exemplified by the story of Bigby Wolf, the political aspirations of the nation are due for a reset, for a move toward less ostentatiousness, but also less openness: as Tannika Wynn explains to Rose Red, Snow White and Bigby create their new ancestral home in the Hesse, as "a project to keep the Patmat safe and comfy, deep in the forest, without fear of being disturbed by outsiders" (22.144). Thus, the fantasy of nation is no longer one of righteous violence, but domestic loyalty.

Styles of Leadership: Geppetto, Flycatcher and Rose Red

At one point during their search for Therese and Darian, Bigby and Stinky touch down in a world inhabited by talking otters. While Bigby questions the otters about whether they remember seeing his cub, Stinky tries to convince them to take up "the Blue Way," as belief in the second coming of Boy Blue will help them "smite the overlords." In response to Stinky's pitch, an otter explains that they have no overlords: "We're a representative litocracy. Pass the reading test, no matter what age, and you can vote" (19.91). This description of government is not only delightful in its confirmation of Willingham's favorable attitude toward careful readers, but also coheres with the focus on the specificities of law, custom, and governmental systems that runs throughout *Snow White* (Vol. 19). While King Cole and others in Fabletown try to mitigate whatever Fable laws support Brandish's claim to Snow White (19.115), Beast exploits his newly acquired knowledge of Fairy laws regarding courtship to delay the Blue Fairy's attack on Geppetto (19.102). A survey of the styles of leadership of Geppetto, Rose Red, and Flycatcher indicates a concern for the way government provides the context for individual rights and the pursuit of justice. While, on the one hand, the dictatorship of Geppetto is critiqued, so too is the flawed republic Rose Red sets up at The Farm. In a text that pays attention to the wishes and fears governing human interaction, it is significant that the most idealized form of government is the absolute monarchy in Haven. While the representation of leadership in *Fables* portrays a resistance to the forces of globalization that would hide governmental systems and increase bureaucracy, it also depicts a deep desire for leadership that is honest, courageous, and embedded in community.

As Jack Zipes notes in *Breaking the Magic Spell: Radical Theories of Folk and Fairy Tale*, the political milieu that imbues the canonical Western tradition can "be linked to concepts of medieval patriachalism, monarchy and absolutism.... The world of the folk tale is inhabited largely by kings, queens, princes, princesses, soldiers, peasants, animals and supernatural creatures." Further, Zipes argues that the "magical" aspects of folk and fairy tales reveals "the social critique latent in the imaginative element," whereby "the impulse and critique of the 'magic' are rooted in a historically explicable desire to overcome [class] oppression and change society" (35–36). For example, in his reading of "Hansel and Gretel," Zipes points out that—although it is the children's stepmother who, upon facing starvation, advises her husband to abandon Hansel and Gretel in the forest—the "villain" in the tale is the witch who lives in a house made of food, and who intends to eat Hansel and Gretel. Thus, Zipes shows, "the witch (as parasite) can ... be regarded here as representative of the entire feudal system or the greed and brutality of the aristocracy, responsible for the difficult conditions. The killing of the witch is symbolically the realization of the hatred which the peasantry felt for hoarders and oppressors" (38). Zipes' political readings—though foundational in the field of folk and fairy tale studies—cannot be deemed monolithic; as Sadhana Naithani points out, the "vast repertoire of narratives [comprising the field] are not unified by an individual author or a common sociohistorical context" (756). Further, different readers may decode tales according to their own ideological consciousness (755). Finally, Naithani argues that— as examples of imaginative discourse—folk or fairy tales are political in that "narration itself is a political act ... what makes the inherently political nature of folktales and fairy tales both interesting and threatening is that folktales have a wide range of recipients" (755). Thus, in attending to the way leadership is represented in *Fables*, it is important to consider how such activity is more than simply a background state of affairs but is incorporated into stories that reach out to the imaginations of readers.

In *Fables*, the generalized feudal setting of canonical Western folk and fairy tale persists via the descriptions of conditions in the Homelands, both with respect to the notable lack of modern technology and weaponry and in terms of class categories, although—in *Fables*—the medieval estate of the Church seems to be replaced by a cadre of more or less powerful sorcerers and magical beings, from the likes of Senior Undersecretary Mudsnipe, who works at the Ministry of Sorcery (6.83), to Lumi, the Snow Queen (6.97). Still, as represented in *Homelands* (Vol. 6), those in the higher classes—such as Captain Chernomor—live in opulence (6.64), those in the peasant class persist as farmers or shepherds or common soldiers, and are mostly voiceless, and the word of the Emperor in meting out rulings is absolute (6.111). When Boy Blue emerges from his disguise as an old woman, scoffing at the way "aristocrats ... never take notice of the peasant class" (6.115), his attack on the Emperor seems to perform a similar social critique as Zipes argues is found in "Hansel and Gretel," although actually cutting off the oppressor's head at the site of government is less "symbolic" than pushing a forest witch into an oven. Of course, Blue's act only appears to be a successful attack on the system, as is revealed during subsequent scenes during which Geppetto admits to being the power behind the Imperial throne. This ironic plot twist shows that Boy Blue's rebellious act does not ultimately exemplify criticism of a social system, which perhaps should not be surprising considering the irrelevance of feudal ideals in the contemporary moment. That said, the styles of government and leadership that are explored in *Fables*—together with the representation of acts taken for or against particular styles of government and leadership—reveal a similar project that Zipes sees in the tales that emerged in 18th and 19th century Germany: "The magic and fantastic elements are closely tied to the real possibilities for the peasantry to change conditions, albeit in a limited way. The emphasis is on *hope* and *action*" (39, emphasis added).

The depiction of Geppetto, the fearsome Adversary, whose rise to immense power is explained to Boy Blue in *Homelands* (Vol. 6), invites comparisons with a number of real world dictators, from Joseph Stalin (whom he physically resembles) to Napoleon Bonaparte to Julius Caesar to various other perpetrators of genocide. Geppetto is calculating and brutal, content to solidify power via regular public "execut[ions] ... [so that] the people will get the message that they'd best not harbor [traitors]" (10.195). His expansionist agenda is not founded on any nationalist, religious or ideological principle; rather, conquest is just something he "develop[s] a taste for" (6.169). This "taste" includes a willingness to commit genocide, as his plans for the conquest of the Mundy world reveal (9.95), though he consistently refers to his mode of rule as "benevolent" (6.169, 10.195). For his part, Willingham does not explicitly associate Geppetto with a historical counterpart, but rather refers to him as an "intelligent evil overlord ... [who] remains safely in the background," and who creates self-supporting "bureaucracies ... [to] take care of the never-ending task of deadening personal freedom" (Nevins, 94). Thus, the critique in *Fables* of Geppetto's leadership style derides power that is hidden, centralized, and essentially administrative. During the war on the Adversary, the Fables first seek to cripple the bureaucracy: though Boy Blue enthuses about the power of Briar Rose's enchantment, referring to the sleeping spell as "a terrific weapon of very potent spellcraft" (11.117), the great value of putting everyone in the Imperial city to sleep is tightly connected to Geppetto's undue dependence on a fussy bureaucratic system and a vast consolidation of power. Importantly, the *action taken* is a crippling of an overbearing system, while the *act* involves "one tiny drop of Briar Rose's blood" (11.117): thus, in this part of the tale, the "magical" element reveals the *hope* that small choices and accomplishments can have political meaning in a world where the workings of power are increasingly occluded.

Similarly, the missions of The Glory of Baghdad flying warship and the Fort Bravo unit involve literal and symbolic attacks against a large target: while the warship works to destroy all the gates between worlds, thus limiting the geographical reach of Imperial power, the troops at Fort Bravo—whose job it is to protect access to the last Beanstalk, the last "escape route out of the Imperial Homeworld" (11.84)—are instructed by Bigby to "hold ... this ... ground" (11.85). Both of these *actions*, thus, reflect a particular attitude toward space, whereby the desire to control large swathes of territory, mostly by proxy, is criticized, while the act of personally defending local territory is prized. Again, one can read the war against Geppetto's leadership style as a challenge to forces of globalization that undermine an individual's or a community's connection to and control over local space and home.

In the days prior to Briar Rose putting the Imperial City under the sleeping enchantment, the Emperor—a massive wooden puppet who acts as Geppetto's figurehead—complains to Lumi about the progress of the Empire's battles with The Glory of Baghdad, saying "Father Geppetto should be here to hear these bad tidings. I'm troubled that he is not" (11.88). Though Lumi makes excuses for Geppetto's absence, the idea of a leader who keeps himself safe in the background, while sending his own people into battle, is disparaged, especially in comparison with the likes of Prince Charming. Though Charming revels in his role as "Director of Homeland Recovery" (11.40), wearing a full dress uniform during a combat mission (11.80), he also sacrifices his own life in order to destroy the final gateway between Homelands (11.161). The critique of Geppetto's cowardice is brought into further relief when he arrives in Fabletown, escorted by Bigby, Boy Blue, and Pinocchio. Upon his arrival, a third-string Fable named Stanley brags "We captured him! We captured the Adversary!" Bigby's response to the boast is to remind Stanley, "you didn't capture anyone. You stayed home during this war, remember?" (11.174). Thus, Geppetto's personal cowardice—which is displayed again at The Farm, when he employs Aspen and Alder as bodyguards (14.119)—is linked to the disapproving representation of his attitude toward leadership, an attitude which denies any sense of responsibility to the community itself. Once he can hide behind the strength of the dryads, he pronounces that, though he "will not serve a pack of dishonored killers.... I will lead you, and protect you, and eventually mold you into good citizens" (14.122). The contrast between "serve" and "lead" in this pronouncement reinforces the critique of any leadership system that does not respond to the interests of the specific collective; ironically, though Geppetto may have a deep understanding of arboreal magic, he has no grasp of the notion that a leader must be rooted within the community.

In the days leading up to the war with the Empire forces, Rose Red and Boy Blue announce to the non-human Fables that they have been given a choice to remain at The Farm or to travel to Haven, where Flycatcher has offered them a place. As Blue explains, in choosing Haven, the non-human Fables will be joining "a real kingdom with old-time vows of fidelity and service and such," and will have to "give up Fabletown citizenship" (11.20). The explicit marking of the difference between living in Haven and living on The Farm (two locations that—as Boy Blue points out—are comparable in size and offer comparable standards of living) draws attention to what it means to live in a kingdom versus a democracy. Further, Rose Red follows up Blue's explanation of Flycatcher's offer with the counsel that "this is one choice that can't be made by groups or families, no matter what subgroupings you still identify yourself with ... no one else has the authority to make [the decision] for you" (11.21). Paradoxically, any Fable who exercises his or her own liberty to make the choice to move to Haven will be giving up future opportunities to act on individual authority. The democratic principles that ostensibly imbue Fabletown are complicated by the undue influence of the old Fabletown executive, though Prince Charming does manage to win an election and thereby wrest power from the triumvirate of King Cole, Snow White, and Bigby (at least until he gets tired of being mayor). The issue of leadership at The Farm is also problematic: as Dun Pig points out to Snow White before the attempted revolution, Weyland Smith was simply appointed to run The Farm, much to the consternation of the non-human Fables (2.27). In the wake of the revolution and the hearings, Rose Red takes over as the administrator of The Farm, seemingly just because she "likes" the job and Snow White has the power to "formalize the arrangement" (2.110). Also, in similar fashion to Geppetto, Rose Red employs Clara the fire-breathing raven as an "enforcer," so as to thwart further attempts at sedition (2.112). Still, though the governing of Fabletown and The Farm clearly departs from the government of the United States, the leadership style of Rose Red is meant to operate as a version of republicanism, not only in comparison to the dictatorship of Geppetto, but also in contrast to the monarchy established by Flycatcher.

When Rose Red warns the non-human Fables against allowing individual decisions to be made by "groups" or "subgroupings," she is pointing out an area of concern that troubled early commenters on the new republican experiment of America. In a series of essays, referred to as *The Federal-*

ist Papers, written between 1787 and 1788, authors Alexander Hamilton, James Madison, and John Jay set out to convince "the young republic [that it] needed a much stronger national government if the nation were to remain free and independent" (Carey and McClellan, xlv). In "Federalist Paper #10," Madison deals with the problem of factionalism in a democracy, noting that the only remedy against the "mischiefs of faction"— whereby the ruling "passions" or "interests" of one group of citizens would undermine "the rights of other citizens" (43)—is the "scheme of representation" in a relatively large republic (46). As he argues, "the representatives must be raised to a certain number, in order to guard against the cabals of a few" and "they must be limited to a certain number, in order to guard against the confusion of the multitude" (47). When Rose Red finally emerges from her self-pitying funk, she asks Clara to call a meeting for "Every faction leader. Every disgruntled Fable" (15.99). A double-page spread shows the various "cabals of a few" that have emerged during Rose Red's absence (15.104–105), while the day listening to grievances of those on The Farm reflects the problem of "the confusion of the multitude" (15.113–115). Rose Red thus decides to create an advisory council made up of representatives from each faction, even allowing for a representative from old Fabletown to "sit in on our meetings from time to time" (15.118). Importantly, however, Rose Red's capacity to enact the republican ideal is founded on the continued presence of Clara, the magical enforcer of decorum (15.109, 15.119). At The Farm, it is the threat of Clara's "dragon fire" that neuters Geppetto's influence. As with the function of Briar Rose's enchantment, the magical element of Clara draws attention to the *hope* that is at the center of this imaginative vision of government, which is that the scheme of representation will keep perverse factions in check, and that enforcers of the republic will act on behalf of the entire community. As a subtle commentary on current debates in the United States regarding federalist overreach versus state rights, *Fables* provides a fantastical picture of the republican ideal.

The fantastical picture represented by Rose Red's leadership, however, is not sustained, as the text also presents some of Rose's decisions as dangerous to the community. In particular, Rose Red's attitude toward crime and punishment is called into question, and is set in opposition to the meting out of justice in Flycatcher's monarchy. Early in her tenure as administrator of The Farm, Rose Red indicates that she has a much more flexible notion of punishment than the Fabletown executive, which is perhaps unsurprising given the way her "punishment" for her role in the plot to stage her own murder and steal Bluebeard's money is to rise to a leadership position at The Farm within a matter of months. As she tells Boy Blue, who has been sent to The Farm to work off the crime of stealing the Vorpal Sword and the Witching Cloak, "the folks down at Fabletown have their agenda, and I have mine" (7.83). For Rose Red, Blue's status as a "bona fide hero" makes her unwilling to follow through with the pre-scribed sentence of hard labor, and it is this tendency to let emotion and whim get in the way of enacting justice that makes her style of leadership problematic. In deciding to release Brandish from being chained in a pit and offering him a "second chance" (20.81), Rose Red behaves like a stereo-typical bleeding heart liberal, whose desire to prove her own "until-the-end-of-my-days purpose" (20.85) endangers the community she is supposed to serve. Again, it is the magical element of Brandish's literal lack of heart, his function as an embodiment of the notion that some individuals are simply evil and cannot be reformed, that reveals the cri-tique of a social system that would place Brandish's rights on par with everyone else's. When Brandish finally slays Lancelot (21.192), the text implicitly critiques the pitfalls of a justice system that promotes restorative measures, or that tries to "err on the side of being too accommodating" (21.150). Thus, the text responds to a cultural moment in which the lum-bering federalist system, while trying to remain free from "the influence of factious leaders," is perceived to pervert the notion of democracy by "accommodating" the marginal rather than protecting the rights of the many.

To oppose the less than satisfactory picture of justice advanced by Rose Red in her quasi-republic, the text explores the idealized monarchy in Haven. In the final arc contained in *Witches* (Vol. 14), a volume that depicts the rise of the various factions that would undermine the govern-ment of The Farm, a seemingly lighthearted tale of a ball game in Haven takes a darker turn. After leading his baseball team, the Gobtown Crush-ers, to victory and spending the evening drinking heartily, Mr. Brump tries to make his way back to Goblin Town; along the way, he meets Mr. Seed-crate—a Fable squirrel—and, in a drunken moment of weakness, Mr. Brump eats Mr. Seedcrate (14.158). In other sections of *Fables*, the text depicts caricatures of justice, as when the Emperor in the Imperial City orders a man's crops to be burnt rather than either dismissing the case as a family squabble or finding a solution in law to deal with his complaint (6.111), or when Bufkin's lawyer congratulates him on receiving the "humane" sentence of hanging under Roquat's demented system (17.83). In Haven, not only is Mr. Brump given Trusty John as his hard-working advocate (14.167, 14.169), but Flycatcher takes seriously the "responsibility" to honor both the law and his citizenry (14.166). After hearing from the defense witness, Ollikander Strikeswift—brother to the scorpion featured in the famous fable, "The Frog and the Scorpion"—Flycatcher must weigh between the forces of law and the forces of nature/culture, which must, ostensibly, be accommodated in a pluralist community. Though Flycatcher admits to being "moved" by Trusty John's defense, unlike Rose Red he does not allow emotion or his own preferences to undermine the principle of citizenship, pointing out that "Mister Brump subjected himself willingly to our law and justice" (14.180). Flycatcher tempers his judgment with mercy, exiling Brump rather than carrying out his execution (14.181). Later, Red Riding Hood advises Flycatcher that exercising such mercy must be a one-time occurrence, as "do it a second time and they'll think you're soft" (14.183). Not only does this comment cohere with the way this arc—again—explores the matter of Flycatcher's complex masculinity, but it confirms the idea that the idealized depiction of a truly benevolent and wise king is a fantasy, one that draws attention to the types of *hope* at the heart of the tale.

The moral perfection that imbues the trial of Mr. Brump is as artificial as the perfect quest to find and found Haven, as was depicted on Fly TV. The explicit framing of Flycatcher's quest narrative as a tale of goodness eagerly consumed by those engaged in all manner of subterfuge, double-crossing, and militaristic behavior, reflects a cultural desire to retain at least the fantasy that we still care about and strive for goodness, fairness, and justice. Like Flycatcher's quest, Mr. Brump's trial is filled with magical elements that reveal the *hope* at the heart of this portrait of leadership. In the first place, the conditions of the trial itself are perfect: both Weyland Smith and Trusty John are dutiful, disinterested, and skilled advocates, as different as possible from the stereotype of the crafty and/or self-serving lawyer whose main goal is to pervert justice and get paid. The submissions of both witnesses—both the Fable bird who observes the crime and Ollikander Strikeswift—are accepted without questions, with no underhanded attempts by either advocate to win the case by discrediting a witness. As Weyland explains at the outset, once the King's judgment has been given "there will be no appeal" (14.170), which reveals a critique of current notions of legal institutions that are perceived to be unduly bureaucratic, costly, and inefficient. Further, Flycatcher's ability to carry out an absolutely just, yet merciful sentence reveals the fantasy of a seat of justice that is inherently all-knowing and fair. Just after Mr. Brump commits the crime of letting his own goblin nature override the citizenship oath he made, the text shows Flycatcher finally overcoming the enchantment that turns him into a frog as a result of nervousness and the guilt he feels about his dead wife and family. As the Frog Prince asserts, "I-I-I-will-not-let-this-thing-rule-me-any-longer. I won't!" (14.160). The magical *act* of breaking an enchantment confirms Flycatcher's ability to remain free of outside influences, which might cloud his perfect judgement. Finally, and most important in terms of this idealized portrait of leadership, the magical figure of Grinder embodies the figure of the perfect citizen. At first glance, Grinder appears to fulfill a similar role as Geppetto's dryads and Rose Red's dragon-raven; when many of Haven's goblin community gather to protest Mr. Brump's arrest, Grinder threatens to "bash in a few goblin heads if you don't all turn around and go home" (14.172). The difference between Grinder and the other enforcers, however, is that Grinder is not concerned with protecting Flycatcher, but with protecting the ideal of freely elected citizenship. Grinder is not appointed as an enforcer, but simply chooses to stand up to the malcontents in his own subcommunity; when Flycatcher thanks him for his display of "loyalty," Grinder's response represents the fantasy of the perfect member of a populace: "An oath is an oath" (14.182).

While the representation of leadership and/or styles of government in *Fables* does—at points—veer toward allegory, the figures of Geppetto, Rose Red, and Flycatcher (along with the old and new Fabletown executive) are never presented as personifications. As is most obvious with the depiction of Flycatcher, but which is also true of other leaders in the text, the point is to critique cultural fantasies about appropriate actions of governments and to lay bare anxieties about the way global political activity is increasingly opaque. It is this anxiety about "hidden" forms of government that gives rise to the persistent figure of the enforcer, as the role of such a figure is to make ostensible differences in styles of government irrelevant, if both the dictatorship of Geppetto and the republic imagined by Rose Red are enacted through displays of force. The representation of Grinder, however, adds another layer to the text's portrayal of the notion that "might makes right." Even more significant than Grinder's physical power to put down any rebellion in Flycatcher's realm is his ability to articulate the rights and responsibilities of citizenship; even more so than Flycatcher is idealized as the perfectly just monarch, Grinder is emblematic of the perfectly accountable citizen. Thus, in depicting the imperfections of various leaders and governmental systems, the text also suggests that a populace made up of self-interested, "perpetually indignant malcontents" (15.116) is likely to get the type of equally self-interested leaders that they deserve.

Fables and Fantasy:
Geography, History, Economy

The starting publication date of *Fables* is May 2002, meaning that the entire series is written in what has been termed the "post–9/11" period. The probability that the events of 9/11 might operate as a cultural touchstone for *Fables* is amplified by the setting, as Fabletown exists somewhere in New York City. That said, in contrast to references elsewhere in the text to "real" historical events—for example the Napoleonic Wars (4.12), the American Civil War (3.7), the rule of the English Raj in India (12.159), World War II (5.33), and the U.S. invasion of Iraq, which is obliquely referred to when Frankie recalls fighting Bigby during "Dubya Dubya Two" (16.10)—explicit mention of 9/11 is absent. Perhaps the clearest echo of those events occurs in *The Dark Ages* (Vol. 12): after Beauty raises the alarm that the Business Office in the Woodland Building has disappeared, Frau Totenkinder advises the Fabletown Executive that, "all of the binding spells in the area have come or are coming undone ... which means none of our buildings are structurally safe anymore" (12.80). Moments after the Woodland Building is evacuated, it collapses, filling the street with clouds of dust and debris in a scene familiar to anyone who watched the news footage of the aftermath of the fallen Twin Towers (12.85–89). Importantly, when the now-iconic New York firefighters appear on the scene, they find no evidence of terrorism, as there are no "survivors" or "bodies" (12.105). The assertion that the aftermath contains only the suspicious results of "deliberate sabotage" (12.106), however, points to the post–9/11 cultural concern regarding the mysterious workings of power in a globalized age. In thinking through the way *Fables* responds to the context of globalization, it is useful to consider the text's relationship to the genre of fantasy as developed in part by J.R.R. Tolkien, whose works have had an enormous influence on the subgenre of sword-and-sorcery comics, and whose interest in history, geography, and materiality was a reflection of his apprehensions about the rise of industrialization and imperial capitalism. The representation of geography, history, and money in *Fables* signals a current cultural concern with matters of security, identity, and livelihoods in the age of global cultural and material flow.

In his discussion of contemporary adaptations of the Western canon of fairy tales, Tom Shippey points out that—while feminist and postmodern writers have attended to the content of the tales of Charles Perrault and the Brothers Grimm—of less concern has been the project that defined the lifetime work of the Grimms; unlike Perrault, whose adaptations of older Italian and French tales were unambiguously bourgeois and literary, the Brothers Grimm were ostensibly concerned with "discovering at once the history of the Germanic languages ... and the mythology which they felt must have overlain those old texts" (271; see also Zipes 2002, 27–29). Though the matter of the "authenticity" of the folk tales in the Grimms' collections is its own area of rich debate among folk and fairy tale scholars, Shippey's point about the way the Grimms intended to map the historical and linguistic "territory" of Germany is important, as is the connection he makes between this intention and the work of J.R.R. Tolkien. As Shippey argues, Tolkien's interest in English folk traditions gave rise to the genre of fantasy, which added to the fairy tale a "history in the form of annals and chronicles; geography in the form of maps; language and linguistic relationships; a guide to non-human species" (272); in other words—as many literary scholars have pointed out—the defining features of fantasy include the portrayal of an intersection of the fantastical and the ordinary, as well as the creation of a detailed "secondary world" in which the adventures take place. In *J.R.R. Tolkien, Robert E. Howard and the Birth of Modern Fantasy*, Deke Parsons describes Tolkien's depiction of the complex geography of Middle-Earth as a moral imperative informing his critique of industrialization, asserting "In [*The Lord of the Rings*], treating nature as intrinsically valueless material useful only to build machines leads to treating people as valueless machine parts" (53). Further, as Andrew Lynch argues in "Archaism, Nostalgia, and Tennysonian War in *The Lord of the Rings*," the critique of industrialization is linked to a condemnation of the type of mechanized warfare waged by Sauron's "conscripts, machines, and slaves," whereby "[t]he desolate Great War landscape of trenches, mud, shell holes, corpses, and total deforestation is associated with Isengard, the Paths of the Dead, or Frodo's and Sam's journey into Mordor" (87). In a similar fashion, the context that informs Willingham's treatment of "territory" in *Fables* are the features of an increasingly globalized world, one in which the ever-increasing flow of communications, capital, bodies, and culture across terrain collides with the ever-increasing concerns about policing borders, defining citizenship, managing information, and protecting local interests. Willingham's text additionally partakes in the deliberate "archaism" of fantasy, which Lynch argues allows Tolkien to engage in social critique without resorting to allegory. Lynch explains that while "evil" becomes associated with the "modern," so too does "good" become associated with the "medieval" (87). Thus, though the mechanized war is condemned, the heroic ideal of "war as an ennobling cultural and moral struggle" is maintained (Lynch 90).

As per the genre of fantasy as it has developed over the past century, *Fables* responds to the apprehensions about the temporary cultural moment via a nostalgia for the power of what Lynch calls "the 'bright swords' of medievalist idealism" (90). When the policing of borders fail, or when drafting a straightforward history becomes too difficult, or when economic systems supporting the community become impossible to parse, the fantasy of medievalism assuages current cultural anxiety.

If Tolkien took great pains to elaborate on the geography of Middle-Earth, comparatively speaking the geography of the Fables' Homelands is rather vague. In *Peter & Max: A Fables Novel*, the narrator explains that the Mundy world "seem[s] to contain miniature versions of every Home-land world they'd originally come from," including "Albion," "The Rus," "Erin," and "Americana" (19–20). Aside from this spare explanation— which in any case still does not provide a sense of the relative location of the many Homelands—what is known is that the various worlds, including the Mundy World, are connected by gateways. Controlling these gateways, thus, emerges as crucial strategic activity, especially within the context of the war with the Adversary. In leaving out the kind of precise world-building activity so central to the genre of fantasy, *Fables* highlights the symbolic importance of the gateways as they are associated with matters of security and cultural identity. The volume *March of the Wooden Soldiers* (Vol. 4), collecting comic book issues that were published during the American war with Iraq in 2003, is anxiously concerned with the threat of infiltration and attack, as reflected in the representation of various gate-ways. In the first arc collected in the volume—"The Last Castle"—Boy Blue describes the final battle with the Adversary before the "last gateway to freedom" (4.13) is deliberately destroyed so that the enemy cannot fol-low the Fable evacuees to their safe haven in the Mundy world (4.51). Interestingly, throughout the series there is no marking of the fact that the Fables are illegal immigrants to the Mundy, as the arc "The Last Castle" focuses solely on the violence and loss associated with leaving the Home-lands. Thus, the Fables retain the status of pilgrims to the New World (as is reinforced in the narrative of Hansel and Gretel's arrival in New Amster-dam, which uses imagery associated with the Puritan immigration to America [9.65–66]). The next arc in the volume, however, begins with another border crossing, showing Red Riding Hood/Baba Yaga's move-ment through northern Saskatchewan on her way to Fabletown (3.55–56). Bigby is immediately (and predictably) suspicious of the new refugee, explaining to Snow White why he suspects she is an enemy spy (4.92–94), and eventually confirming that the enemy has infiltrated the North

Canada Gate (4.153). By this point in the narrative, Red Riding Hood's cohort—the wooden brothers, Hugh, Lou, and Drew—have also crossed the border to prepare for an armed invasion of Fabletown (4.155, 4.170–171). In opposition to the focus on how the fleeing refugees get *out* of the Homelands in "The Last Castle," the focus of the narrative arc, "March of the Wooden Soldiers," and the core of Bigby's suspicions, is the matter of how the enemy can get *in*, not via a battle but via subterfuge and a failure at the border. The distinction between the worthy Fable refugees who once arrived in the New World and the clearly malevolent enemy forces who have infiltrated an already established community is confirmed when the wooden brothers deliver Boy Blue's broken body and read the Adversary's manifesto, which calls for submission to the Empire (4.160–161).

The anxiety regarding enemy infiltration and borders continues during the war with the Adversary, in which a primary goal is to destroy the gateways between Homelands and to show the difference between a local commitment to territory and the bureaucratic overrun of power. Once this war is over, however, the issue of borders and travel becomes more complicated, suggesting an even deeper cultural anxiety about the efficacy of security measures that protect states, or even about the very meaning of nation in the globalized era. On the one hand, the threat of Mr. Dark makes the significance of a security border hyperbolically literalized. When Bigby returns to Haven after seeking out possible sites for a new Fabletown, Flycatcher takes him to the border of the kingdom so that Bigby can see Mr. Dark "trying to get in" (16.46). Flycatcher explains that he is—with more effort every day—able to "[keep] the barrier intact" via his magic (16.47), and the pictorial elements in this scene reinforce the point that Haven's borders are supernaturally protected. Mr. Dark—who is drawn using a darker palette of colors than the figures in Haven—tries to scratch down the barrier, singeing his fingers on its magical energy. On the other hand, after Mr. Dark is defeated by the North Wind, there are increasing instances in the text of Fables travelling between worlds by way of magic. For example: in *Cubs in Toyland* (Vol. 18), Therese and Darian make their way from Wolf Valley to Toyland via magical means, Therese on the enchanted Toy Boat and Darian on the back of Lord Mountbatten, who is only allowed one step in each of many diverse lands (18.28, 18.48–49); in *Snow White* (Vol. 19), Stinky and Bigby attempt to track down the cubs' trail using Briar Rose's enchanted car, which is able to move between worlds and which is really "the evil destroyer witch, Hadeon" (19.62–63); in *Camelot* (Vol. 20), not only does Rose Red send Commander Arrow and other Fable birds with a message to be delivered across worlds about "her new order of knighthood" (20.62), but Winter—in her guise as the new North Wind—is shown moving about her world-crossing realm, monitoring the way Rose Red has begun to attract massive amounts of magical power (20.171). The second half of the series, thus, transitions away from the representation of gateways that, though obviously fantastical, still mimic to some extent the real world function of a security checkpoint or border crossing, which can be guarded and/or infiltrated. The increasing prevalence of magical barriers and magical movements situates the second half of the series more firmly within the genre of fantasy, where magic— as Parsons puts it in his commentary on Tolkien—represents "desire" and "a method to gain perspective" on contemporary issues (28). The representation of magic in *The Lord of the Rings* is often associated with "technology clothed in demonic form" (Parsons 28); in *Fables*, the context of globalization produces representations of magic that reflect both the fervent hope for security in a world where the "borders" of war are impossible to locate, as well as the fear of becoming lost in a world where the meaning of locality and belonging is diminished.

In the final narrative arc of *Cubs in Toyland* (Vol. 18), Ambrose Wolf, now fully grown and living with his wife, child, and Fable cat, Flanders, is depicted as the writer of the multi-volume "A History of Fables in America, the Mundy World and Beyond" (18.154). Ambrose's focus on chronicling the history of his community and his forebears to some extent echoes the roles of Bilbo and Frodo Baggins, who collect their own histories in the volumes that make up *The Red Book of Westmarch*, the ostensible source of Tolkien's *The Hobbit* and *The Lord of the Rings* trilogy. Lynch argues that much of the archaism and appeal to "folk" forms of storytelling in Tolkien's mythos connects to a desire to affirm continuities with England's past (82), so that the author's lament about the horrors of mechanized warfare is also a lament about the cultural tendency to consider the Great War as a site of catastrophic rupture—an ending point for ideals such as nobility and heroism and sacrifice. In *Fables*, Willingham veers between wry cynicism and a similar nostalgia to that which imbues Tolkien's search for a continuous history, although—as per the context of globalization— desire is now directed toward a comprehensible sense of history's "storyline," especially in the face of such contemporary exigencies as overwhelming data, "real time" reporting, and heterogeneous narratives. In *Legends in Exile* (Vol. 1), the site of Fabletown's originary violence is marked during the Remembrance Day speech given by Mayor King Cole. Beginning his history lesson like a fairy tale—"Once we were a thousand separate kingdoms, spread over a hundred magic worlds" (1.85)—Cole articulates the grand narrative the community uses to make sense of itself, whereby "it took an invasion to unite us" (1.86–87), and whereby the "end" of history will marked by a "return" to the Homelands (1.90). The narrative pattern of a nation's violent founding and of its noble endeavor at unity echoes the mythology of American exceptionalism and the nation's status as the incarnation of the "City Upon a Hill." Even the intrinsic promise of dissolution through transcendent return might be related to strains of millennialism, which, since the 18th century, have occupied those Americans convinced of their nation's role in the coming of the next world. Most importantly, Cole's Remembrance Day speech provides the community with an easily digestible and repeatable sense of their own "nation's" history. At the same time, the very coherence of the history Cole reiterates is called into question, as the speech itself is framed as a fundraising gambit. As Mayor Cole reminds Snow White, "Remembrance Day is more than a big party. It's when we get most of our contributions—our operating budget for the next year" (1.64). That Cole gives Snow White this reminder after pages of pictorial evidence that he—as mayor—lives in a lavish apartment undermines the integrity of his speech, even before he gives it. This instance of dramatic irony, however, also confirms the notion that history is not—in fact—a story, except that we often need to use it as such.

As the final narrative arc included in *Super Team* (Vol. 16), the tale "Waking Beauty" describes the attempts of Jubilee Mirant to establish himself as the "First Emperor of the Restored Empire" (16.131). Though Mirant's aspirations are no different from any of the other upstart emperors—who are "springing up nearly every day, proclaiming themselves the rightful new lord of lords" (16.129)—his plan is unique in that it includes waking up Briar Rose with a true love's kiss, and thereafter taking charge of "the bureaucrats who actually ran things" (16.133). Before Mirant can go about "manufacturing" the true love requisite for his scheme to work, however, the sleeping beauty is stolen by a squadron of goblins and the thorns surrounding the Imperial City are set afire (16.145–146). As the external narrator of "Waking Beauty" affirms, "Most historians agree that this day marked the final death rattle of the Old Empire" (16.148). Here, and elsewhere—for example, in the "The Last Sinbad Story" (21.48–50) and "The Last Story of Prince Charming" (21.132–134)—the proliferating narrative of *Fables* acknowledges the idea that even empires will wax and wane, perhaps commenting on America's diminished power in an increasingly globalized world. In "The Boys in the Band," the final narrative arc in *Camelot* (Vol. 20), an external narrator points out that Fabletown is ultimately wrecked "by the idea of why it was created in the first place"

(20.252), which is the idea that the refugees from the various Homelands will eventually return home. Significantly, though depictions of dissolution undermine the notion of history as a grand narrative of continuous progress, the fantasy that history can still be massaged into a usable story is maintained. Despite Mirant's very practical justification for "manufacturing" the conditions to wake Briar Rose, a valuable outgrowth of his plan is the creation of a suitably compelling origin myth for his new empire; once the issue of the need for bureaucrats is long forgotten, the story of true love's kiss will persist. The reliance on the compelling meaning of origin is also present in "The Boys in the Band," in Danny Boy's insistence that Seamus need not return to Fabletown, unless "that other world owns you now" (20.252); Danny's notion of return, however, depends on a rather retrograde understanding of nation whereby people "belong" somewhere specific, and that therefore rejects the forces of globalization. Even the twinned "last stories" of Sinbad and Charming reduce the complexity of a new war between an emerging Arab empire and an opposing guerrilla force to a fantastical battle between former allies, friends, almost brothers (11.70).

As noted above, the figure of King Cole is initially presented as an incarnation of the grasping, corrupt politician: his energy is apparently all directed toward fundraising activities, living large off state resources, and trying to make potentially explosive problems—such as Bigby's investigation of Rose Red's murder—go away. Indeed, when Prince Charming decides to trigger an election for the position of mayor, his primary goal is to take charge of Fabletown's vastly increased fortune following Bluebeard's demise (3.165). As the text progresses, however, Cole's interest in money matters is shown to be far more community-oriented than Charming's, or at least more practical. As Snow White points out to Bigby when he derides Cole's fixation on money, "No government can work without it. You shouldn't be so quick to impugn his character" (4.95). The connection made here between "character" and "community work" is developed most fully in "Fair Division," a tale about King Cole collected in *1001 Nights of Snowfall*, which describes the way Cole takes charge of the non-human subjects of his realm who, like him, have taken refuge in an abandoned mine in order to escape the invading hordes of the Adversary (*1001*, 121). The ending of "Fair Division" highlights the bitter irony of the moment in the early 17th century when Mayor Cole—a former champion of the non-human Fables—signs the law banishing them to The Farm (*1001*, 135). The bulk of the tale, however, depicts the King's attention to matters of survival, as "even under these dire circumstances, he counted it his most solemn responsibility to look after the welfare of even his most humble subject" (*1001*, 122). In direct opposition to the way he is portrayed in *Legends in Exile* (Vol. 1), Cole's practice in the mine is to divvy up the food among his subjects first, leaving little to nothing for himself (*1001*, 124). This abiding concern with the well-being and continuity of his community is, arguably, what animates his focus on "mundane" matters of money in the new world, though—especially in the contemporary moment—the need to acquire and share out supplies necessary for survival cannot be resolved simply by stealing food from a nearby farm (*1001*, 131). After the fall of the Woodland Buildings and the disappearance of the Business Office, Cole becomes consumed with the loss of the Fabletown fortune, and his distress is shown to have nothing to do with personal greed. Just before she transitions into her guise as Bellflower, Frau Totenkinder allows Cole to follow her into the woods, a space she seeks out because "all fairy tales take place in the woods ... even those that don't" (14.58). The reference here to the context of "fairy tales," with their ahistorical focus on symbolic matters of exchange, puts into more stark relief Cole's eminent practicality. When Totenkinder admonishes Cole for "mourn[ing] the loss of money," he replies, "do you have any idea how much it costs to keep The Farm going for a single day?" (14.59), going on to itemize such expenses as seed, animal feed, utility bills, gasoline, and property taxes (14.60).

Cole's unequivocal assertions about the complexity of keeping a community afloat in a complex economy appears at first to signal a break with the genre of fantasy, which—despite emphasizing the "ordinariness" of the secondary world—frequently resorts to a fairly simplistic, quasi-medieval economic structure in which peasants try to eke out a subsistence-oriented existence, wicked characters loot and hoard, and virtuous characters rise in stature and are rewarded, often with treasure. In Tolkien's world, mundane notions of money are less important than symbolic notions of treasure, which can be stolen, hoarded, given as a reward, or renounced, as in Frodo's destruction of the One Ring. As Ishay Landa argues in "Slaves of the Ring: the Political Unconscious," Tolkien's reaction to the Great War, not only as a mechanized series of battles of attrition but as a war between various imperialist powers, formed the context for his creation of the complex image of the Ring, which distills "all the immeasurable contradictions of the capitalist system: the enormous productivity with the annihilating destructiveness, the unlimited power of the few with the utter impotence of the many" (122). In *Fables*, money is less symbolic, as is indicated by the fluid but largely prosaic transfer of wealth from Bluebeard's treasure room to the community coffers (3.161), or in the representation of Bigby and Beast's expenditures as they prepare for war with the Adversary (10.84–85). When Bigby transfers his power as sheriff to Beast, he introduces him to Gudrun, the Goose who lays the Golden Eggs, explaining that her eggs allow him to "finance my unauthorized operations," as Bigby also knows a guy "who converts [the eggs] into untraceable funds" (5.107). Here, gold is not a symbolic treasure figuring in a heroic tale of sacrifice and/or reward, as is further evidenced by the image of Bigby casually tossing an egg to Beast; rather the depiction of an "off the books" source of financing points to the text's concern with the inscrutable flow of money in a world characterized by complex and hidden power networks. While the focus in Tolkien's work on the possession of treasure points to his anxiety about the corrupting nature of property (Landa, 125), the persistent representation in *Fables* of magical sources of endless money reinforces both the text's entrenched validation of capitalism and its relationship to globalization. When Frau Totenkinder provides King Cole with the magical bag filled with a seemingly limitless supply of golden coins (14.109), he is thrilled not because he intends to hoard the treasure but because he intends to spend it. Further, while *The Lord of the Rings* focuses on the exhausting, treacherous process of transporting the One Ring to Mordor, this moment in *Fables* shows a contrasting image of the magical, apparently effortless transfer of gold from Mr. Dark's former holding room in another world to The Farm. Here, the text not only shows how it is situated in a globalized world, already defined by the quick, though sometimes mysterious flow of capital, but also confirms a fantasy whereby this complex flow still benefits the local community.

As noted above, various scholars have explored the way Tolkien's development of the fantasy genre was connected to his desire to mark a continuous history of England, whereby the return to medieval ideals of "ennobling cultural and moral struggle" (Lynch 90) is meant to mitigate the rupture produced by the rise of industrialization and imperial capitalism. Especially as the comic book series progresses, imagery associated with medieval warfare suggests a similar move in *Fables* to recapture a romanticized past. Lynch argues that "in seeking to reconnect the present to the Middle Ages, [Tolkien] therefore binds himself to the intervening ages as well" (82). The problem with this potential correspondence between Tolkien's works and *Fables*, however, is that the idea of "medievalism" isn't actually relevant to the history of America; rather, the continuity marked by images of swords and armor in *Fables* links the series with the genre of fantasy as it has emerged as a literary framework for thinking through moral binaries. Thus, the final battle between the two sisters, though not necessarily a battle between good and evil (or even between medieval and modern), rests solely on the notion of straightforward opposition. In a globalized context, when ideas of borders, histories, and economies are anything but straightforward, the retreat into fantasy marks not a wish for the continuous, but rather a wish for the straightforward.

Race: East versus West, Pure versus Mongrel

In Tom Shippey's analysis of the way the so-called "core" group of fairy tales became the subject of several critical studies and revisionist adaptations, he notes that for a long time the attitude among English-speaking critics and writers to such narratives was decidedly non-serious, especially in comparison to late twentieth-century critics and writers who began to consider the category of the postmodern fairy tale (254–255). When finally turning their attention to the folk and fairy tale, critics and writers honed in on a relatively small group of tales which, Shippey suggests, are only linked by their similar plots elements (261). Though many folklorists point out that the phenomenon of folk and fairy tales has a lengthy history and is a global practice, it must also be noted that the "canon" of tales that has been repeatedly adapted and critiqued—especially within English-speaking Western culture—is made up of those nineteenth-century European versions of the tales that were eventually translated into English: as Jack Zipes comments, "The Grimms' *Children's and Household Tales* was not the culmination of the oral and literary tradition, but it did bring together representative tales in a style and ideology that suited middle-class taste throughout Europe and North America, and the subsequent value of the tales has been determined by the manner in which people throughout the world have regarded them as universal and classic" (Zipes 2001, 868). As a survey of Jess Nevins' *Fables Encyclopedia* shows, most of characters Willingham makes use of in his revisionist adaptation of tales emerge from the "universal and classic" European tradition, though the text is also indebted to Arthurian legends, English nursery rhymes, and canonical nineteenth-century literary works (and, in some of the *Fables* spin-offs, figures from American, African, Indu, and Japanese folklore traditions are introduced). The most striking exception to this Eurocentric focus, of course, is the introduction of the "Arabian Fables," who come to serve important roles during the war against the Adversary. In its representation of cultural difference, *Fables* appears to deny the need for accommodation, while still promoting the importance of tolerance of cultural difference. That said, the text rejects xenophobic attempts at racial purity, mostly because such goals get in the way of the day-to-day functioning of the community.

In Ulrich Marzolph's entry on the *"Arabian Nights,"* collected in *The Greenwood Encyclopedia of Folktales and Fairy Tales*, he goes over the evidence for Indian or Iranian origins of the text, especially of the famous frame tale, in which a woman tells tales in order to postpone her execution; the oldest surviving version of some of the collected tales is "a three-volume Arabic text that most probably dates from the middle of the fifteenth-century" (56). Though research into the origins of the *Arabian Nights*, or of *The Thousand and One Nights* as the collection was called at least since the mid-twelfth century, is important, Marzolph also notes that it was Antoine Galland's translation of the work into French in the early eighteenth-century that cemented its stature in the history of world folk and fairy tale. Galland not only translated the fifteenth-century Arabic text—which broke off after the 282nd tale—but integrated other Arabic stories into the work, including those that have become popular among Westerners, such as the stories of Sinbad, Ali Baba, and Aladdin (Marzolph, 57). After Galland, Arabic and European scholars worked to recover other editions and translations, leading to the text's enormous impact as "an integral constituent of European and world culture" (Marzolph, 59). The references to the *Arabian Nights* in *Fables* fall into three categories: first, some of the most famous characters are used: Sinbad, in *Fables*; Ali Baba, in *Fairest*; and Aladdin, in *Cinderella: From Fabletown with Love*. In working with these figures, little to no reference is made to the stories out of which they emerge; for example, in *Fables*, Sinbad is an emissary from the Arabian Homelands, only incidentally portrayed as the famed mariner and merchant from the source text; Aladdin meets Cindy as they pursue the same spy mission, while Ali Baba—though still depicted as a thief—gets wrapped up in a story of Briar Rose and Lumi. Second, Willingham adapts the famous frame tale of King Shahryar and Scheherazade in *1001 Nights of Snowfall*, though in his version it is Snow White who uses the stratagem of storytelling to delay her death. Finally, there are various Arabian characters—including a number of harem girls, a D'jinn, and such figures as Yusuf and Hakim—who appear out of the generalized world of the *Arabian Nights* rather than from particular tales. Thus, with the exception of the rewriting of the frame tale, the use of Arabian characters does not operate as revisionist adaptation, as the source tales are not referenced enough for a "critical examination of the original work" (Zipes 1994, 10). The reason for the focus on the characters as simply "Arabian" rather than as figures from archetypal narratives is that the text's interest in these non-European characters is related to politics, not plot.

The volume *Arabian Nights (and Days)* (Vol. 7) collects issues that were published between December 2005 and May 2006, although the second narrative arc—"The Ballad of Rodney and June"—is only thematically related to "Arabian Nights (and Days)" as an additional exploration of Otherness, as will be discussed below. The publication dates reflect the way this portion of the series responds to the aftermath of the 2003 American war with Iraq, in particular the years of political destabilization and insurgency in Iraq, the reports of prisoner abuse by Americans at Abu-Ghraib, the mounting number of American casualties, and the election of a transitional and then permanent Iraqi government. The text makes explicit reference to this context, for example, in the images of American soldiers on patrol in Baghdad (7.57), in the representation of the Arabian "prisoners" of Fabletown, who are depicted in shackles, with sacks over their heads (7.68), and in the complicated matter of allies versus enemies that animates Yusuf's first wish to the D'jinn (7.51, 7.73). As Wilson Koh argues in "'Put Not Your Trust in Princes': *Fables* and the Problematisation of Everyday Life," the volume might be read as a challenge to popular discourse that regarded the war's aftermath as evidence of an insurmountable rift between Western and Eastern cultures, as it

> restages the motives and outcomes of the real-life Iraq war in gloriously utopian tones: the Fabletown heroes suffer no casualties, the Grand Vizier becomes the victim of his own hubris, Sinbad willingly learns English to better co-operate with the main Fabletown outpost, and the motivations of the American Fables for helping the Arabs are born mainly from (meta)human decency [147].

Koh additionally argues, however, that the "carnivelesque" qualities of this utopian vision are undermined by the way *Fables* ultimately affirms "the superiority of the neo-conservative American way of life" (147). In considering the representation of the Arabian Fables not only as part of a satirical response to the particulars of a political situation but also as an exploration of the more general issue of cultural difference, it is helpful to look at the representation of language play and power structures.

From the first pages of *Arabian Nights (and Days)*, the related issues of language, translation, and meaning are shown to be central thematic and plot elements: while the Arabian Fables speak another language—as evidenced by the use of a distinct font in their speech bubbles (7.7)—Prince Charming's first "words" in the volume are a series of noises he makes upon waking in his prison-like sleeping area (7.8–9); even the scene showing how the new mayor has reached the nadir of his civil service career highlights the way language use is never straightforwardly related to communication, as phrases such as "thank you so much for your patience," "we're working on it," and "I'll look into it first thing" (7.10–11) are clearly meaningless. The text also appears to challenge the stereotype of the parochial American, as the inability to make heads or tails of a foreign language or culture is referred to as "idio[cy]" (7.16) and "insan[ity]" (7.20). Even worse than a total lack of communication, however, are the text's representations of partial communication: Charming and Yusuf's halting conversation about "rooms" and "slaves" almost results in violence (7.20), while Miss Safiya—former harem girl—embarrasses Flycatcher and infuriates Red Riding Hood with her inadvertently sexually charged mistranslations (7.86–97). Thus, the text appears to chastise Westerners for their own unwillingness or inability to develop better modes of communication, while also suggesting that the work of comprehending and surmounting cultural difference is laborious, complicated, but worthwhile, as shown in Beauty's nascent attempts to converse with Hakim (7.94). That said, the representation of the way King Cole utilizes his absolute command of Arabic language and custom destabilizes progressive notions of cross-cultural communication and accommodation. When Cole is called upon to act as interpreter during discussions with the Arabian Fables, he immediately performs his mastery of Arabic nuance and poetic embellishment, appropriately exalting Sinbad and Allah and colorfully cursing the Adversary (7.25). Cole's impeccable abilities as an interpreter, however, do not result in precise translation, but rather in a series of language tricks: when Prince Charming states that Sinbad will keep his slaves "over my dead body," Cole "translates" this response as "My honoured mayor (may Allah bless him with sons in abundance) agrees that we must recognize and respect each other's ways"; when Cole then asks Sinbad to respect the American "custom to hang slavers," Sinbad is delighted by Cole's rhetorical dexterity, ignoring Yusuf's outrage and challenging King Cole to a game of chess (7.39–40). The narrative arc's depiction of the enormous power of language tricks reaches its apex in the revelation that Frau Totenkinder "alter[s Yusuf's] language," in order to thwart his use of the D'jinn as a weapon (7.73). Further, the representation of Beauty's "pretty speech" to Charming, in which she tries to deflect responsibility away from her own participation in their kiss (7.32), and the way Rose Red selectively interprets Fabletown directives with respect to Boy Blue's punishment (7.83) confirms the text's skepticism as to the possibility of ingenuous cultural exchange.

The focus on the necessarily imperfect course of translation in *Arabian Nights (and Days)* (Vol. 7) counters the idea that cultural accommodation will eventually eliminate the practice of "Othering," or of considering those who are not Western, not only "other," but also "inferior." The freeing of the Arabian slaves in Fabletown does not in any way reduce how they are exoticized or framed according to Western expectations: despite Beauty's attempts to speak his language, Hakim remains committed to the hackneyed role of the Eastern master of painful assassination techniques (7.94), while the harem girls retain their stereotypical garb and continue to function as objects of sexual titillation (7.97). Further, the pictorial depiction of the Homelands version of Baghdad entirely conforms to Western stereotypes of ancient, mystical "Arabia" (7.93). That said, the representation of King Cole—the new ambassador to Fabletown East—wearing a Victorian British Army pith helmet shows the text's self-awareness of its own hyperbolic orientalism. Though Koh's point that *Fables* confirms "the superiority of the neo-conservative American way of life" is well-taken, the very obviousness of this confirmation—together with the very obviousness of the moral high ground Prince Charming takes with respect to the issue of slaves—highlights the text's meta-critique of hierarchical power structures. As noted above, Frau Totenkinder foils Yusuf by "alter[ing ...] language," though as she explains to Beast, she is only able to change Yusuf's words "within the bounds of what he'd actually wish on his enemy" (7.77). That the Fabletown executive express distaste for the horrifying nature of the D'jinn's slow torture of Yusuf appears pointedly hypocritical, as just down the hall Sinbad languishes in a dark cell (7.79). In the scene depicting the interrogation of Sinbad, Willingham again emphasizes the issue of language, drawing particular attention to the matter of "intention," a concept that Sinbad first mistranslates as "interjection" (7.84) and—later—mistranslates as "invention" (7.86). As with the language trick involving the D'jinn, the idea of intention is presented as a crucial site of possible mediation: while Frau can change the target of Yusuf's destructive intentions, Cole and Charming can strategically accept Sinbad's "interjection," his "invention," that he meant Fabletown no harm in bringing with him a highly magical weapon. Once the matter of "intention" has been settled—i.e., once the leaders of Fabletown West decide that Sinbad and the other Arabian Fables would make useful allies in the war against the Adversary—the status quo, which includes being served food by one of Sinbad's harem girls, prevails (7.88–89). Thus, the text decisively celebrates the preservation of a narrow worldview, one in which Riding Hood gushes about Flycatcher's gift of candies (7.95) and fumes about the way the Arabian females dress (7.96–97); this celebration ensues within the context of acknowledging that the West's habit of racist Othering never gets in the way of the formation of political alliances.

Thus, the critique imbedded into the representation of East-West relations in *Fables* is that difficulties of cultural accommodation at the social level don't preclude necessary political maneuvers, and that—as long as the notion of "intention" remains flexible—strategic relations of power can be maintained and strengthened. The notion that high level political relationships are necessarily distinct from ordinary social relations is underscored in the opening sections of "The Ballad of Rodney and June," also collected in *Arabian Nights (and Days)* (Vol. 7). Though the bulk of the letter the wooden soldier Rodney writes to "Father Geppetto" focuses on his affection for June and his desire that they both be transformed into flesh, he begins by noting his current military role patrolling a garrison at the edge of the Arabian Homelands (7.103). From Rodney's point of view, the Adversary forces are occupying Arabian territory, which the Arabian Fables continue to try to reclaim (7.105). In other words, in direct opposition to the standard American perspective on events occurring in Iraq in 2005 and 2006, the reader of *Fables* is invited to view the occupying army as the antagonists and to sympathize with Arabian forces who, as they attack, shout "Death to the Infidels!" (7.100–101). The inclusion of this inversion in Rodney's letter is doubly significant, as the text's second most explicit examination of race is in the representation of Geppetto's wooden soldiers, who continuously boast about their "racial" purity. When the wooden brothers Hugh, Lou, and Drew first arrive in New York, they are offended when a street vendor tries to sell them hotdogs, noting that "the meatheads of this world will eventually have to learn how to respect their betters" (4.89). In their insistence on their status as "the chosen elite of the empire" (4.151), the wooden brothers are likened to members of past and present white power movements, a connection made explicit in a scene when a Mundy family comments on the sight of the full battalion of wooden soldiers marching toward Fabletown. While the adult male first notes that the participants on parade are "too white to be Black pride, or Latino pride, or Asian pride," he comes to the conclusion that they are a group of "young Republicans"; when the man's son wonders if his mother is confusing the group with "the Nazis," his mother replies, "Is there a difference?" (4.185). Elsewhere in the series, Willingham reiterates his antipathy toward the privileging of racial purity, for example in the representation of the World War II Nazi scientists, who refer to themselves as members of "the master race" (5.53), and in *Werewolves of the Heart-*

land, which acts as a kind of sequel to this narrative arc in *Fables*; despite occasional pictorial depictions of a racially diverse population in Story City, the graphic novel draws attention to the problematic course of staying inside the same "breeding pool" (*Were*, 66). As Bigby points out to Harp, the town is "doomed" because of its insistence on sameness: "You have the wolf mind, multiplied by thousands ... added to that, every single member of the community is a natural killer" (*Were*, 71). Also, the representation of Ghost reflects a condemnation of the fear of miscegenation: when he first finds out about Ghost, who—ironically—is referred to as a "pure zephyr," the North Wind suggests that Snow White is "tainted" (15.145). Ultimately, however, North develops a plan to destroy himself rather than fulfill his promise to kill Ghost, thus confirming the text's denunciation of race-based eugenics.

The battle between the wooden soldiers and Fabletown is finally decided when Bigby arrives and destroys the wooden army with his "huff and puff" (4.209); while this act represents one of the most successful performances of Bigby's masculine role as a community protector, it is also significant that the "pure" wooden soldiers are beaten by a mixed-species character, one who immediately starts directing an orderly clean-up of the battle area. Though the text's representation of the Arabian Fables maintains a highly suspicious attitude toward notions of accommodation or authentic cross-cultural exchange, the idea of tolerating difference is promoted, especially if—at the social level—everyone can agree to just get on with the practical matters of co-existence. Such practical matters are connected throughout the text with the representation of appropriate performances of citizenship. In part 2 of "The Ballad of Rodney and June," June describes the fulfillment of their wish to be made flesh and their new life, living close to Fabletown and working as agents for the Empire: as June notes, despite their ambivalence about some of their work, they proceed with "every terrible deed. Because we are loyal to our Empire" (7.142). The issue of Rodney and June's loyalty to the Empire is again raised just prior to Fabletown's attack on the Homelands, when Pinocchio pleads with his two "younger siblings" to rethink their notion of what is constituted by loyalty: as Pinocchio puts it, acting in their father's "best interest" means helping Fabletown undermine his position as "the bloody goddamn Emperor of the bloody goddamn Empire" (11.75). The point of this scene is again to show that dealing with the finer points of cultural difference is less relevant than dealing with the practical matters of living within a complex polis. Thus, it is not surprising that the final appearance of Geppetto's wooden soldiers occurs when they are sent to attack Haven, the new

kingdom that Flycatcher sets up in opposition to the Empire, and in opposition to the idea of a "chosen elite."

In the lead up to the confrontation between Flycatcher and an army
of wooden soldiers—the so-called "Golden Horde"—Geppetto rejects the
advice of his largest puppet, the figurehead Emperor, to "simply [ignore]"
Haven and allow the community to co-exist with the Empire (10.198).
Geppetto, instead, orders genocide, whereby the Golden Horde will
"slaughter everyone, even onto the smallest child" (10.199). When the
Golden Horde arrives at Haven, Flycatcher surrenders to them and his
sacrifice produces a magical effect: first, the wooden soldiers are turned
back into trees, able to find "rest" after "so many ages as the Emperor's
elite killers" (10.210); second, Flycatcher's sacrifice breaks the spell of loyalty that binds the wooden soldiers to Geppetto, a spell that was first produced by the Blue Fairy (6.158), but which is eventually synthesized by
Geppetto who keeps the Blue Fairy captive (6.162). When Flycatcher is
asked whether he in turn will create his own army of wooden soldiers "and
send them out to conquer other lands" (10.216), the horrible image of an
army of Flycatchers once again confirms the text's denunciation of sameness, which is thus linked to a denunciation of loyalty that is enforced. On
one end of the spectrum are the likes of Geppetto, who manipulates trees
from the living Sacred Grove into unnaturally loyal puppets, or Mr. Dark,
who retains the service of his witherlings by eating their teeth, or Roquat,
who makes use of such motivational mottos as "Unquestioning service is
the least you owe him!" (17.77). At the other end of the spectrum is the
ideal of "choice" that Flycatcher continues to affirm (10.226). As Flycatcher
points out, the trees in the Sacred Grove have the status as "subject[s] of
my kingdom" (10.215) and—as discussed in Chapter Three—the construction of Haven functions as a fantasy of the perfect community, one in
which every subject chooses to abide by the laws of the land, and where
a multicultural citizenry can co-exist, as long as there is no expectation
that particular cultural differences—such as the goblin appetite for Fable
creatures—will be accommodated.

Thus, the fantasy of Haven works in a similar fashion to the utopian
vision that Koh describes as a "restag[ing of] the motives and outcomes
of the real-life Iraq war": just as the elite of Fabletowns West and East
perform "co-operation" and "decency," so too does the King of Haven perform his openness to goblins, non-human Fables, and ghosts. That said,
just as the entire run of *Fables* uses a normative cast of characters who
are European in origin, an arrangement that ensures that the Arabian Fables
will be read in political, rather than literary terms, so too is the image of

perfect multiculturalism shown in Haven predicated on the willingness of Flycatcher and his all white, human, and European advisory council to be tolerant. During the baseball game between the Frog Bombers and the Gobtown Crushers, it is clear from the depictions of the crowd that the goblins represent the "Other" team. While the text denounces any hint of the desire for "purity," linking such desires with the forces of tyranny, the European perspective of *Fables* is never decentered.

Simplicity, security, and stability: these are the political aspirations that are highlighted in *Fables* and that point to the text's function as a response to an increasingly globalized world. *Fables* explores the relationship between community and bureaucracy, between leaders and citizens, and between notions of national identity and of cultural difference. Throughout, *Fables* appears to advocate for the recentering of the citizen identity and for the shoring up of local power as a bulwark against the amplified complexity of systems and against competing historical and cultural narratives. This fantasy of working out political tensions—simply and effectively—brings us to the topic of magic, as *Fables*—like other wonder tales—makes use of the depiction of extraordinary happenings in order to bring the culture's hopes and fears into relief.

4

Magic, Metaphysics and Metafiction

In the wake of the final battle between Cinderella and Frau Totenkinder, at the end of which all the spells that hide Fabletown from Mundy eyes are destroyed, King Cole decides to embrace the new normal and create the "Totenkinder Memorial School of Magic" (22.135); later, the Magic Mirror admits to Frankie that, indeed, he has been asked to teach at the school (22.138). Though the Mirror's admission may operate primarily as a gentle joke on Frankie, who can't understand why he, a self-professed genius, has not been asked to teach, the scene also brings to mind the provocative idea that magic itself is a teacher; that magic—like a story—exists as a mirror to help us see things more clearly or differently. It is an agent of defamiliarization, which forces us to look at our own reflections with fresh eyes.

In *Fables*, the subject of magic is explored as it relates to the notion of systems that guide human action and sense of being: moral, technological, political, and epistemological. The representation of magic allows the text to explore how the inexplicable might be explained, or how a desire for the irrational might be rationalized. The key issues explored in this chapter are the way magic is related to questions about power, the way the system of magic compares to systems of technology, religion, and language, fortune, and fate, and the way the function and force of magic is always connected to meditations on the role of story as a means by which individuals and communities make sense of themselves.

Magic and Power in the Age of Anxiety

During the party he throws to celebrate being elected the new mayor of Fabletown, Prince Charming approaches Frau Totenkinder to discuss with her and the other witches of the 13th floor an election promise he made, which is "government sponsored glamours and transformations" (5.90). Frau Totenkinder demurs at the notion of a "volume discount" on spells, explaining "We're already nearly at the limit of our ability to craft spells.... We aren't able to mass-produce our workings like some Mundy factory" (5.90–91). Here and elsewhere in *Fables*, magic is described as being a limited commodity, whereby, for example, Ozma describes the tactic used by Frau Totenkinder/Bellflower to use a number of spells in succession in order to battle Mr. Dark as "spending her power lavishly" (15.153). Further, there is a distinction made in the Fables universe between the "Great Powers," or those whose magic is elemental, such as the North Wind or Mr. Dark, and practitioners of magic, whose knowledge of the craft and/or access to magical objects makes them more or less powerful. Thus, when the wooden soldiers deliver Boy Blue's wounded body to the Woodland Building, they make it known that—on behalf of the Emperor—they intend to "take possession of all magic property illegally removed from our lands" (4.161). In *Postmodern Fairy Tales*, Cristina Bacchilega notes that in older tales "the fairy tale's magic act requires ... a careful balance of threats and rewards," whereby even in the potentially liberating folk tale, the representation of magic will "rely on and reinforce social norms" (6–7). While it is tempting to try and dissect the details of the scheme governing magic in *Fables*, the system is never perfectly outlined, leading to the sense that—in the end—magic here represents the anxious *desire* for such a thing as comprehensible social norms, or for an ordering principle in the universe that might overrule arbitrary politics and petty struggles. As shown, for example, in the representation of magical objects and of the Great Powers, the text strives to imagine ways in which power might be limited, thus promoting the fantasy of finding the parameters of an anxious age of proliferation and excess.

In their discussion of the representation of magic in folk and fairy tales, scholars often begin with the matter of classification, pointing out that tales that include instances of magic are known as wonder tales. Jan Ziolkowski explains the relationship between wonder tales and magic thus: "Wonder is the effect that such tales seek to achieve, while magic is the means that they employ to attain this goal" (64). The wonder tale is defined by its cultural history: as Jack Zipes notes, though the literary tradition of the fairy tale does include wonder tales, the discussion of the genre is often connected to oral tellings of "the folk": "During the Middle Ages, most people in *all* social classes believed in magic, the supernatural, and the miraculous ... [wonder tales] were told and retold because they had some connection to the material conditions and personal relations in their societies" (2006, 53). Due in large part to the foundational work of Vladimir Propp, scholars also discuss the wonder tale in terms of its structure. In the 1928 work, *Morphology of the Folktale*, Propp discusses the character types found in wonder tales and the sequence of actions—or functions—that make up the standard plot. Finally, as Zipes points out in *Why Fairy Tales Stick*, the crucial element of the wonder tale is that they produce in readers a sense of amazement:

> It is this earthy, sensual, and secular sense of wonder and hope that distinguished the wonder tales from other oral tales such as the legend, the fable, the anecdote, and the myth.... In the oral wonder tale, we are told to marvel about the workings of the universe where anything can happen at any time, and those *fortunate* and *unfortunate* events are never really explained. Nor do the characters demand an explanation—they are instinctively opportunistic and hopeful.... They have not been spoiled by conventionalism, power, or rationalism. In contrast to the humble characters, the villains are those who use words and power intentionally to exploit, control, transfix, incarcerate, and destroy for their own benefit [50–51, emphasis in original].

Zipes' argument is relevant to an exploration of *Fables* in a couple of ways: first, the simple contrast between "humble characters" and "villains" does not hold in the comic book series, not so much because of an absence of villainy, but because of a dearth of humility: the "good" characters in *Fables* are almost never portrayed as innocents, having all lived long enough to be highly rational, if not downright scheming, very much attuned to and invested in the workings of power, and often stubborn and set in their ways. Further, the opportunism and hopefulness of characters such as Jack, Prince Charming, or even Rose Red is usually represented as problematic. Second, Zipes asserts that—in the typical wonder tale—characters do not seek an "explanation" for marvelous occurrences, which runs counter to the response to magic portrayed throughout *Fables*, as shown, for example, in Ozma's decidedly rational approach to building the Super Team (16.31). Significantly, it is the widespread aspiration to make magic comprehensible—to consider it as a system—that makes almost every character in *Fables* a potential "villain" who would "use words and power intentionally" and "for their own benefit." Thus, the representation of magic in *Fables* is equally a representation of our interaction with systems of power, which are often displayed as morally ambiguous.

Crucial in the scholarly descriptions of the wonder tale is the fact that magical occurrences produce awe, a sense that something out of the

ordinary has happened, usually with the effect of changing the social condition of the central character. As discussed early in Chapter One, most
folk and fairy tales are wish-fulfillment narratives that project a desire to
challenge unfair social conditions by representing an individual who
miraculously, though deservedly, rises in status. As also noted, however,
this standard plot structure is not pertinent to *Fables* because of the text's
emphasis on characters that have already "come-of-age," as well as its focus
on a complex community rather than a single protagonist. The "wonder"
produced by the magical occurrences in *Fables*, instead, is often related
to protecting or performing a status quo, or—in contrast—is associated
with power and war. As noted above, one of the basic services offered by
the witches of the 13th floor is to help wealthy Fables who purchase magical spells keep their non-Mundy appearance a secret (1.15); likewise, the
Fabletown witches are also responsible for setting up various binding spells
that connect the rooms of the Woodland Building (12.79–80), and consistently work to keep Fabletown magically invisible to the Mundys (4.173).
Like many folk and fairy tales, the series includes examples of magical
transformation; however, whereas Propp's conception of transformation
or enchantment is often linked with the plot functions of punishment or
reward, as well as with the rising status of a protagonist (Propp, 62), the
magical transformations of such figures as Bigby, Beast, Grimble, and
Hobbes are connected to their capabilities as "big fighters" (4.192). Such
representations of transformation are more in keeping with the tradition
of superhero comic books, whereby these characters generally retain their
human "identities" unless required to do battle. The other main source of
transformation in *Fables* is Blue Fairy magic, which Geppetto synthesizes
and exploits in order to create his enormous regime of puppet adminis-
trators and wooden soldiers (6.162). Importantly, this transformation
magic is likewise unrelated to narratives about what an individual character deserves, but is mass-produced so that Geppetto can assert and
retain administrative power. *Fables* also includes various representations
of magical travel, for example via the Witching Cloak, magic carpet, gateways between worlds, and so on. In this most explicit version of what Zipes
calls "the workings of the universe where anything can happen at any
time," the point is to focus on the largeness of the world inhabited by these
characters, and to draw attention to an important dynamic explored in the
text that opposes expansiveness with limits.

The concern with the relationship between expansiveness and limits
relates to the fantasy of comprehending a governing system for behavior
in an anxious world, as also is shown by the text's depiction of magical

objects. In his summary of some of the basic Proppian components of the folk tale, Zipes notes that the hero will a) encounter a magical helper or antagonist, and b) have to "prove him- or herself and acquire gifts that are often magical agents, which bring about a miraculous or marvelous change or transformation" (49–50; see also Propp 39–44). In *Fables,* the figure of the magical helper or antagonist is incredibly complicated given, for example, the monstrous history of such "helper" figures as Frau Totenkinder or Bigby, or given the distinction made in the text between the Great Powers and the practitioners of magic, which will be discussed below. The representation of the magical object, however, is more straightforward and often connects to the standard function of such items in folk and fairy tale. Stith Thompson notes in his seminal work *The Folktale* that "A general pattern is found in nearly all stories of magic objects. There is the extraordinary manner in which the objects are acquired, the use of the objects by the hero, the loss (usually by theft), and the final recovery" (70). As Propp further suggests, the "transference" of the magical object to the hero "very often [has] the character of a reward" (44). In contrast, according to Propp, when a villain acquires a magical agent, "the actual movement of the tale is created" (30–31), meaning that a plot is initiated in which the villain will eventually be vanquished and punished.

The most significant magical objects in *Fables* are the Witching Cloak and Vorpal Sword, which are "acquired" (that is, ostensibly stolen from the Fabletown Business Office) by Boy Blue (5.129) and used by him during his quest in the Homelands (see *Homelands*, Vol. 6). The magical property of the Vorpal Sword—an object that is mentioned in Lewis Carroll's nonsense poem "Jabberwocky," which is included in *Alice's Adventures Through the Looking Glass*—is its ability to chop off the heads of enemies (an action accompanied by the sound "snicker snack" [6.61], in another allusion to "Jabberwocky"). As Boy Blue acknowledges to Flycatcher, "the sword does most of the fighting for you" (10.32) and, indeed, in his battle with Baba Yaga in the lost Business Office, Bufkin can barely hold the Vorpal Sword and yet manages to chop off Baba Yaga's head (14.137). Boy Blue and Bufkin's use of this object seems to conform to the convention that deserving, humble characters make use of a magical object to defeat their enemies, thus proving themselves worthy of the transformation into hero (though, as discussed in Chapter One, Boy Blue's quest narrative is a bit of a trick). Other examples of magical weapons in *Fables* include the Eastermark Blade, Brandish's magical sword (14.64), which is "actually a hundred magic weapons conquered and absorbed over the ages into the one which rules them all" (19.142); the magical armor worn by Flycatcher, including Excalibur, famed sword from Arthurian legend that allows the ghosts of the Witching Well to "maintain [their] solid living forms" (10.204); and the magical armor that Snow White and Rose Red acquire as they move toward their fateful showdown. While the contrast between the Eastermark Blade and Excalibur is an example of the text's clear-cut contrast between the use of a magical object by a villain versus by an innocent, the contrast between Snow White's blade "Ice" and Rose Red's blade "Thorn" is morally ambiguous. In the text's development of the standard wonder tale's conventions, an important plot function of acquiring and controlling magical weapons is not necessarily related to the representation of worthiness (or villainy), but to the exploration of a more complicated dynamics of power.

Boy Blue's second magical object is his Witching Cloak, an object with a far more intricate history and meaning than the Vorpal Sword. Thompson notes that "Seldom in folktales does any thought seem to be given to the process by which magical objects may be constructed: their existence is merely taken for granted" (78). In the case of the Witching Cloak, however, the text provides some detail about its history, which is parceled out to the reader only after Mr. Dark vows to "punish those who made use of" the Witching Cloak (12.56). As Mr. Dark explains in *Witches* (Vol. 14), he once had a "bag of endless nightmares and infinite screams," into which he tossed all those who sought to battle with him (14.26–27), but whose first purpose was to "[hold] naughty children" (14.29). After Mr. Dark is boxed, the bag is turned into a cloak, though Mr. Dark explains that "my bag was part of me, and so I was never fully trapped" (14.29); also according to Mr. Dark, he "manipulated" those who used the Witching Cloak to defeat the Adversary, thus bringing about his own release from the box (14.29). Mr. Dark's motive of vengeance is not particularly logical, as the Brotherhood of Boxers who trap him serve the Empire and are not affiliated with Fabletown; still, as the prophetic head of Colin Pig explains to Rose Red "there was always going to be a price for using the Witching Cloak" (12.95). That "price" amounts to Fabletown becoming the object of Mr. Dark's ire and losing Boy Blue, whose absolute confidence in the magical properties of the Witching Cloak cause his downfall. In using the cloak to try and block a magical arrow aimed at Bigby during the final battle with the Adversary's army, Boy Blue is wounded and, as Doctor Swineheart eventually discovers, the wound is infected with "a tiny piece of thread from the Witching Cloak" (12.66). Even before the story of the Witching Cloak's history and Boy Blue's death are narrated, however, the text explains that Flycatcher is able to "copy" the magic of the cloak, which he uses to magically transport himself (and sometimes others) across worlds (10.227). The significance of the complex, achronological narratives involving the Witching Cloak relate to the text's sidestepping of a purely oppositional system of reward and punishment, as well as its exploration of how power is commodified and—ideally—limited: as Colin Pig notes, the use of magic has a "price" and even an object like the Witching Cloak has a threshold of power. Further, the backstory of Mr. Dark's magical bag, together with the idea that the Good Prince Flycatcher can "copy" the fundamentals of a magical object, suggest that there is a balanced system of elemental magic or universal power that transcends the limits of human use. Interestingly, in place of the wonder tale's standard depiction of magic to reinforce a "careful balance of threats and rewards," the depiction of magic in *Fables* reflects an anxious desire to *find* balance, to be assured that some kind of governing system of meaning or justice is actually in place.

Before her duel with Mr. Dark, Bellflower has a discussion with the North Wind, in which she explains her theory of "the fundamental nature" of magic: that "it's the raw stuff of chaos that desires order" (15.143–144). Bellflower claims that her superior knowledge of the ordered conventions of the duel will give her an edge in the battle with Mr. Dark. What is important in Bellflower's pronouncement is the way it connects to her practitioner's concern with the ordering principles of accumulation and spending. As explicated in "The Witch's Tale," included in *1001 Nights of Snowfall*, Frau Totenkinder/Bellflower accumulates power via blood sacrifice (*1001*, 103), and spends it—first, according to her own sense of whim and vengeance (*1001*, 105–107)—and then, according to her sense of duty toward the community associated with Snow White and Rose Red, who saved her from the oven (*1001*, 94, 116). In *Witches* (Vol. 14), Frau Totenkinder transitions into Bellflower in order to "follow a trail of gold to a world that finds itself overburdened [with magic]" (14.68), thus embarking on a prepatory period of accumulation. The focus in this volume on accumulation and spending is reinforced by such images as the magical bag full of gold coins sent to King Cole, which connects matters of magic to mundane issues of money (14.108), as well as by the narrative of Ozma's challenge to Geppetto's increasing authority at The Farm. As Ozma stresses to the remaining 13th floor witches, "we have to move quickly to confound Geppetto's scheme [to run The Farm], before it can take root among the gullible and miserable populace"; to do so requires that "for once we must forget prudence and thrift to spend lavishly" (14.128). Using magic borrowed from all the other witches, Ozma publically transforms

Reynard the Fox into a human (14.132), thus impressing on her audience her prodigious power. However, while Ozma is able to fool her Fable community, the representation of her fussy and ultimately pointless preparations to battle Mr. Dark (16.123), not to mention her subsequent failure to prevail against a deranged Bigby (21.85–86), show that the "careful balance of threats and reward" does not hold in the *Fables* universe. Likewise, despite Bellflower's careful planning and wise spending of spells, including one that makes use of thousands of golden coins (15.183), she too fails to defeat the Great Power of Mr. Dark (15.198). Again, the hero/practitioner's failure reflects the text's dubiousness about trusting any system that is too simplistic, as there are no longer any clear "social norms" that can be relied upon or reinforced.

During Bellflower's excursion back into the Homelands, she first visits the box that once contained Mr. Dark (14.88), and then seeks out Dunster Happ, former commander of the Brotherhood of Boxers (14.118). As is described in the first narrative arc of *Witches* (Vol. 14), the Brotherhood is a quasi-religious order made up of sorcerers who—like the witches of the 13th floor—are concerned with "husband[ing]" magic and "expending" power "only in the course of duty" (14.13). Their main task in serving the Empire is to capture those whom Mr. Dark refers to as "the weirds" (14.18); once such conduits of pure magic are captured, the practitioner sorcerers make use of their power (14.29), an arrangement even Bellflower deems "unworthy" (14.88). Still, Bellflower asks for Dunster's help, stating her intention to kill Mr. Dark, not box him (15.20). As Dunster notes, however, "killing" one of the Great Powers isn't really possible: "his dark spirit would manifest in a new person. Creation cannot abide a permanent loss of this force. It's like that with any of the Great Powers" (15.106–107). It is sometimes unclear which figures in *Fables* qualify as one of the so-called Great Powers. During the crisis with the Arabian Fables, Frau Totenkinder explains to Beast that—unlike a D'jinn, which is almost "pure magic" (7.41)—practitioners and even "your average elder gods" are a "mixture of magic and mundane material" (7.42), which suggests that it is not magical ability that defines a Great Power. After all, even Mr. Dark can't get through Flycatcher's magical barrier in Haven (16.46) and a D'jinn, the revived Baba Yaga, and her three servant knights are all beaten by a flying monkey, some wooden heads, and several tiny women (14.93, 14.137). The closest delineation of the Great Powers comes in Dunster Happ's explanation that "each of the Great Powers has his own personal magic box artifact" (15.110), a theory that leads to the construction of the boxes to begin with. Indeed, it is the North Wind's use of his own box artifact—his "casket of primordial winds" (16.116)—that traps both Mr. North and Mr. Dark. Likewise, as is suggested in the first narrative arc of *Happily Ever After* (Vol. 21), the fated showdown between Snow White and Rose Red has caused each sister to become a "container" for the magical energy that animates their family history (21.13).

On the one hand, the notion that the Great Powers will always exist, even if a particular manifestation of that power "dies," confirms the fantasy explored throughout *Fables* regarding balance and stability: that the universe makes sense, even if human politics and social relations are filled with chaos, pain, and foolishness. This fantasy is confirmed in the representation of Winter Wolf's emergence as the new North Wind, as her Great Power is connected to basic genealogy and is simply "reveal[ed]" (17.86): as Dunster Happ comments, her elemental status appears "naturally" (17.74). On the other hand, the mythical notion that each of the Great Powers can be "boxed" or limited—a circumstance that creates periodic imbalance, as shown by the rise of the Empire and by the horror leading up to the confrontation between Snow White and Rose Red—paradoxically adds to the fantasy of stability. The extended narrative of the D'jinn indicates the way this particular strand of the fantasy manifests: as Frau Totenkinder explains to Beast, the D'jinn are "wild things, with no sense of good or evil" (7.42) and no limit to their power. It is only via the human ingenuity of Sulymon and Daedalus that the enormous power of the D'jinn is limited, ostensibly for "constructive use" (7.43). The problem, of course, is that humans are as likely to be destructive as constructive, as shown by the wishes of Yusuf, who wants only to destroy his enemies and cement his personal prestige (7.71). Later in the series, when Bufkin is trapped in the lost Business Office, he tricks the D'jinn into returning to his bottle by mimicking the greediness of Yusuf, telling the D'jinn he intends to wish for a way out of the Business Office, for "riches," and for "a harem of hot flying monkey babes, of course" (14.92). However, while the text subverts a key principle of the folk and fairy tale as wish-fulfillment narrative by pointing out that humans generally wish for stupid or dangerous things, it also celebrates the idea of cleverness, both in the story of Sulymon and Daedelus and in the representation of Bufkin. The fantasy that the governing principles of the universe can be balanced, stable, and limited is ultimately a fantasy that humans themselves will strive to find limits to their own greed and destructive tendencies.

In her discussion with the North Wind about the nature of magic, Bellflower declares that "Magic yearns. It's the raw stuff of chaos that desires order" (15.144). This pronouncement coheres with the basic scheme underpinning the way magical power is presented in *Fables*: certainly in the representation of magical "spending" and magical objects, but even in the representation of the Great Powers, the text tends to focus on the way massive forces can be limited. This fantasy that magic belongs to a system that is balanced and that provides limits operates in tension with anxiety about a world in which systems are inscrutable and in which money, information, threat, and chaos proliferate. Bellflower's notion that magic "yearns" also recalls the key element of the wonder tale, which is that it will produce in readers a sense of awe and, maybe, hope; this gesture toward the emotional impact of stories of magic relates to a corollary response to anxiety, which is the hope that humans themselves will manage to think their way out of chaos, as do the likes of Sulymon, Daedalus, and a wise monkey named Bufkin.

Magic versus Technology, Religion and Language

One of the narrative arcs braided into *Sons of Empire* (Vol. 10) depicts a meeting among various Imperial forces who come together to discuss— as Lumi, the Snow Queen puts it—"the final fate of the rebel Fabletown" (10.26). The proposal put forth by Lumi describes not simply an attack on Fabletown, but the apocalyptic destruction of the entire Mundy world via four phases: a plague of pestilence, spread by the likes of the sorcerer Tom Harrow (10.33); a plague of fire, spread by dragons (10.34); a plague of cold, spread by Lumi herself (10.36), and a plague of famine, which, as Lumi explains, "will proceed automatically from the others" and make for an effortless occupation of the Mundy world (10.39). A counter-argument to this proposal is presented by Pinocchio, whose main point is that "advanced technology" will allow a Mundy army to take down any and all of the Homeland worlds (10.87). As Pinocchio asserts, the Empire's sorcerers can be defeated with a "five-point-six-two round travelling at 3282 feet per second" (10.85). Pinocchio's vision, thus, is not only an attempt to undermine Lumi's horrifying plan—though ostensibly from a position of wanting to "save" his father, the Emperor (10.90)—but is also a self-reflexive acknowledgment of a widespread convention of the sword-and-sorcery fantasy text, which is the pre-industrialized setting. As a fervent comic book reader, Pinocchio would be familiar with this convention, as is made clear from the belittling reference in his presentation to figures from the vast Homelands as "Meevil[s] ... short for medieval people" (10.84). In *Comic Book Crime: Truth, Justice, and the American Way*,

Nickie D. Phillips and Staci Strobel assert that, "comic books provide readers with a means of processing existential dilemmas in an age of anxiety and threats that reach global proportions" (220). In its oppositional representations of magic versus technology, and magic versus religion, *Fables* counters basic principles of the sword-and-sorcery genre, i.e., that the simpler world of swords and magic offers greater potential for justice, and that so-called progress produces moral regression. However, the collision in *Fables* of primary and secondary worlds, associated respectively with the contemporary period and an imagined pre-industrial period, allows for the complex exploration of such "existential dilemmas" as the use of advanced weaponry as a means of imperialist conquest, the function of religion in the contemporary moment, and the important place of scholarship in a world of competing narratives. Paradoxically, when magic is contrasted with technology, organized religion, and elitist scholarship, the textual insistence that magical power is superior to these influences reflects concern about their ascendency, especially in terms of an amoral attitude toward community.

In his introduction to the *Historical Dictionary of Fantasy Literature*, Brian Stableford discusses J.R.R. Tolkien's oft-quoted 1938 lecture "On Fairy Stories," in particular his point that, by providing an "imaginative sidestep ... [into] imaginary worlds," such narratives allow the reader to "recover a proper sense of perspective" on reality (xlv). The method by which this "imaginative sidestep" is achieved is a combination of mimesis and the fantastic: as Stableford explains,

> most fantasy novels begin naturalistically, adopting the pretense that the worlds they contain are simulations of some aspect of the reader's experienced world, albeit one that is carefully distanced geographically, and perhaps historically. In the most discreet variety of fantasy literature, a singular element of fantasy is introduced into this seemingly mimetic context so that its disturbing effect can be observed and measured [xlvii].

Further, Stableford argues that the secondary world presented in fantasy includes elements—often supernatural or magical—that are portrayed as having become lost over time, whereby the "representation of the primary world as a product of long-term magical erosion contrasts sharply with the representation of the primary world as the product of progress, one in which a wealth of knowledge and technological apparatus has been accumulated" (xlviii). Arguably, whereas the representation of magic in the wonder tale is meant to produce awe, all the while confirming existing social structures, the representation of magic in fantasy is meant to produce a sense of loss, whereby magic isn't an avenue for wish-fulfillment so much as for nostalgia. In heroic fantasy comics, especially the sword-and-sorcery genre epitomized by *Conan the Barbarian*, the sword-wielding barbarian is generally pitted against a problematic, proto-civilized world, in which the use of magic is often diabolical. Though the main point of sword-and-sorcery comics may be to feature as much drinking, wenching, and fighting as possible, the straightforward battle between forces of barbarism and civilization suggests a type of resistance to the more hidden politics of the modern world. In his discussion of Robert E. Howard, the creator of Conan, Deke Parsons notes that "Howard held onto so many historical animosities that even he could not keep them straight" (68); in the representation of Conan's barbaric violence, Howard displays his own "rage, justified and made clean by the environment of the Hyborian Age" (101). In *Fables*, however, the collision between a secondary world of sorcerers and a primary world, associated with Mundy technology and culture, provides the opportunity for a doubled "imaginative sidestep," as both a fantastical pre-industrialized space and our own reality are under scrutiny. Also, whereas Stableford outlines a relationship between the primary and secondary worlds in which the secondary world of fantasy includes magical elements that have eroded over time, in *Fables*, the ascendency of magic in the primary world (i.e., the Mundy world inhabited by the refugee Fables), draws attention to the ways in which we have become numb to pervasive technological and rhetorical influences.

The counter-narratives presented at the meeting of Imperial forces in some ways foreshadow the narrative of the war against the Adversary; as Boy Blue explains in his external narration, "This time we'd cheat.... This time we brought guns to a swordfight" (11.80–81). Throughout *War and Pieces* (Vol. 11), and at numerous other points in the text when Mundy technology is described, Willingham displays his high-level knowledge of military discourse and weaponry. To some extent, the stockpiling of weapons and the emphasis on military training, as shown for example when Beast and Bigby start preparing for the war by securing the exclusive use of a "private special forces and commando training school" (10.85), echoes the late-twentieth century vigilante approach of a comic book figure like The Punisher. As Tyler Scully and Kenneth Moorman note, with his massive personal arsenal and military background, "The Punisher was not a man hindered by the ineffective systems of the law but a relentless vigilante, bringing images of cowboy justice to mind" (646). Like The Punisher, who rarely displays moral compunction about his weapons-based pursuit of extra-systemic justice, when Fabletown turns to Mundy tech to fight the Adversary, the scheme is referred to as a "cheat." The issue of morality in relation to weapons technology is complicated in *Fables*: on the one hand, a character like Cinderella, a self-professed master of "all the Mundy advancements in espionage over the years," who has had centuries to "perfect [her] tradecraft" (11.59), is presented as a "white hat" (11.61), one who makes use of knowledge and tech to undermine the enemies of Fabletown's freedom. Further, in contrast to the scenario Pinocchio presents at the Imperial table—and despite Prince Charming's assertion that the goal of the war is to "write an end to [the] filthy Empire, once and for all" (10.76)—the phases of "Operation Jack Ketch" primarily seek to incapacitate the enemy. Phillips and Strobel argue that, "Comic book narratives routinely include the use of incapacitation as a means of (temporarily) halting criminal behavior" (207), a route that operates in contrast to the typically apocalyptic and genocidal plans of super villains. Thus, at many points in the narrative, the primary world that is conversant with advancements in weapons technology is presented as a world that properly makes responsible use of that knowledge in a battle against evil wizardry.

On the other hand, the primary world of advanced military technology does not always represent a fairer playing field, despite the conceit that in the war against the Adversary, the members of Fabletown are the good guys. First: whereas the possibility of using magic is confined to those with the capacity to engage in such activity, Mundy weapons can simply be purchased, and not just by the likes of Beast and Bigby. A crucial aspect of the initial plan to attack Fabletown, as presented in *March of the Wooden Soldiers* (Vol. 4), is the purchase of guns (4.122), and Big Ned's insistence on the safeguard of the "three-day waiting period" (4.126) is depicted as absurd and ineffectual. Second: in both the vision Pinocchio presents to the Imperial council and during preparations to take on Mr. Dark, the notion of using military grade weapons as a means to conquer the Homelands persists. As Pinocchio points out, the opportunity to conquer the Homelands will "probably unite all the nations of the Mundy world for the first time in history.... Why war with each other while there are thousands of new lands fresh for the picking?" (10.89). This attitude toward armed conquest is not restricted to the Mundys; as Snow White explains to Beast, the incentive to be dangled in front of Fables willing to battle Mr. Dark is likewise the prospect of armed conquest: "Basically we turn them loose to carve out a new kingdom or two" (14.115). The pictorial image of heavily armed men wandering through the burnt-out remains of a pre-industrial Homeland (10.88) echoes eerily with images of American soldiers in Iraq, whereby the slur "Meevil scumsuck" (10.89) becomes a code for the way any conquered "enemy" is dehumanized as part of the imperialist process. The text's periodic critique of contemporary forms of imperialist military actions thus undermines any notion that progress in weapons technology represents moral advancement. While, as Phillips and Strobel put it, "one of the major attractions to comic books is the emotional resonance of retributive justice" (216), Snow White's glib assertion that "Land for service is a time-honoured tradition" (14.115) indicates her callous attitude toward the anonymous violence intrinsic to her plan. In this way, the dichotomy between (technological) temporary incapacitation and (magical) apocalypse is complicated, as the desire for conquest has little to do with notions of justice.

Perhaps an even clearer signal of the way *Fables* presents the use of advanced weapons technology as an "existential dilemma" is the virtual disappearance of such activity as the comic book series progresses. While the contemporary Fable community continue to depend on magic to supplement their technological know-how, with Briar Rose's sleeping enchantment and the use of the beanstalk as vital to the war effort as the use of guns and bombs, the narrative arcs that focus on Mr. Dark and on the fated feud between Snow White and Rose Red deal with magic, not technology. Further, even during the war with the Adversary, the Fables make use of Mundy weapons, but not other sorts of advanced technology, for example tech that is associated with surveillance and communications. As discussed in Chapter One, *Fables* depicts various magical means of surveillance in order to reflect on current questions about the way political power is enacted. Further, as noted in Chapter Three, the focus on magical movements in the second half of the series coheres with the context of globalization and the attendant concerns about the meaning of borders and belonging. This gradual disappearance of scenes that focus on the difference between technology and magic serves as an ironic reminder of the way tech has become such a ubiquitous presence in the contemporary moment that we forget to reflect on the way our lives are organized by advances in weaponry and telecommunications.

Likewise, the text deals with another "existential dilemma," which is the way religion operates in the current era. Jack Zipes argues in *Why Fairy Tales Stick*, that "it is only with the gradual rise of the Christian Church, which began to exploit magic and miraculous stories and to codify what would be acceptable for its own interests, that wonder tales and fairy tales were declared sacrilegious, heretical, dangerous, and untruthful" (53). Thus, Zipes points out, a contrast was established between the "trivial" wonder tale and the "true world of belief" (53). Inverting this paradigm,

Fables presents figures from folk and fairy tale taking up residence in the "real" world (a world represented as nominally Christian, insofar as there are celebrations of Christmas), only to have one of their own—Stinky, the badger—create a new, possibly heretical and dangerous, religion. The text's critique of religious rhetoric, which is presented as generally illogical and self-serving, reflects contemporary concerns about the rise of fundamentalist groups who frame their political aspirations in religious terms. And, as is the case with the gradual intensification of the fantasy of a world ruled by magic, the representation of religion's failure to take hold—paradoxically—reflects anxiety about its present-day influence.

As it happens, prior to crafting his own religion, Stinky is an amateur philosopher of magic, showing enough intuition about Fable nature that Frau Totenkinder invites him to begin studying "the craft" (12.136). Stinky misunderstands Frau's invitation, assumes that she is mocking him, and refers to himself as a court jester (12.136). Though Frau Totenkinder may well have been taking Stinky seriously, after he reinvents himself as Brock Blueheart, proclaiming the good news of "The Blue Way" (13.15), he is more and more associated with foolishness. In the early positioning of his "new found purpose in life" (13.25), Brock emphasizes the political dimension of his new religion, pointing out to the likes of King Cole and Snow White that "this is the last errand I'm running for any of you self-appointed members of the gentry" (13.27). Most early followers of "The Blue Way" are other non-human Fables, suggesting that this religion—like the Puritan religion of early American settlers—champions the cause of those who feel oppressed by the establishment. However, the seriousness of "The Blue Way" is called into question almost immediately, as Brock and his brethren misinterpret the sounds coming from Rose Red and Jack as they have sex. In response to Rose's persistence in calling out "Oh, Blue!" during the act, Brock makes two pronouncements: first, that Boy Blue clearly needs "to take a wife" before he returns (13.91) and, second, that Jack must be Blue in "disguise ... rather than in your true form of glory" (13.93). The representation of Brock's absurd religious "reading" of events satirizes the tendency of evangelicals to interpret things so as to satisfy a predetermined set of values, paying no attention to logic or reality; this satire coheres with the rest of *The Great Fables Crossover* (Vol. 13), which focuses on such metafictional issues as the role of the author and the power of story conventions.

Later in the series, the satirical critique of Brock Blueheart's religion gives way to other sorts of critiques. During a clandestine meeting of Ozma, Geppetto, and Brock, one of Geppetto's dryad bodyguards insults

Brock, disparaging his status as an "animal" (15.94); Brock responds by
growing into a massive, armed badger, proclaiming himself the "First
brother of the sacred returnists! Wielder of the Blue Magic!" (15.95).
Brock's ability to transform reflects the idea that—no matter the degree
to which religious rhetoric might be satirized—those who "wield" this
rhetoric are enlarged, and thus may gain access to political power. In this
scene, Brock is defeated by Alder's arboreal magic, as the text pits so-
called "true power" against "magic based on collective [belief] structures"
(15.96–97). As with other textual references to the notion of the Great
Powers, Alder's act reflects a desire for a transcendent ordering principle
that will provide balance and limits to political machinations. The final
blow to the new religion occurs when Boy Blue and Bigby have a discussion
in the transitional space leading to the "Lands after Life," during which
Blue expresses his displeasure with Stinky: "if you can get him to ditch the
nonsense and the blue scarves, I'd appreciate it" (20.114). On the one hand,
this scene counters the way religious rhetoric often claims to simply repeat
the words of a deity, as here the ostensible godhead directly undermines
the words and actions of his prophet. On the other hand, the reproach of
Stinky precedes the final turn of the discussion between Boy Blue and
Bigby, in which Blue offers his own philosophy of life's meaning: "concen-
trate on what's important [and] … fight for … those who matter to you"
(20.115). In juxtaposing Blue's critique of Stinky's religion with the ideal
of "fighting for those who matter to you," Willingham suggests that the
problem with religion is its tendency to become institutionalized and self-
serving: indeed, while "The Blue Way" may have emerged from Stinky's
desire to fight for the rights of the non-human Fables, the couching of
those moral values in the rhetoric of religion undermines the cause.
Importantly, the dwindling of "The Blue Way" as a religious force in *Fables*
is meant to draw attention to the dominance of such rhetoric in our own
reality.

A third "existential dilemma" that *Fables* sets in relief by way of its
portrayal in relation to magic and notions of justice is the dilemma of
knowledge acquisition in the contemporary moment. In their conclusion
to *Comic Book Justice*, Phillips and Strobel note that "one thing that readers
were keen to point out is the way, as with any other form of literature,
they use comic books narratives to work through their own understand-
ings of the world" (220). In its varied representation of scholarship, especially in relation to magic, *Fables* suggests that a crucial counterweight to
the persistent influence of technology and religious rhetoric is knowledge,
though Willingham's ideal of knowledge is the sort that helps a person

determine "what's important ... [for] you to fight for." In the contrast, for example, between Ozma's dependence on scholarship as she prepares to battle Mr. Dark and Bufkin's use of scholarship in his own fight against a D'jinn and Baba Yaga, the text promotes the ideal that all power (technological, spiritual, scholarly) should serve the community.

Ozma rises to prominence in *Fables* after the apparent disappearance of Frau Totenkinder (who will later return in her guise as Bellflower). In *Witches* (Vol. 14), the power dynamics of the 13th floor collective are explored, as is Ozma's leadership style: she is shown to be eminently practical and canny, quickly assigning Maddy the job of gaining intelligence about Mr. Dark (14.113) and cleverly countering Geppetto's own bid for renewed power with a judicious "spending" of impressive transformation magic (14.132). In other words, Ozma is very task-oriented and—in her own words—she insists that the Fables "live in the real world ... not some fantasy we'd like to construct for ourselves" (15.18). Despite Ozma's commitment to clear thinking and cleverness, an attribute she admires in Frau Totenkinder/Bellflower (15.175), her approach to the problem of Mr. Dark is depicted as excessively scholarly. In *Super Team* (Vol. 16), Ozma's meticulousness is portrayed as a shortcoming, suggesting that effective and ethical knowledge occurs only within the context of community need. Throughout the volume, Ozma—whose preparation involves stringent testing of possible candidates for the battle against Mr. Dark, as well as a clear vision of how best to avoid Mr. Dark's practice of feeding on his opponent's fear—shows an exaggerated independence. Though she occasionally concedes a point of argument to Pinocchio, who is convinced that following the conventions of superteam comics will give the Fables a competitive edge, she views the undertaking as "my great task—my justification for taking over the witches of the 13th floor" (16.123). This largely strategic, self-serving attitude is contrasted throughout the volume with, for example, the attitude of Pinocchio, whose somewhat absurd reliance on comic book conventions are meant to serve the community by providing a sense of belonging; as he censures Ozma, "even if they can't help, you still need to honor their willingness to sacrifice" (16.67). Ozma's disconnected mindset is also juxtaposed with Flycatcher's: whereas Flycatcher will not remove Bigby or Beast's family from harm's way out of a sense of fairness, Ozma's bloody-minded focus on the task of defeating Mr. Dark gets in the way of her "caring" about anyone's safety (16.58). Finally, the thoroughness of Ozma's scholarly preparation ultimately comes to nothing, as Mr. Dark is defeated by the Great Power of the North Wind, who sacrifices himself because of love—love for his grandchildren and for his son. The failure of

Ozma's magical craft here indicates that knowledge in the form of information, statistics, data, and so on must function within a context of care in order to be meaningful.

In the representation of Bufkin, Willingham presents an idealized vision of the scholar, one whose application of practical and magical knowledge is flexible, analytical, matter-of-fact, and generous. In *Witches* (Vol. 14), the portrayal of Frau Totenkinder's disappearance and the jockeying for power among the 13th floor witches, Geppetto, and Brock Blueheart is braided with the narrative of Bufkin's adventures in the lost Business Office, which Mr. Dark has succeeded in unbinding from the rest of the Woodland Building. Bufkin is constructed as a cross between two conventional figures from folk and fairy tale: the clown, or fool, and the unlikely hero; in fact, Bufkin is very much like the typical protagonist of what are known in folklore studies as "Jack tales," in that he proves beyond all expectation to be a clever and lucky champion of a folk community (McCarthy 509–510). The motley community of the lost Business Office consists of Frankie (Frankenstein's monster's head), the Magic Mirror, several wooden heads left behind after the Battle of Fabletown, and a crew of newly hatched Barleycorn women. The narrative of the battle between this community and the D'jinn and Baba Yaga explores the unique nature of Bufkin's scholarly persona, which is—in the beginning—portrayed in bathetic terms: when the Mirror criticizes Bufkin's ability to ask questions in the form of a rhyme, Frankie points out that the attempts are "pretty good for a monkey" (14.41). Likewise, when Bufkin first confronts his enemies is his guise as "Bufkin the Brave," they simply laugh at him (14.72). However, as his magical helper the Mirror advises him, "You have read almost every book in our library. High time to finally put that vast wealth of information to use. And you've got friends here. Rally them" (14.76). Even more significant, Bufkin's scholarship is presented as its own kind of magical power: when Baba Yaga queries the Mirror about Bufkin's powers, the Mirror responds, "He reads. He reads everything" (14.96). The crucial difference between the depiction of Ozma-the-scholar and Bufkin-the-scholar hinges on the manner in which they make use of knowledge: whereas Ozma's approach is elitist and unduly theoretical, Bufkin is humble, practical, and happy to rely on the advice and help of his colleagues. Whereas Ozma's motives are personal, Bufkin is focused on his community; as he declares after the battle, "No one threatens my people in my house" (14.138). In other words, Bufkin's knowledge manifests as magic because his attitude toward scholarship is that it is one tool among many and because his approach to confronting adversity is moral.

In her own "battle" with a D'jinn, which is really a confrontation with Yusuf's destructive wishes, Frau Totenkinder prevails because of her ability to manage language: being unable to directly oppose the D'jinn's magic, she simply changes the words Yusuf utters (7.73). In fact, in the representation of technology, religion, and scholarship, everything comes down to the "magical" power of language: Pinocchio wins the day at the conference table because he presents a more convincing narrative; Brock Blueheart is temporarily able to attract followers because his description of "The Blue Way" is moving and effective, though he loses his moral high ground when he turns into a poor "reader"; Bufkin's gambit against the D'jinn, as well as his ability to rally his motley army, likewise depends on his astute use of language. *Fables* suggests that the complexity of the contemporary world makes it impossible to revert to sword-and-sorcery versions of justice, simply because justice may be difficult to recognize behind the influence of technology and rhetoric. Rather, the text suggests, the key is look beyond the surface of language use and consider the relationship between tools for control and those they serve.

Fate, Fortune and Freedom

Though it is in the final volume of *Fables* (*Farewell*, Vol. 22) that the conclusive showdown between Snow White and Rose Red takes center stage, a burgeoning conflict is foreshadowed at least as early as *Camelot* (Vol. 20), when Rose Red, against the express wishes of her older sister, chooses to allow Brandish a chance at redemption (20.86). Though the moment is portrayed as a choice, whereby Rose Red pleads with Snow White that offering redemption is "my absolute, until-the-end-of-my-days purpose in life" (20.85), later scenes in the volume suggest that the decision Rose Red makes is irrelevant. As the Lady of the Lake intimates to Morgan le Fay, Rose and Snow are simply acting their parts in another story, one that takes precedence even over the Camelot script (20.156). As a wielder of fate, Lake is intensely conscious of its effects, so much so that having a glimpse of her own leads to self-induced temporary incapacitation: after seeing Ambrose, who she will eventually wed as shown in the final pages of *Cubs in Toyland* (18.187), Lake starts drinking heavily, depressed by the idea that she is "just another one of the controlled" (20.161). For his own part, Ambrose is also keenly aware of being controlled, having been saddled early on with Ozma's prophecy about the cubs (17.32). Though Ambrose eventually comes to understand his own part in the prophecy, he also knows that the very notion of prophecy is complicated, later referring to

his life as "bits and pieces of other stories" (19.148). Throughout the series,
the workings of fortune and fate are explored, especially insofar as these
forces undermine personal freedom, though it is often suggested that an
individual can choose whether or not to be overwhelmed by outside influences, even influences that appear beneficial.

In a comic book series that plays with the conventions of a number
of literary genres, it is unsurprising that characters would have to negotiate
both the quirks of fortune and the constraints of fate, as each principle
might be thought of as belonging to the traditions of fairy tale and fantasy,
respectively. In his description of the wonder tale, Jack Zipes refers to the
generalized setting in which "anything can happen at any time, and these
fortunate and *unfortunate* events are never really explained" (2006, 51,
emphasis in the original). Though many folk and fairy tales make use of
the structuring principles of reward and punishment, whereby virtue is
rewarded and defects such as greed, laziness, and cruelty result in punishment, the magical elements in these tales show that the powerful fantasy
of just desserts depends a great deal on the workings of luck. As Stith
Thompson points out, though a character's actions throughout his or her
adventures may mark him or her as deserving in some way, the initial status of the character as a locus for a fortunate transformation is often arbitrary or symbolic; in his discussion of the motif of the "Successful Youngest
Child," for example, Thompson notes that "the [primary] distinguishing
quality of these heroes and heroines is the fact that they are the youngest"
(125). In other words, the folk and fairy tale—though often portraying the
wish for social justice or personal fulfillment—pits such wishes against a
largely implacable set of circumstances, and one's relationship to those
circumstances is only altered via the mechanisms of fortune. In contrast,
a key convention of fantasy is that events proceed not according to luck,
but according to fate. As Brian Attebery notes in *Strategies of Fantasy*, the
"formula" for the genre appears to include the following steps:

> Take a vaguely medieval world. Add a problem, something more or less eco-
> logical, and a *prophecy* for solving it.
> Introduce one villain with no particular characteristics except a nearly all-
> powerful badness. Give him or her a convenient blind spot ...
> To the above mixture add one *naïve and ordinary hero* who will prove to be
> the *prophesied* savior; give him a comic sidekick and a wise old advisor who
> can rescue him from time to time and *explain* the plot [10, emphasis added].

While fantasy shares with the folk and fairy tale the figure of the
"naïve and ordinary hero," one who may have no readily apparent special

qualities, the key element that distinguishes the fantasy hero's adventures is that they are determined by fate rather than initiated by luck. Further, while the folk and fairy tale often features a magical helper or donor who provides the hero with the means to effect his or her personal transformation, the fantasy narrative conventionally includes some figure whose role it is to "explain the plot," i.e., to show how the hero's actions are connected to the fate of his or her world, and to rehearse how any events that take place are in line with a prophetic script.

Arguably, both sorts of narratives undermine the idea of choice: the folk or fairy tale is closed down in the sense that fortune is arbitrary, a matter related to wishes and hopes rather than self-determination, while fantasy is closed down by the script of fate. In making use of elements from both generic traditions, *Fables* seeks to confront the meaning of such closure, especially because the text is so concerned with the ideal of individual freedom. In his sidebar comments on Bigby Wolf, included in Jess Nevins' *Fables Encyclopedia*, Willingham notes that, "In the adventure-writing trade, it's those you like best who get dumped on the most.... There's a very good reason 'happily ever after' is only possible when the story's over" (30). As discussed in Chapters Two and Three, the complex treatment of Bigby Wolf throughout the series sheds light on such social and political themes as the role of the modern father, changing conceptions of masculinity, and the position of America on an increasingly globalized political stage. The character of Bigby, however, is not solely or even primarily a social and political animal, but is a figure that looms large within the realms of the magical, metaphysical, and metafictional. Two of the embedded tales that focus on Bigby—"The Runt," included in *1001 Days of Snowfall*, and "The Destiny Game," the final narrative arc in *Cubs in Toyland* (Vol. 18)—demonstrate the way the comic book series makes use of the oppositional notions of fortune versus fate, showing the text's concern with how both concepts operate in tension with freedom, a principle tenaciously championed by Willingham's much abused hero, Bigby. Paradoxically, Bigby's attempts to outwit both fortune and fate do not culminate in the representation of a newly freed, more powerful hero; rather, in the main narrative, Bigby's self-determination—which occurs when he goes "off-script," following his own story—often results in a type of weakening, which the text suggests is a cost of freedom.

As per its source, the frame tale of *1001 Nights of Snowfall* portrays the undertakings of a clever woman who, in order to delay her execution at the hands of a jealous Sultan, tells him stories every night, continually piquing the Sultan's interest and giving him reason to let her live one more night. Further, the frame tale in *1001 Nights of Snowfall* resembles the frame of *The Arabian Nights* in that the clever woman's ultimate purpose is to help heal the Sultan from his murderous jealousy and anguish about being once betrayed in love. After hearing the tale, "The Runt," however, the Sultan concludes that it is a "grim story" (85), and, indeed, the narrative of the North Wind's abandoning of a white she-wolf, her subsequent death from despair, and the rage of her youngest cub who, in preparing to seek revenge on his father, develops into a bloodthirsty, pitiless monster, recalls the mode of mythology more so than fairy tale. Still, "The Runt" makes use of the motif of the "successful" youngest child whose personal situation is transformed through magic, though—in this case—the magical donor, the North Wind, is also the tale's antagonist. Snow White informs the Sultan that the "lesson" in this story is that even terrible acts can be forgiven, as the monstrous wolf is "now a trusted and loyal member of our community in exile" (85). However, the embedded narrative itself has nothing to do with forgiveness: in fact, the conclusion of "The Runt" explains that the Great Wolf never forgave his father, but only accepted that he could not avenge himself upon him (84). In other words, "The Runt" is not in any way a story of healing, but rather one of horror, one that confirms Bigby's complicated identity as a flawed and perhaps only temporary hero. With respect to the issue of fortune, what "The Runt" explores is the awful perversity of luck; for example, when the Great Wolf rescues a maiden from a dragon, she assumes that a "fortunate" event has befallen her, only to find out that the wolf intends to eat her because he doesn't fancy dragons (80). Further, the vow the wolf makes to become "bigger and stronger than anything" (77) goes unfulfilled, as he never becomes more powerful than his father. In its play with the motif of fortune in this rather gory fairy tale, the text succeeds in allowing more room for self-determination, as the young wolf is bent on acting rather than being acted upon. That said, the incoherence of the clever woman's assertion that the tale is about forgiveness draws attention to the way, in the main narrative of *Fables*, Bigby's increasing movement away from his monstrous identity manifests as weakness, whereby in forgiving his father, Bigby feels defeated (16.128). This sense of personal downfall, however, is presented as the cost of living freely among his community.

Like "The Runt,*" the story "The Destiny Game" is an embedded tale conveyed within the context of a larger narrative, this time Ambrose Wolf's multi-volume "A History of Fables in America, the Mundy World and Beyond" (18.154). The notion of a "historical" context, together with the emphasis in "The Destiny Game" on the workings of fate, connects the tale with the genre of fantasy although—as with "The Runt" with respect to folk and fairy tale—certain aspects of the formula are destabilized. In the first place, the figure of the "naïve and ordinary hero" is clearly problematized, as the Great Wolf is both cunning and extraordinary, perhaps having more in common with the conventional figure of the "villain with no particular characteristics except a nearly all-powerful badness" (Attebery, 10). The Great Wolf's monstrosity, however, is set in tension with what the reader already knows about Bigby as a protector of the Fable community and of his family; this tension is especially prominent because "The Destiny Game" is included as the final narrative arc in *Cubs in Toyland* (Vol. 18), a volume that describes Bigby and Snow White's anguish in the face of their missing cubs (18.113), and that depicts the death of the child who most resembles his father (18.132). The issue of prophecy itself is also subverted, as the plot of "The Destiny Game" revolves around the turtle's revelation to the despondent Great Wolf that the whimsical Green Woman (otherwise known as the Lady of the Lake) does not "reveal fates, she assigns them" (18.169). In exchange for her life, the Green Woman swaps the dreadful fate she assigned to the Great Wolf with a superior fate she had previously given to Magus Atlantes (18.180), a move suggesting that fate is as arbitrary as fortune. Unlike the conventional formula for fantasy, in which the savior hero is prophesized to act in some scripted way so as to salvage his or her community, the assignation of fate must here be disrupted in order for the individual—once monster, and now hero—to discover a context for community service. "The Destiny Game" thus suggests that individuals should not only fight against fate (in similar fashion to the way "The Runt" requires that the young wolf direct his own fortunes), but also should avoid inquiring too closely into its prescriptions. It is, after all, the Great Wolf's curiosity about his own destiny that causes the Green Woman to consign him to an ignominious death (18.161); further, as Ambrose Wolf records, the wolf never learns about his new fate: "He learned the details of his life only as they occurred" (18.186). Here again, the play with the convention of prophecy emphasizes a certain kind of freedom, even if it is the freedom to become less than a great and powerful monster.

In considering *Fables* in its entirety, it becomes clear that Willingham is more concerned with the limiting function of fate than he is with the arbitrary processes of fortune, as the final "act" of the series explores the way Snow White and Rose Red negotiate the fate defining their familial identity. That said, it is also important to bear in mind how fortune is associated in the text with the quality of hope. Most of the figures that inhabit the Fables universe have ostensibly already been affected by the workings of fortune in the past, before we meet them: these are the persons from the Homelands who have been enchanted, elevated from poverty, advantageously married, magically rewarded, and so on, so much so that their "story" has allowed them to transcend Mundy mortality. Even after escaping the Homelands, however, the Fables still occasionally find themselves targets of and participants in "*fortunate* and *unfortunate* events": for example, Snow White is able to defeat the revolutionaries at The Farm via the magical aid of the three giants and a dragon (2.86–87), not to mention a wily fox (2.57); Bigby and Snow White are placed under a spell, transported away from their home and, after defeating the malevolent Goldilocks (4.156), eventually end up marrying one another (8.98–99); months after receiving a strange gift from Frau Totenkinder, Beast learns from Beauty that, after untold years of waiting, they are to have a baby (14.73–74), which will affect Beast's own curse (16.65); and Winter—the most childlike of the cubs—completes a task she is magically prepared to undertake, and after becomes a King (17.89). These events show that arbitrary things still occur to elevate certain characters over others, though, within the context of *Fables*, such events produce a sense of unease rather than the comfort borne of a good wish-fulfillment narrative.

Along with these and other similar stories, *Fables* examines a crucial corollary to the way events unfold in the folk and fairy tale, which is the notion of hope. In the text, Hope is a character, explicitly identified by Dunster Happ as one of the Great Powers (15.110). Though Hope first speaks to Rose Red in the guise of Rose's mother, sharing enough information about the past to give Rose Red the strength to get out of bed and reassert her leadership of The Farm (15.89), the complexity of the power of Hope is fully explored only after Mr. Dark has been defeated by the North Wind and Rose Red asks to meet with Hope, who has chosen Rose Red as one of her "paladin[s]" (15.125). As the Great Power points out, "hope isn't destiny. Left passive, it's nothing more than disappointment deferred" (15.125). In other words, hope doesn't act as a script for activity, but represents a vision for the future, a vision in which implacable circumstances are in some miraculous way transformed. Further, Rose Red is visited one Christmas by a cricket, a guardian angel figure from Charles Dickens' Christmas book "The Cricket on the Hearth." The journey he takes her on forces Rose Red to confront other aspects of hope: that "hopes [can] get crushed" (17.100); that the concept of justice might be interpreted simply as "the hope that things will turn out all right in the end" (17.105); that hopes for the future sometimes operate to camouflage present misery (17.112–113); and that hope is morally ambiguous (17.118). When Rose Red resolves to become "the paladin of second chances" (20.134), the new roundtable becomes a context for the hope of forgiveness, not only for the likes of Lancelot, Mr. Wellstuffed, and Mr. Brump (20.182), but also for Rose Red who, at this point in the narrative, is still searching for redemption. However, the new Camelot also proves a failure, mostly because the miracle of forgiveness never occurs and what Rose Red comes to realize is that pursuing redemption isn't actually her "end-of-[her]-days purpose in life" (20.85). Rather, she decides to let "loose the demons and monsters and gods of war" (21.194). Though Rose Red is by this time at least halfway convinced that it is her "destiny" to war with her sister, the text leaves room to interpret her actions as a type of freedom, the freedom to "fight like I've got a chance" (21.187). Thus, on the one hand, *Fables* undermines the idea that hope is meaningful, suggesting instead that hope is a sop for those caught within unjust or unhappy circumstances; on the other hand, the freedom to "fight against" one's circumstances is not sentimentalized or shown as necessarily virtuous.

As noted above, though *Fables* interrogates the perversity of fortune, calling into question both the value of hoping or wishing and the default heroic interpretation of self-determination, its exploration of the way the ideal of freedom comes into conflict with the vicissitudes of story convention mostly occurs in relation to the rules of fantasy. Perhaps because the inhabitants of Fabletown and The Farm emerge from the sort of tales that are structured around luck, their more pressing concerns in this narrative relate to dealing with "ecological" problems and "all-powerful" villains (Attebery, 10). When Brian Attebery provides his satirical description of "formula" fantasy, the term "ecological" clearly harks back to the work of J.R.R. Tolkien, whose famous novels are thematically focused on the rise of industry and the destruction of natural England; thus, this term seems irrelevant to the comic book series which is purposefully set within an urban space and which doesn't often consider environmentalist issues. However, the term "ecology" also refers to the study of human groups in relation to their physical environment, an idea of great thematic concern in *Fables* and one related to the exploration of how notions of fate come into conflict with notions of freedom. The "nature" of Fables, as a group, is at odds with their environment: while the community's dearest wish is to remain both hidden and free to govern themselves, their more-than-Mundy status is defined by the fact that they are widely known and that they are associated with the controlling mechanisms of story. Attebery suggests that, moving beyond formulaic versions of fantasy, the capacious genre is not well-served when scholars try to define its boundaries; rather, fantasy "may be approached as a 'fuzzy set' ... defined not by boundaries

but by a center" (12). For Attebery, the "center" of fantasy has three features: the genre is concerned with "the impossible" (14); the typical plot
"begins with a problem and ends with resolution" (15); and the purpose
of the fantasy text is to produce an "awareness of a pattern for meaningfulness" (17). In *Fables*, however, the "pattern for meaningfulness" is a
burden, not a "resolution," as the freedom to live hidden and free is pitted
against the relentlessness of story convention.

The undermining of freedom in this text, whereby the true villain is
not the Adversary, Mr. Dark, or any other all-powerful villain but rather
the story scripts that characters cannot escape, culminates in the idea of
a final showdown destined to occur between Snow White and Rose Red.
Even before this conflict, however, the representation of prophecy shows
Willingham's concern with how personal freedom is weakened when cultural scripts become too familiar. For example, when Colin Pig warns
Snow White about the impending attack on Fabletown, he initiates a narrative in which the problem of the Wooden Soldiers and Baba Yaga are
eventually resolved; however, the resolution is hardly akin to the type of
"recovery" that enlivens the fantasy text (Attebery, 16), except that the
battle's end provides the impetus for Snow White's acceptance of her love
for Bigby (4.216). Rather—as intimated by the juxtaposition of the funeral
for those who were killed during the Battle of Fabletown (4.225–227) and
the meta-awareness of Kevin Thorn (4.222–223)—the battle is mostly
meaningless, except that it operates as a conventional way to end a story
(or, as is the case for the Mundy news team, to ignore a story). Similarly,
Santa Claus activates a plot arc of problem-battle-resolution when he presents Flycatcher with a prophecy, telling him that he can "save" his community from being destroyed in the coming war (9.129). The "resolution"
achieved by the founding of Haven does resemble a type of meaningfulness, as the new monarchy is idealized as the perfect coming together of
a multi-ethnic community. As discussed in Chapter Three, however, the
kingdom of Haven does not afford its citizens the kinds of freedom associated with a democratic republic, and is thus portrayed as a mostly
romanticized space. Though the inhabitants of Haven are hidden and safe,
they do not possess the opportunity for self-determination, which is perhaps why the initiative of the Super Team seems bound to fail. The most
far-reaching prophecy represented in *Fables* is Ozma's prophecy about
the Wolf cubs, which she communicates to Ambrose (17.30–31). Like his
father, Ambrose is keen to hear about the future, despite Ozma's caution
that prophecy "seldom helps and often harms" (17.31). As in "The Destiny
Game," the communication of prophecy has the potential effect of "closing

down" the story, as the life of each cub—and in particular the lives of Therese and Darian—is hereafter read according to a script. However, while the reader knows that "the third will do an evil thing" and "the fourth will die to stop her" (17.32), Therese and Darian are unburdened by this knowledge, which allows for their adventures in Toyland to retain a moral meaning. Thus, the text suggests that excessive knowledge of, or perhaps dependence on, the idea of fate deprives an individual from the opportunity to become truly distinctive.

In the final volume, *Farewell* (Vol. 22), "The Last Lake Story" shows this character up to her old tricks (and Gene Ha's art here is certainly meant to help readers recall his equally remarkable work in "The Destiny Game"). As she explains to the Mountain King—a Great Power who apparently owes Lake a favor—she is on "one last journey of acquisition" (22.98), using her magical power and her collection of debts for her own shrewd purposes. In "The Last Christmas Story," Lake is shown surrounded by her family on Christmas morning, as she and Ambrose explain to their six children that she has managed to collect a number of good fates: as she notes, "in your package is the best possible fate I could find for each of you" (22.105). What is important about this scene—and others like it—is the way the issue of a child's fate is connected to the matter of good or bad parenting, which amounts to whether or not a parent teaches a child how to make the best use of his or her opportunities for choice. Just as Bigby assures Winter that her new fortune-determined status as the North Wind still allows for her to decide what sort of king she wants to be (18.14), Lake and Ambrose leave the decision about whether or not to accept their gifted fate up to each child. On the one hand, Lake feels it is important to offer her children the "guarantee" of a "safe and happy" life; on the other hand, the emphasis in this story on choice indicates that a life controlled by fate, even a safe and happy life, is perhaps at odds with an authentic life, which is a life of not knowing. Here again, the series undermines the notion of "happily ever after," not in the sense that happiness is not possible, but in the sense that the goal of happiness is misplaced; to be controlled by the search for a "happy ending" is to live at odds with the ideals of personal choice and community belonging.

Metafiction and Absorption
(the Rise of Ambrose Wolf)

Included in the penultimate volume of the *Fables* series, entitled *Happily Ever After* (Vol. 21), are nine "last" or "final" stories of various Fables, from Babe the Miniature Blue Ox to Prince Charming. Few of these narratives, however, seems definitive or in keeping with the notion of "happily ever after." For example, "The Last Flycatcher Story," which consists of a single splash page, shows Fly and Riding Hood relaxing together, still very much in love though it is "Many years later, in the Kingdom of Haven"; this tranquil picture is marred by a question asked by Tadpole, one of the couple's children: "Trent and Lucy and Bobby and I were talking. When you die, who inherits the kingdom?" (21.29). Thus, the seeds of another narrative, one that has the potential to be filled with conflict and misery is hinted at, even before Flycatcher's "story" has really ended. Likewise, "The Last Beauty and the Beast Story" does not present an ending, but a kind of beginning, as Beauty and Bliss—who has inherited her father's enchantment—engage in their fledgling business as "champions," scaring off ne'er-do-wells for a "reasonable" fee (21.153). Though Beauty is pleased that the scoundrels they threaten "always run," Bliss warns her mother that "my growly nature will almost certainly have its due someday" (21.155), again insinuating the inevitability of strife. Before this volume, and certainly before *Farewell* (Vol. 22), which includes several other "Last" stories, the text presents one tale that not only appears to end, but to end happily, which is the story of Bufkin and Lily. These adventures are narrated by their compatriot, Hangy the Rope, who once saved Bufkin by simply "refus[ing] to cooperate" in his hanging" (19.16). Bufkin and Lily have countless children, who are all reported to be thriving, and get to retire near "that beloved lunchbox tree"; Bufkin is said to have "lived out his final days in peace and plenty," and Bufkin and Lily are buried side by side (19.59). Hangy contrasts this apparently truthful, idyllic account of Lily and Bufkin's adventures with the "fabricated nonsense ... written by the disreputable Marcus Thomas Buckingwill" (19.49). In this metafictional moment, Hangy's use of an almost-anagram for the names Bill Willingham and Mark Buckingham draws attention to the way creators of fictional texts are responsible not only for happy endings, sometimes referred to as burdensome scripts by scholars of folk and fairy tales, but also for introducing conflict and misery. In its most metafictional moments, *Fables* exposes the twin pressures of dealing with the convention of the happy ending and with the convention in comics of the proliferating narrative, whereby the only "closure" that is offered works to provide readers of the series—the fans—with a sense of belonging.

Various folk and fairy tale (and literature) scholars have pointed out the close relationship between contemporary retellings of folk and fairy tales and the postmodern. In his introduction to *Contemporary Fiction and the Fairy Tale*, Stephen Benson explores "why the fairy tale has exerted such an influence on recent prose fiction," suggesting that it is because the fairy tale is "instantly recognizable," and therefore especially open to practices of "defamiliariz[tion]" (4). Further, Benson states that "the bareness of the form" and the "striking archaisms of the context ... serve as creative stimuli" (4–5), especially for those authors wishing to explore contemporary notions of agency, history, social identity, and power. As Vanessa Joosen suggests in *Critical & Creative Perspectives on Fairy Tales*, the connection between postmodern fairy tales—such as those written by Angela Carter, Margaret Atwood, and Robert Coover—and postmodern criticism might be referred to as an "intertextual dialogue" (17), whereby authors not only work to revise traditional tales, but engage in their own "critical impulse[s]" (35). In other words, authors will highlight an engagement with scholarly conversations about, for example, the role of the author or the stability of meaning. Joosen argues that, in some cases, meta-criticism is introduced in order to express "dissatisfaction with criticism" or—conversely—to "escape the ethics and rules of acceptability that apply to literary criticism" (41). A twin tendency in some metacritical postmodern fairy tales is to mock or critique scholarly activity, which is viewed as overly reductive, unnecessarily convoluted, and a generally inferior, uncreative type of work, while at the same time making use of scholarly or theoretical ideas "without any obligation to finish an argument" (Joosen 2011, 42). In *Postmodern Fairy Tales*, Cristina Bacchilega examines the way postmodern fairy tales "expose the [traditional] fairy tale's complicity with the 'exhausted' forms and ideologies of traditional Western narrative, rewriting the tale of magic in order to question and re-create the rules of narrative production, especially as such rules contribute to naturalizing subjectivity and gender" (23). Arguably, however, while postmodern strategies allow the authors of contemporary tales to destabilize cultural scripts and challenge the tyranny of fixed subject positions and conventional endings, the postmodern age is also exposed as an age of chaos, featuring the emptying out of symbols and the circulation of anxiety and helplessness. The desire in *Fables* to leave certain theoretical arguments unfinished reflects a contemporary uncertainty about the implications of rewriting a culture's stories, especially those that provide the comforting fiction of the happy ending.

In his discussion of Grant Morrison's highly metafictional take on DC's *Animal Man*, published in the late 1980s, Matthew Pustz points out in *Comic Book Culture* that "for comic book fans unfamiliar with contemporary metafiction, Morrison's *Animal Man* was truly innovative" (127);

other readers, Pustz writes, "may have seen *Animal Man* as a relatively simple exercise in postmodernism of the sort that had occurred decades earlier in traditional literature" (129). Whether comic books might be late-comers to postmodern strategies, however, is less important than the dis-tinctive ways comic book authors reach out to those readers Pustz refers to as "comics literate" (110). While the postmodern fairy tale might work to unsettle its readers via the destabilizing retelling of familiar tales, the postmodern comic book not only works to revise conventional comic book content, but also works to "depict the world of readers themselves" (147), acknowledging that, as a group, consumers of comic books participate in a unique culture, one that is bounded by a specific industry and market-place. Comic book readers are not just readers, they are "fans," and—as Pustz argues—"Fans both set themselves apart from and are set apart by the rest of the cultural world. They may be marginalized and ridiculed by mainstream society, but identifying as a fan can also give an individual a certain amount of 'collective identity'" (20). As the number of what Pustz calls "literacy-dependent comics" (156), such as *Fables*, increases, comic book readers are required to wrestle with reflexive and critical commen-tary on conventional comic book content—for example violent or sexist content—and also required to consider their own participation in a specific community, one that provides emotional and intellectual freedom and safety, as well as a sense of being recognized.

As a contemporary, highly literary-dependent, metafictional, and metacritical comic, *Fables* engages with many of these matters. As noted in Chapter One, the representation of Literature as one of the Genres called upon by Kevin Thorn during *The Great Fables Crossover* (Vol. 13) is an example of double-edged metacriticism: on the one hand, Literature's tendency to use the jargon associated with literary theory (13.66) indicates Willingham's scorn for certain kinds of scholarship, on the grounds that such work is elitist and alienating, not to mention a bit boring. Likewise, the characterization of Goldilocks as an angry young woman who consis-tently couches her violent tendencies in radical political rhetoric reflects the text's critique of the rise of literary theory in the postmodern age. For all its scorn, however, *Fables* engages with many of the same questions as Morrison's *Animal Man*: much as Animal Man becomes aware of his status as a fictional character, beholden to the whims of readers (the market), his creator (Morrison), and convention (DC's fictional universe), the Fables who live in the Mundy world are acutely aware that the conditions of their own existence in that world are unusual, because—as Ambrose Wolf so succinctly puts it—"Aren't we the people in stories?" (19.165). Further, as the multiple explicit, reflexive references to the notion of "happily ever after" show, *Fables* seeks to interrogate the "'exhausted' forms and ideologies of traditional Western narrative." When the newly married Mr. and Mrs. Wolf cross the threshold of Wolf Manor (8.101), the text offers a hyperbolic traditionalism, as the door shown in the final panel of the narrative arc "Happily Ever After" implies closure and stability. In keeping with the convention of the proliferating comic book narrative, however, this door remains closed only temporarily, as the familial idyll is threatened from a number of directions, though the value of this paradigm is not questioned. Thus, in contrast to the politics that informs many postmodern fairy tales, the continuing story of Snow White and Bigby Wolf evokes a retrograde celebration of the nuclear family, the members of which would have stayed "happy" had that door stayed closed. And yet, it is not necessarily a radical politics that undermines happiness, but rather the burdens of story and marketplace: as Willingham notes in the original script for "Happily Ever After," which is included in *Wolves* (Vol. 8), the final page of issue #50 included a caption thanking "readers" for their "loyalty, encouragement and reliable 'what happens next' interest" (8.159). This gracious acknowledgement of the fans is predicated on the problematic idea that stories will not end so long as further conflict can find a consuming readership.

Ambrose's idea that the Fables are "stories" is raised at various points in the series, as the relationship between the tales that circulate in the Mundy and the lives of the refugees from the Homelands is elucidated. In general, the system works like this: first, within Willingham's fantasy text, the various Homelands are "real"; as per the settings of most folk and fairy tales, these secondary worlds are populated by quasi-medieval people and are filled with magic, including magic associated with the Great Power of The Fates. As Lake explains to Rose Red, when Rose is trying to recreate the story of Camelot, The Fates are "like children, [in that] they mostly want to hear the same comfortable and beloved stories over and over again" (20.151). Second, during the years of the Adversary's imperial conquest, refugees from the Homelands crossed a magical gateway to Earth, a non-magical "mundane" world that proved safe for many years, mostly because—as the Adversary puts it in a letter he sends prior to the Battle of Fabletown—"our eyes are turned elsewhere for now, to other distant Fable lands" (4.160). Third, during the centuries of exile in the Mundy, the "real" histories from the Homeland begin to circulate as stories, a process most fully described in Willingham's novel *Peter & Max*: "shortly after Fables arrived, mundys all over the world began telling stories about them; stories no one knew were based on actual people and everyone assumed were simply creative and occasionally clever works of fiction" (21). In *Witches* (Vol. 14), Frau Totenkinder marvels at this process, declaring "How wonderful the way they absorb our stories" (14.58). An important outgrowth of "absorption" is that, in the Mundy world, the Fables acquire a new kind of magic, one that is related to how popular their circulated stories have become. This new magic makes figures like Snow White and Cinderella practically invincible, but leaves someone like Boy Blue vulnerable. Interestingly, it is not only those in the Mundy who are entertained by the "histories" emanating from the Homelands: during a visit to the North Wind's castle, the Wolf cubs are shown gathered around their grandfather as he reads them tales of adventure (16.63). Thus, *Fables* emphasizes the idea that story is extremely powerful; that certain characters and plots become ubiquitous and recognizable, not because of the designs of tellers—who may wish to enforce certain ideals or lessons—but because of the desires of listeners or readers, who simply can't get enough. Story itself is magical, like the pot that produces delicious porridge for the hungry child.

In the Grimms' folk tale "Sweet Porridge"—which is itself a version of a widespread "magical item" tale type—a hungry girl is given a magical pot by an old woman; as per instructions from the old woman, when the girl says a certain phrase, the pot will immediate begin cooking porridge and, when the girl says another phrase, the pot will stop. The girl is thus able to keep her mother and herself from starvation. One day, however, the girl is away and the mother wants to make porridge; though she knows the first magical phrase, she doesn't know how to make the pot stop. The pot continues to cook porridge until it spills out of the house, into the streets, and so on, until the girl finally returns and can tell the pot to stop cooking. In this tale, the true owner of the pot is a master of language, not only knowing how to create something nourishing and delicious, but also how to control excess. During a discussion following the funeral for Boy Blue, Frau Totenkinder, Ozma, and Stinky the Badger explore the magical properties of story and, in a highly metafictional moment, Stinky wonders whether there exists "some sort of separate master storyteller ... one who created both us and the tales about us" (12.136). Though this idea is not pursued further—mostly because Stinky assumes that Frau is making fun of him—the issue of a creator's control over this world is complex, as Willingham's comic book is at once an open and closed book. On the one hand, the status of *Fables* as an adaptation of folk and fairy tales depends on the way stories become part of public culture, so that the issue of "authorship" is almost meaningless: if anyone can tell the story of Cinderella, without knowing (or caring) about the difference among Giambattista Basile's, or Charles Perrault's, or the Grimms', or Disney's version of the tale, how can one speak of a "master storyteller"? The story simply "exists" for anyone's pleasure. On the other hand, the continued publication of the comic book series *Fables* depends on Bill Willingham's ability to write a specific book, one which readers will want to consume: the market requires that the storyteller, and the story, somehow remain "separate," as only the true creator has the power to provide nourishment and to control excess. As a creator-driven comic book series, *Fables* also operates both along and against the grain of the convention of proliferation and— at different points in its thirteen-year run—the question of calling story into being was more or less determined by a combination of creative energy and market demand, so that the "end" of the main series occurs even as the video-game/digital comic *The Wolf Among Us* appeals to a new set of consumers and requires the work of a new set of creators. To extend the (admittedly overdetermined) analogy further, the "Sweet Porridge" tale also suggests that something like language magic—or story magic—is not necessarily benign, as shown by the image of the porridge that threatens to overwhelm the village. Particularly in the last "act" of *Fables*, the diabolical power of a story that won't stop is explored via the growing conflict between Snow White and Rose Red, as both appear to be trapped by the age-old fascination with dueling sisters or with the motif of "Kind and Unkind Girls." Also, in "The Summer Prophecy" and "The Last Toy Story," both included in *Farewell* (Vol. 22), an anguished response to the problem of story magic is addressed: in the empty space associated in comic books with the absence of a story world, Dare can only plead with readers to let him know whether or not his "ending" had meaning (22.118), while—in Toyland—the motley group of readers of Darian's story hope that in nourishing themselves, they too can become "magical" (22.124–5).

The representation and reification of a specific group of hungry readers is a crucial metafictional component of *Farewell* (Vol. 22), as is the portrayal of the literary work of Ambrose Wolf. As noted in Chapter Three, in the discussion of how *Fables* makes use of conventions from fantasy fiction, the portrayal of Ambrose Wolf as the writer of "A History of Fables in America, the Mundy World and Beyond" is comparable to the portrayal of Bilbo and Frodo Baggins as writers of the histories of Middle Earth. Ambrose's role as a writer figure is introduced at least as early as *Inherit the Wind* (Vol. 17), when Ozma reveals the prophecy to Ambrose that "the sixth will judge the rest" (17.32), and is further explored in *Cubs in Toyland*

(Vol. 18) in the narrative arc entitled "The Destiny Game." The narrative voice Ambrose uses to write the tale of The Great Wolf and the Green Woman is elevated, as the persistent use of the phrase "In those days" (18.155, 18.160, 18.166) recalls the delivery of an archaic tale from folklore. In the narrative arc "Farewell," the conceit of Ambrose's "true history" book is given its fullest treatment, as evidenced by the comparatively prosaic diction employed. Before he begins the final volume, Ambrose provides a series of caveats to stress the veracity of what follows:

> Most of this is credible (and I hope authoritative) history, supported by facts and testimony from those who <u>witnessed</u> it directly. Of course not everyone <u>survived</u> these events to give testimony. In those cases, I've had to rely on conjecture and extrapolation. But in every case it was <u>informed</u> conjecture [22.2, emphasis in original].

The conspicuous use of phrases associated with the genres of memoir and history serve to highlight the way readers are trained to respond differently to different types of stories, a theme further emphasized by the juxtaposition of Ambrose's solemn narration and the image of the children's books he writes, the most prominent of which is titled "Maestro Mouse cuts the cheese" (22.2). The not-even-very-subtle reference here to a fart joke jars against the headiness of Ambrose's ostensible history project, as if to suggest that the distinction between a multi-volume history filled with "facts" and "testimony" may as well be a kid's book about a gassy mouse: in both cases, a world is created out of language.

However, as is frequently pointed out in *Fables*, language is a powerful magical force, as shown when Frau Totenkinder plays a language trick on Yusuf, spoiling his desire to use the D'jinn against Fabletown (7.73). Following up on the metafictional gambit introduced on the first page of the "Farewell" arc, one can interpret the various instances of magical action as they relate to the text's consideration of story. For example, Ambrose's narration of the final battle between Cinderella and Frau Totenkinder includes metacritical commentary on how to create a good story. In an explication of some of the magic that goes into creating a satisfying plot, he notes that—in a good story about a duel—the beginning "look[s] like nothing at all" (22.19); just as Cindy and Frau are masters of controlling various forms of power, so too must the author know how and when to use forms of "parry and riposte" (22.19). In his narration of Grimble's journey toward Brandish's hidden heart, Ambrose draws attention to the smallness of the bluebird, which allows him to slip past monsters and guards, as he is "not even worth noticing" (22.28). Here, the metacriticism illuminates the magical work of a good reader who, in the spirit of the departed administrative comptroller Muddlecock, takes the time to notice small things, and who is also able to delve into the many layers of story, in order to get at the heart of things. Later still, Ambrose introduces the scene of Rose Red's nighttime walk amongst her troops before the fated battle between her and her sister's forces, noting "Reams have been written on exactly what inspired Rose Red to take her walk that night. I have my own theory, but since this is supposed to be a history, I'll save my speculations for other venues" (22.70). These metafictional notes raise a number of issues related to what might be called literature magic: first, as pointed out in Chapter Two during the discussion of Rose Red's redemption narrative, the scene itself is an intertext for Act IV, scene i of Shakespeare's *Henry V*, showing the way literature is built out of other literature, as well as the way the examination in literature of the notion of "history" is an age-old concern. Further, the reference to the "reams [that] have been written" about the event connects to the field of literary criticism, as Willingham concedes to the creative potential of even "speculative" critical work. Finally, the highly literary intertext augments a highly intratextual moment, as those readers firmly ensconced in the *Fables* community will recognize Rose Red's interlocutor as Boy Blue. Thus, the plot "trick" of Rose Red's flash of insight into the way her familial fate might be interrupted is all the more resonant because this new understanding coheres with her emotional desire to become "worthy" of Boy Blue's respect (12.137).

An additional type of story magic hinted at in the "Farewell" arc, which reverberates throughout the entire *Farewell* volume, is "fan magic." In his narrative notes introducing the last chapter of the arc, called "The Last Battle" in another intertextual reference, this time to the final volume of C.S. Lewis's Narnia series, Ambrose states, "They met at the place we now know as Treaty Rock ... [a] main destination for Fables who make the pilgrimage to the Mundy World" (22.74). The "we" Ambrose refers to is a proleptic fantasy, pointing toward a future community, perhaps a community of fellow scholars, who maintain nuanced and ongoing discussion about their past, their culture, their touchstones (pun intended). Also, as the allusion to Lewis's series reinforces, a connection can be made between community identity and the sacred desire for common symbols, such as a "rock" on which to build a history and mythology. This imagined "we" is thus expanded to include those who would "make a pilgrimage" to commune with an important monument to their sense of identity and history. In conjuring up the notion of the sacred pilgrimage, Willingham indicates

that—if so inspired—communities will choose to do the work of reinforcing themselves and that this work will, at its best, resemble an act of love.
In his Afterword to the series, Willingham—whose "artist portrait" in the
top left-hand corner of the page is identical to the drawing of Ambrose
Wolf, completing his work on the "History" (22.78)—directly acknowledges the importance of the community of *Fables* fans. The Afterword
not only playfully discusses the unique "demographics" of the readership,
but asserts that "Stories don't exist until they've been read or viewed or
heard, and fleshed out within the minds of an audience.... If anything's
missing, it's left to you to keep going until you can fill it in" (22.153). Even
before this assertion, *Farewell* (Vol. 22) calls out to "you," tying up a number of loose narrative threads in ways that satisfy and legitimize long-time
readers; in particular, the arc entitled "Blue Skies, Blue Moon, Blue Suede
Shoes and Forever Blue" demonstrates the complicated relationship among
a fan community, the object of their devotion, and an outsider audience.
Before his open tryout at the "Tower of Song," a music club in what is
apparently the "music lover's heaven" (22.112), Boy Blue comments that
the new audience represents a "tough room" (22.111): Blue must prove
himself to be one of "the best" (22.111), even within the context of an art-
form that has been in action "for a thousand years" (22.113). When Blue
announces the names of his compositions—"Flies for Breakfast" and "One
Bad Arrow Blues" (22.114)—only true fans of the *Fables* series would understand the intratextual references.

   The metafictional elements of *Fables* touch on many of the same questions touched on in similar such texts in literature and in comics: what is
the relationship between author and story? Who controls a text? Why is
story so powerful, especially considering it is made up of mere language?
What does it mean to identify with a made-up character, or with a community of readers whose love for the made-up helps to provide a sense of
home? Among the many familiar characters from the series revisited in
the last volume is Santa Claus, provider of spiritual guidance, paladin of
Hope, servant of the North Wind: in "The Last Christmas Story," Santa
Claus is up to his more customary work, sharing cookies and milk with
Ambrose before delivering gifts. As he notes to Ambrose, his sack is filled
with the children's books Ambrose writes, to which Ambrose responds,
"They pay the bills, so I can afford to write the histories" (22.101). In this
metafictional moment, Bill Willingham's avatar calls to mind the long-
standing discussion of how to deal with comic books and their readers: are
these books simply for "children," or rather for adults who persist in reading non-serious literature? In this scene—and at various points throughout

Fables—the text argues that comic books are also a magical history, telling the tales of a culture's complex anxieties, concerns, and hopes.

A system or a story; a meaningful fate or a maligning of freedom: the extraordinariness of magic as represented in *Fables* helps to frame the way we try to come to terms with our ordinary lives, our own remoteness from the occluded sites of power. Magic asks: where does power come from? Does it gather over time, like the magic woven into the Witching Cloak? Is it conferred on to the great, or just on the lucky? Do systems of power even make sense? Throughout the series, the benefits and constraints of magical power are weighed against the personal freedoms of individuals, not only in terms of the way they choose to wield or become beholden to such power, but also in terms of how the freedom of choice itself becomes a kind of magic. And freedom of choice is shown to be most significant—most magical—when it serves the community or when it creates a sense of belonging and safety and family. For all that is extraordinary about these almost immortal characters—characters taken from tales that exist over huge swathes of time and space and culture, characters that have fought or become monsters and heroes—their moments of happiness look pretty ordinary: Christmas morning, a sprawling family reunion, the chance to create art.

5

Spin-Offs

This chapter surveys the numerous spin-offs (to date) of the main *Fables* series, providing a few comments about each text or series that are in keeping with this study's focus on adaptation, theme, and plotting. With the exception of the *Fables/Unwritten* crossover, described below, the spin-offs are conceived of as "canon," in that they work to fill in details of character histories without contradicting the events described in the main series; the spin-off series *Jack of Fables*, for example, portrays events that occur contiguously with the action in *Fables*, while *The Wolf Among Us*— both the video game and the digital comic book series—is written as a prequel to *Fables*. While some of these texts are the creative work of Bill Willingham, it is increasingly the case that new writers are entering into the *Fables* universe, mining it for its as yet unrecorded stories.

Peter & Max

So far, *Peter & Max* is the only *Fables* novel; it was written by Bill Willingham, illustrated by Steve Leialoha, and published in 2009. The novel shifts back and forth between two parallel plots: in the first plot, which is set a couple of years before the start of the war against the Adversary, Peter Piper leaves his wheelchair-bound wife, Bo, back at The Farm and travels to Hamelin, Germany in order to confront his older brother, Max, who is the famed and terrible Pied Piper. Thus, in similar fashion to the way he amalgamated the separate tales "Snow White and the Seven Dwarves" and "Snow White and Rose Red," Willingham here combines elements from three English nursery rhymes—"Peter Piper Picked a Peck of Pickled Peppers," "Peter, Peter Pumpkin Eater," and "Little Bo Beep"— with the legend of the Pied Piper, which tells of a ratcatcher who, after being cheated out of payment by city officials, used his magical pipe to lead the children of Hamelin away from the town, after which they were never seen again. According to Bernard Queenan, the legend first appeared in writing in the sixteenth century, and this version spoke of a real incident that occurred in Hamelin in 1284 (107); in the nineteenth century, the legend was retold by the likes of Johann Wolfgang Goethe, the Brothers Grimm, and Robert Browning (111). The second plot in *Peter & Max* is set in centuries prior, in Hesse, a quasi-Germanic continent: in this plot, the Pipers—a family of travelling musicians—have their lives turned upside-down when the Adversary invades their Homeland. Even before the invasion, conflict enters the family when Johannes, the elder Piper, bequeaths the family's magical flute—Frost—to his younger son, Peter, thereby infuriating his elder son, Max. In response to this slight, Max seeks revenge on his own family, as well as on Bo Peep, Peter's childhood friend and, later, his sweetheart. The Hessian plot follows Max's rise as the diabolical Pied Piper, as well as the adventures of Peter and Bo in the conquered city of Hamelin. Along with these relatively unfamiliar figures from the *Fables* universe, the Hessian plot also features glimpses of Bigby, who is still a ravenous, giant wolf living in the forest, and a girl who refers to herself only as "the Black Forest" (238), but who is readily identifiable as Bellflower/Frau Totenkinder. The Black Forest girl becomes an ally for Max, giving him his own deadly, magical flute, which he names Fire.

The novel deals with several themes familiar to readers of *Fables*, including: the destructive nature of sibling rivalry; the healing nature of long-abiding romantic and married love; the way an oppressive political system will give rise to unusual allies and underground communities; and the moral complexity of wielding magical power. This last theme is of paramount importance in the novel and, in particular, the relationship between Max and Frau Totenkinder draws attention to the degree to which those with power must use it responsibly, lest they become complicit in the circulation of violence and evil. In the representation of the two flutes, Frost and Fire, the novel continues to examine the function of magical objects in the *Fables* universe, suggesting that—unlike those objects found in the standard wonder tale, which have no history and are simply acquired and used—all magical objects can act as mirrors, taking on the qualities of those who make use of them. Interestingly, the subject of the lost children, a central, traumatic motif in the source tale, is only gestured toward in the novel, and is not a site of emotional resonance. Finally, the novel explores the way desire is sometimes interchangeable with greed, and the way the community offers a space for healing and justice.

Jack of Fables

The first issue of the spin-off series *Jack of Fables*—co-written by Bill Willingham and Matthew Sturges—was published in September 2006; the series ran for 50 issues, and featured the adventures of two Jacks: Jack Horner, who, as Willingham notes in the *Fables Encyclopedia* is "the bad boy who never learned" (Nevins, 115), and his son, Jack Frost, who is as naïve and honorable as his father is vulgar and untrustworthy. Willingham notes that "Jack was sort of an ongoing experiment to see how many different characters from fables, fairy tales and folklore we could shoehorn into a single character" (Nevins, 115), and—indeed—the character name "Jack" appears so frequently in folk and fairy tales that he is a kind of archetype. In his introduction to the collection, *Jack in Two Worlds: Contemporary North American Tales and Their Tellers*, Carl Lindahl notes that the earliest English versions of so-called "Jack Tales" were "obscene and scatological" (xiv), and that he was presented as a "working-class hero," popular with English readers (xv). Also central to the English "Jack Tale" tradition is the idea of the journey, during which Jack encounters magical helpers and fights enemies before returning home (xviii). Lindahl argues that the specific identity of the North American version of Jack was solidified by Richard Chase who—in 1943–published *The Jack Tales*, a collection of Jack folk tales from North Carolina. Chase's enormously influential version of Jack is characterized by his status as a "cultural outsider" (xxiv) and by his interest in "material success" (xxiv). In keeping with the American ethos of self-reliance and rising social status, "The American [Jack tales] ... foreground the individual, but not without offering him a social order that ensures his success" (xxxi).

In *Jack of Fables*, the figure of Jack Frost resembles a sci-fi version of the English Jack: for much of the series, his appearances show him using a magical sword, being aided by a magical helper—the wooden owl, MacDuff—and having noble adventures in space. For their more complex portrayal of Jack Horner, Willingham and Sturges exaggerate key features of the American Jack tradition: whereas the English Jack often uses magic to defeat a powerful enemy, such as a king, the American Jack has no magic, and must rely on resourcefulness to overthrow his magical foe (xxvii). Even in the narrative arc that marks his transition away from Fabletown—"Jack Be Nimble," collected in *Homelands* (Vol. 6)—Jack Horner is aware that the most useful magic he can access is magic associated with popularity, which is why he goes to Hollywood to produce blockbuster films about himself; by the time Priscilla Page picks up Jack as he hitchhikes his way out of Tinsel Town, his popularity makes him "the most famous and powerful Fable of all" (*Escape*, 11). The issue of magical popularity is especially crucial to the *Jack of Fables* series because, even more so than the main comic book series, *Jack of Fables* explores the meta-levels of storytelling, featuring such key characters as the Page Sisters, three Senior Librarians of the Golden Boughs Retirement Home, which is actually a well-guarded prison for Fables; Mr. Revise, the Head Librarian, an incredibly powerful figure whose self-assigned task is to "neuter" Fables, censoring all aspects of their stories that make them "memorable and distinct" (*Escape*, 49); and the Pathetic Fallacy, otherwise known as Gary, who is Mr. Revise's grandfather; Gary has the power to temporarily give life to inanimate objects and is Jack Horner's long-suffering sidekick throughout the series.

The relationships between Jack Horner and these figures—collectively referred to as Literals—form a loose context for Jack's adventures, which include escaping from the Golden Boughs (*Escape*); battling the blood-thirsty Lady Luck in Las Vegas (*Hearts*); searching for gold in the Homeland known as Americana (*Americana*); and joining Mr. Revise in his battle against his brother Bookburner (*Book of War*). Also, these figures, along with Kevin Thorn, the Literal responsible for writing the universe inhabited by Fables, show up in *The Great Fables Crossover*, volume 13 of the regular series; in that adventure, Jack turns to Fabletown for help dealing with Kevin, who intends to write them all out of existence. Thematically, this metafictional context draws attention to the question of who "controls" a story: Is it the author? Is it editors, censors, or librarians, all of whom regulate access to texts? Is it the piling on of story conventions, which no author can escape from, no matter how ingenious? Or will a trickster figure like Jack Horner always manage to exceed the limits imposed by authors, editors, and conventions, perhaps by reaching out to the imagination of readers? At the end of many issues of *Jack of Fables*, Jack Horner narrates a final caption, hinting at his next series of incredible adventures, which usually promise to involve lots of sex and/or outlandish heroism: for example, the final caption of "Viva Las Vegas," collected in *Jack of Hearts*, declares, "Next: I take this crazy, brain-sucking bitch to task, play a round of golf, and even find time to take out a dozen Nazi vampires with my bare hands" (*Hearts*, 74). Importantly, Jack's metafictional promises to his readers prove completely delusional, as the next issue "Heaven or Las Vegas" features neither Nazi vampires nor golf.

Another important convention of the American Jack tradition that *Jack of Fables* plays with is the focus on "material success" as a reflection of self-reliance: the series begins with Jack Horner bemoaning the loss of the greater part of his Hollywood fortune (*Escape*, 9) and follows his various attempts to enrich himself. The convention of a context of "social order" within which to enjoy this success is destabilized, as Jack Horner's desire to hoard treasure causes him to transform into a dragon (*Jack and Jack*, 100). In contrast, Jack Frost moves from adventure to adventure, spending all the money he earns to provide his companion MacDuff with a new body after his wooden one is burned (*The End*, 33–37). Thus, an important theme that runs through *Jack of Fables* is the changing conception of the hero, as the text juxtaposes the activities of a rich, conniving scoundrel with those of a poor, honest champion. The two Jacks finally meet in the final volume of the series—*The End*—when Jack Frost decides to come out of a short-lived retirement in order to fight a dragon, who is really Jack Horner, his own father (*The End*, 37). Before the battle, which also involves the Page sisters who are after Jack Horner's hoard of books, and some stragglers from the Golden Boughs who fight against their former captors, Jack Horner is shown as a cartoon dragon, trading bad jokes with Gary about eating Gary's dates (*The End*, 19) and the problem of how to deal with all the dragon poop (*The End*, 52). These allusions to the American history of the comic strip funny pages reflect the degree to which Jack Horner represents a hyperbolic distillation of the American Jack tradition; in contrast, when Jack Frost first presents himself to the dragon, his overblown language and chivalric stance recalls a European romance tradition, as this Jack is no longer just an ordinary bloke turned hero. In the battle's decisive moments, the two Jacks seem to destroy one another (*The End*, 132–133) and various devils appear to fight over their ownership of Jack Horner's soul (*The End*, 137–139). The ever wily American, however, doesn't wait around to see which devil wins; thus, the series seems to suggest that the adventures of scoundrels are more satisfying, are more in keeping with our own degenerate, consumption-oriented age, and have more potential for renewal than tales of noble heroes.

Cinderella Graphic Novels

The spin-off comics included in the collections *Cinderella: From Fabletown with Love*, published in 2010, and *Cinderella: Fables Are Forever*, published in 2011, were written by Chris Roberson and drawn by Shawn McManus; while McManus also worked on issues of *Fables* (primarily drawing the adventures of Bufkin in Oz) and *Fairest* (drawing Cinderella again), Chris Roberson's connection to the *Fables* universe derives from his membership in the Clockwork Storybook writing collective, an Austin, Texas, based organization that included Roberson, Willingham, Sturges, and science fiction and fantasy writer Mark Finn. As is made clear from titles that reference the adventures of James Bond, the *Cinderella* volumes play up the lead character's status as Fabletown's most adept and glamorous spy, and show her jet-setting to exotic locales such as Dubai, the North Sea, and a Homeland known as Ultima Thule (*Love*) and Russia, Thailand, Burkina Faso, and the Deadly Desert of Oz (*Forever*), engaging in remarkable feats of surveillance and combat, and enjoying amorous moments with Aladdin (*Love*) and Ivan Durak, a figure from Russian folklore (*Forever*). As noted in *The Great Fairy Tale Tradition*, "There are thousands of oral and literary versions of 'Cinderella,' one of the most popular fairy tales in the world" (Zipes, 444). The commonalities that connect many of the variants—from Duàn Chéngshì's "Yè Xiàn," written in China in the 9th century, to Giambattista Basile's "La gatta Cenerentola," written in the early 17th century—include: the basic plot, in which a young girl's inheritance or rightful place in the household is threatened by her stepmother; the figure of a magical helper, whether in the guise of the girl's dead mother or godmother or birds; and the use of a shoe test to prove the girl's identity. Given the tale's popularity, it is unsurprising that it has been the subject of much scholarly criticism, including feminist criticism, which focuses on the way the patriarchal system produces females who are either cruel or passive, and psychoanalytic readings that examine the tale's rendering of maternal absence.

In the *Fables* universe, including the spin-off texts, Cinderella is totally different from the passive, neglected heroine of the source tale, except in terms of her association with shoes (though not with a shoe test), and in terms of her fraught relationship with her own magical helper, Frau Totenkinder, who in supplying the super agent with various magical gadgets, calls to mind the character Q in the James Bond canon. For all Cinderella's claims that "it's a business relationship, plain and simple" (*With Love*, 15), her mysterious promises to Frau in exchange for magical help recalls the way the most interesting and complex relationships in the source tale are among female family members. Indeed, despite the presence of Aladdin and Ivan throughout *From Fabletown with Love* and *Fables Are Forever*, respectively, the central conflict in both volumes is with another woman, Cinderella's erstwhile Fairy Godmother in *From Fabletown with Love*, and Dorothy Gale in *Fables Are Forever*. The figure of the Fairy Godmother allows Roberson to explore the twinned themes of "disappointed girls" and the way "every blessing [is turned] into a curse" (*With Love*, 123), themes that are amplified by the back-up story of Crispin, the shoemaker's elves, and the magic shoes, and by Safiya's tale of exchanging the captivity of the harem for the "illusion" of freedom in the Mundy world (*With Love*, 91). In *Fables Are Forever*, Dorothy Gale is presented as Cinderella's nemesis, connected with her insofar as they are both associated with shoes and they are both accomplished agents: Dorothy often makes the point that "You're the same as me, Cindy. A killer" (*Forever*, 105). Cinderella, however, justifies her own activity on the grounds that she is a "patriot. I do what I must to protect the people of Fabletown" (*Forever*, 136). Thus, in *Fables Are Forever*, Roberson playfully adapts the source tale's basic plot, in which a persecuted heroine attains her rightful inheritance, in order to examine the issue of rightful or righteous political or military action.

Fairest

The spin-off series *Fairest*, which ran from May 2012 to March 2013 and included 33 issues plus the graphic novel *Fairest in All the Land* (published in November 2013), was described by Willingham as "a series of miniseries," with each narrative arc focusing on one of the female Fables (Renaud, "Willingham and Vertigo"). A number of different writers and artists worked on the series, including: Phil Jimenez, who contributed the art for the issues collected in *Fairest: Wide Awake*, which describes the waking of Briar Rose and Lumi, who were stolen away from the sleeping Imperial City following the defeat of the Adversary (see *Super Team*, 16.145); Lauren Beukes and Inaki Miranda, who, respectively, write and draw *Fairest: The Hidden Kingdom*, a prequel to the events recounted in the main *Fables* narrative portraying Rapunzel's attempt to recover her lost children and her journeys to modern and ancient Japan; Sean E. Williams and Stephen Sadowski, the respective writer and penciler of *Fairest: The Return of the Maharaja*, a narrative set in the Indu Homeland in the years following Prince Charming's apparent death when he destroyed the final gateway between the Homelands; Marc Andreyko, who writes *Fairest: Of Mice and Men*, another Cinderella story, drawn by Shawn McManus, this time pitting Cinderella against one of her stepsisters and a mysterious army of mice men; and Mark Buckingham and Russ Braun, though in *Fairest: The Clamour for the Glamour*, a narrative arc about Reynard the Fox's adventures as a man and a lottery for glamours held at The Farm, Braun draws and Buckingham takes on the role of writer. The graphic novel *Fairest in the Land* is written by Willingham, with its many tales drawn by twenty-four different artists. The graphic novel is a murder mystery, narrated by the Magic Mirror and staring Cinderella as the detective, an unfamiliar role for her; in the absence of Bigby, who is at this point in time a collection of glass shards, Mayor Cole calls on Cindy to solve the mystery of who is murdering Fables. All of the narratives included in the *Fairest* spin-off either precede the timeline of the main series, or occur between the time of the Empire's fall and the return of the predatory, shattered Bigby, allowing for an extended exploration of Cinderella's many exploits, for stories featuring such secondary figures as Briar Rose, Rapunzel, Bo Peep, and Reynard the Fox, and for the introduction of Nalayani, the protagonist of *The Return of the Maharaja*; also, both *The Hidden Kingdom* and *The Return of the Maharaja* explore non-Western folklore traditions, contributing to the idea raised in *Peter & Max* that every region of the Mundy world has its own parallel Homeland. Interestingly, though the initial conceit of the spin-off series was that it would focus on "the fairest flowers of many lands" (*Wide Awake*, 7), male characters such as Prince Charming (in *The Return of the Maharaja*) and Reynard (in *The Clamour for the Glamour*) often take center stage.

While the narrative arcs in *Fairest* usually refer to events in the main *Fables* narrative, the series itself contains fewer braided narratives, with each individual "mini series" remaining relatively self-contained. Still, there are a number of formal and thematic patterns that emerge across the various narrative arcs. First, there is often a thematic exploration of the power of story, for example: in *Wide Awake*, Lumi's fascination with Ali Baba's storytelling prowess is juxtaposed with Briar Rose's attempts to master the story constraints placed upon her at her birth; in *The Hidden Kingdom*, the force of story is thematically connected to the trauma of memory, as Rapunzel struggles to recall the tale of her lost children; in *Fairest in All the Land*, story is explored at a meta-level in a way that recalls *Legends in Exile* (Vol. 1), as detective Cinderella must piece together various bits of fragmented testimony in order to find a pattern in the Fabletown killings. Next, as might be expected in a series that focuses primarily on those figures from folk and fairy tale whose stories end in a declaration of true love or in an advantageous marriage, the pursuit of love is often a central plot element, though often the aim is to destabilize convention: in *Wide Awake*, Ali Baba's ability to awaken Briar Rose—which is supposed to signify "true love" (*Wide Awake*, 26)—jars not only against the failure of love to take hold between the two adventurers, despite conditions/conventions that favor romantic attachment, but also against Ali Baba's growing affection for Lumi; in *The Hidden Kingdom*, Rapunzel's fraught love affair with Joel Crow, her hairdresser, is explored alongside her equally fraught, centuries old love affair with Tomoko, who is a kitsune, a figure from Japanese folklore who is part woman/part fox; as a bakeneko—a supernatural cat, who initially recalls the Catbus from Hayao Miyazaki's *My Neighbor Totoro*—tells Joel, "Whatever. She loves you. She just loves someone else more" (*Hidden*, 133). In *The Return of the Maharaja*, Prince Charming fails to charm Nalayani, the Indu warrior whose deepest love is for her village, and Nathoo's homoerotic desire for Charming is accepted as natural (*Maharaja*, 135), while in *Of Mice and Men*, Cinderella's love affair with Ramayan, a Hindu god, ends once Marcel's mice monster children are defeated—as Snow White puts it to her, "So, men are like shoes? You get new ones for every adventure? (*Mice and Men*, 134). Only in *The Clamour for the Glamour* does the series portray a "happily ever after" tale of love, as Reynard the Fox and Meghan, a Mundy girl from Louisiana, have a mixed-species child, named "Fair," and express their desire to live as a happy family (*Clamour*, 134).

As the name of Reynard and Meghan's child highlights, another focus in the series is—unsurprisingly—the issue of what constitutes being "the fairest in the land," and how culturally accepted notions of "prettiness" operate. When Fair is born in the back room of a fast-food restaurant, a customer sees the baby's fox tail and calls her "a monster! A devil child" (*Clamour*, 113); the issue of the way difference is considered to be monstrous, and therefore in need of disguising, coheres with the central theme of *The Clamour for the Glamour*, in which the non-human denizens of The Farm demand that the Fabletown executive follow through on Prince Charming's ill-advised election promise of glamours for all who desire them (*Clamour*, 20–21). Further, the image of the so-called monstrous female with a fox's tale in this relatively comic volume of *Fairest* recalls the similar image of Tomoko in the much darker *The Hidden Kingdom*; Tomoko, along with her fellow yokai (or monsters, as per Japanese folklore) are banished from the emperor's kingdom (*Hidden*, 39), while the beautiful Mayumi has her mouth slashed open by power-hungry Ryogan, and eventually becomes a monster who haunts mirrors (*Hidden*, 78). The cultural tendency to vilify monstrosity or ugliness and celebrate the prettiness of women is explored most fully in *Fairest in the Land*, in which Goldilocks proves to be the villain with a special nut against "all of you pretty ones ... [because] every one of you gets pushed to the top of the food chain, entirely due to your looks" (*All the Land*, 130). Thus, Goldilocks concocts a plan to use the magical sword Regret, which always finds its intended target, but which also requires a second victim as "a price for its miracles"; significantly, Regret allows that one of each pair of victims may be brought back to life, if that wish is expressed in time (*All the Land*, 104). Though Cinderella refers to Goldilocks' position on the advantages of beauty as "crap," in keeping with Willingham's general disdain for what he perceives to be overly dogmatic radical feminist argument, this challenge is only partial. In the aftermath of Cinderella's vanquishing of Goldilocks, Snow White meets up with her to discuss Cinderella's choice to "save all the pretty girls" (*All the Land*, 137), i.e., to bring back to life those of the murder victims who comfortably fit into the category of "fairest" at the expense of such figures as Mrs. Ford, an oracle of death; the Moon from nursery rhyme, Edward Dantes, Ali Baba, Dunster Happ, Aspen, Beauty's Lamia, and the Blue Fairy. Though the Magic Mirror assures Cinderella that she has made "objectively good choices" (*All the Land*, 149), the witch car Hadeon's comment about the way the Fables act as "slave owners" (*All the Land*, 143) draws attention to the way power in the community flows via cultural systems—including systems of what "fair" means—that are morally indeterminate.

The Unwritten Crossover

The Unwritten is another highly metafictional comic book series published by Vertigo, written by Mike Carey with art by Peter Gross. The volume, *The Unwritten Fables*, co-written and drawn by Willingham and Buckingham, collects *The Unwritten*, issues 50 to 54. Unlike the crossover between *Jack of Fables* and the main comic book series in *The Great Fables Crossover*, the events that take place in *The Unwritten Fables* are not "canon," in that they have no explicit impact on the *Fables* narrative, though—in a 2013 interview with *Comic Book Resources*—Willingham explained to Jeffrey Renaud that "the story that is being done in 'The Unwritten' is possibly, and even likely, to have ripples within the 'Fables' storyline" (Renaud, "Carey and Willingham"). *The Unwritten* recounts the adventures of Tom Taylor, the son of a great children's books author, who is often thought to be the living incarnation of his father's greatest creation, boy wizard Tommy Taylor. In the crossover—which presents a parallel *Fables* universe, one in which the North Wind does not defeat Mr. Dark—Tommy Taylor is summoned by the gathering of 13th floor witches; along with his fictional wizarding companions Sue Sparrow and Peter Price, Tommy becomes Fabletown's best hope of defeating Mr. Dark. *The Unwritten Fables* is primarily focused on exploring the relationship between story and reality, as Tommy, Frau Totenkinder, and Mr. Dark work to understand the relationships among the colliding fictional worlds. In these conflicts,

knowledge is (predictably) presented as the greatest power, though there
is a concomitant suggestion that there is safety or strength in maintaining
an ability to be surprised by story. In terms of its connection to the main
Fables narrative, the "ripples" produced by *The Unwritten Fables* are subtle, as the relationships among Snow White, Bigby, Rose Red, the North
Wind, and the Cubs, and among Flycatcher, Red Riding Hood, and Boy
Blue are explored in a world gone "topsius turvius" (*Unwritten*, 107). Also
thematically important is the exploration of parents and children (especially fathers and sons), as Pinocchio pointedly asks Tommy, "you think
flesh-and-blood kids don't come with strings attached?" (*Unwritten*, 50).

The Wolf Among Us

In October 2013, Telltale Games released the first of a five episode
graphic adventure video game called *The Wolf Among Us*; the action is set
years before the events recounted in the main *Fables* comic book series
and the main player is Bigby Wolf, Sheriff of Fabletown, who is back to
solving mysteries as he did in *Legends in Exile* (Vol. 1). After the success
of the video game, Vertigo created a digital comic book series—written
by Dave Justus and Matthew Sturges, and drawn by a variety of artists,
including Stephen Sadowski, Shawn McManus, and Travis Moore—which,
more or less, covers the same narrative ground as the game though with
room for more detail: each chapter of the game translates into 12 issues
of the comic book series. In both forms of *The Wolf Among Us*, Bigby
encounters a Fable named Faith when he breaks up an argument between
her and The Woodsman (Faith is eventually identified as the protagonist
from Charles Perrault's tale "Donkeyskin"); later, Faith's head is found on
the doorstep of the Woodland Building, leading off an investigation into
her murder.

The video game is played from Bigby's point of view, which results
in an emphasis on his role as a street detective, as the game play necessarily
involves looking for clues, making narrative choices, and unlocking secrets,
including those related to the "Book of Fables," in which character back
stories are explained as the game progresses. In *The Wolf Among Us* comic
book, Bigby contrasts himself with a figure like "Miss Marple," asserting
he's not "that kind of a detective" (Justus and Sturges, *Wolf Among Us* #8);
for example, the smell of Faith's blood "awakens something ancient and
powerful" in Bigby, which is the desire "to hunt" (Justus and Sturges, *Wolf
Among Us* #4). Similarly, the game more so than the comic emphasizes its
urban setting, making continuous reference to issues such as poverty,

prostitution, racketeering, and drug use in its deliberate contrasting of the "seedier" areas of the Mundy with the "luxury" of the Woodland Building; in general, the characters that populate the video game are unhappy, angry, downtrodden, and perpetually suspicious of one another, setting up various kinds of resistance that Bigby-as-player must negotiate or battle against. The comic book, in contrast, includes much more humor and play with the notion of story, and is thus reminiscent of Sturges' work in *Jack of Fables*. For example, in the video game, the story of "Donkeyskin" is quickly recounted as a dark tale of incest, marking Faith as a woman with an unhappy past in order to reinforce the general setting and tone (*The Wolf Among Us*). In the comic book, the tale of Donkeyskin is retold in rhyming couplets over twelve pages, drawing attention to such story elements as the female protagonist's ability to disguise herself and the complex relationship between love and enchantment (Justus and Sturges, *Wolf Among Us* #5). Also important in the comic book is the historical relationship between Ichabod Crane and Bigby Wolf, who occupy the roles of teacher and student in 17th century Salem, Massachusetts, as Justus and Sturges connect the arrival of Bigby in the Mundy with the plot of Arthur Miller's *The Crucible* and with an exploration of the relationship between magic and the American witch hunt. The comic book is thus more explicitly intertextual and metafictional: when Prince Lawrence asserts that he wanted to write "The End" to his and Faith's unhappy story, Bigby responds, "Looks like you got a 'To be Continued' instead" (Justus and Sturges, *Wolf Among Us: #7*); when Grendel retells the story of Little Red Riding Hood, he makes use of as many expletives as possible, drawing attention to the way our response to story depends on the telling (Justus and Sturges, *Wolf Among Us: #10*). The game, in contrast, deliberately highlights action, as the recounting of plot is employed as a connecting piece between the opportunities for player interaction, which usually comes in the form of deciding how Bigby will approach a situation or fighting opponents like The Woodsman, the Tweedles, Grendel and so on. Also, the "magic" offered by the Crooked Man and his crew resembles nothing so much as cheap drugs, as the Crooked Man's empire operates as a counter force to the uncaring bureaucracy of Fabletown.

The most conspicuous themes underpinning *The Wolf Among Us*—in particular the game version of the narrative—are, first, the issue of class difference and, second, the exploration of decidedly "mundane" dark environments, in which poverty will give rise to social vulnerability and a criminal class that is more than willing to abuse, exploit, and control the vulnerable. Also prominent—and problematic—is the representation of the violence done to women; unlike the main comic book series, which features a complex range of women characters, *The Wolf Among Us* video game presents several unhappy, abused, and dead women, thus conforming to an unfortunate convention in comic books (and video games) whereby violence done to women operates as a plot device to motivate male protagonists to heroic action (Robbins, 216). Finally, in the video game the issue of Bigby's integrity is an open question. In the comic book, the backstory of Crane and Bigby in Salem explores the development of Bigby's moral compass and attitudes toward truth, features of his character that align with the main series; in contrast, the video game offers the player various avenues for character development, whereby Bigby can be more or less violent, more or less honest, and more or less compassionate. An important feature of the game is the gathering of statistics on "Player Choices," as players can make comparisons about the way they have "written" Bigby's character.

In an interview with Vaneta Rogers, in which Willingham and Buckingham discuss the publication of the final volume of *Fables*, Willingham rehearses the idea that "stories do go on" (Rogers). Willingham here not only refers to the possibility of further spin-offs or a return to the *Fables* universe, a possibility that is particularly relevant in the comic books industry, but to the way story "goes on" in the minds of readers, in their musings, discussions, debates, and daydreams. As per usual, Willingham takes the time in that interview to denigrate the work of literary critics, again making use of the descriptor "pointy-headed academics" (Rogers). Rather than feel insulted, my response to this assessment is to note that academics too are readers: we are the Muddlecocks who look for patterns across a sprawling set of texts. As a relatively wide-ranging introduction, *A Tour of Fabletown* is necessarily limited in terms of the depth of argument and, no doubt, certain analyses have been left unfinished, various holes require further investigation, and some paths of argument (into the more worrisome parts of the forest) might require a total change of direction. In other words, the story and the response go on.

In *A Tour of Fabletown*, I offer an introduction to some of the plots, patterns, and themes in this expansive series and its offshoots. The complexity and ingenuity of *Fables* allows for any number of frames for analysis, including those I have focused on: the relationship between *Fables* and the literary history of adapting the folk and fairy tale; the portrayal of social roles and of politics; and the meaning of magic in this fictional world. Throughout this study, I have tried to consider how a close reading of *Fables* illuminates various current anxieties, as well as various possibilities for social cohesion, whereby the anxious exploration of the rise of increasingly opaque political dynamics, or of the shifting nature of gender, or of the weakening of nation, is mitigated by narratives that champion the ideals of redemption, community belonging, and choice.

Works Cited

Andreyko, Marc. *Fairest 4: Of Mice and Men*. New York: DC Comics Vertigo, 2014.

Ashliman, D. L. "Father." *The Greenwood Encyclopedia of Folktales and Fairy Tales*. Ed. Donald Haase. 3 Vols. Westport, CT: Greenwood, 2008. 334–336.

_____. *Folk and Fairy Tales: A Handbook*. Westport, CT: Greenwood, 2004.

_____. "Magic Object." *The Greenwood Encyclopedia of Folktales and Fairy Tales*. Ed. Donald Haase. 3 Vols. Westport, CT: Greenwood, 2008. 598–599.

Attebery, Brian. *Strategies of Fantasy*. Bloomington: Indiana University Press, 1992.

Bacchilega, Cristina. *Postmodern Fairy Tales: Gender and Narrative Strategies*. Philadelphia: University of Pennsylvania Press, 1997.

Benson, Stephen. "Introduction: Fiction and the Contemporaneity of the Fairy Tale." *Contemporary Fiction and the Fairy Tale*. Ed. Stephen Benson. Detroit, MI: Wayne State University Press, 2008. 1–19.

Bobby, Susan Redington. "Introduction: Authentic Voices in Contemporary Fairy Tales." *Fairy Tales Reimagined: Essays on New Retellings*. Ed. Susan Redington Bobby. Jefferson, NC: McFarland, 2009. 5–12.

Boucher, Geoff. "'Fables' Writer Bill Willingham Finds a Happy Ending Despite 'That damned Shrek.'" Interview with Bill Willingham. *Hero Complex: Pop Culture Unmasked*. Jan. 17 2010. http://herocomplex.latimes.com/uncategorized/fables-writer-bill-willingham-finds-a-happy-ending-despite-that-damned-shrek-1/ Accessed Oct. 2 2014.

Brown, Lisa. "The Speaking Animal: Nonhuman Voices in Comics." *Speaking for Animals*. Ed. Margo DeMello. New York: Routledge, 2013. 73–77.

Carey, George W., and James McClellan, eds. *The Federalist: A Collection by Alexander Hamilton, James Madison, and John Jay*. Indianapolis: Liberty Fund, 2001.

Carey, Mike, and Bill Willingham. *The Unwritten Fables*. New York: DC Comics Vertigo, 2014.

Chaney, Michael. "Animal Subjects in the Graphic Novel." *College Literature* 38.3 (2011): 129–149.

Copeland, Rita, and Peter T. Struck. "Introduction." *The Cambridge Companion to Allegory*. Eds. Rita Copeland and Peter T. Struck. Cambridge: Cambridge University Press, 2010. 1–11.

Davidson, Hilda Ellis. "Helpers and Adversaries in Fairy Tales." *A Companion to the Fairy Tale*. Eds. Hilda Ellis Davidson and Anna Chaudhri. Cambridge: D.S Brewer, 2003. 99–122.

"Diamond Announces Top Comic Books & Graphic Novels for 2014." *Diamond News*. Jan. 9 2015. http://www.diamondcomics.com/Home/1/1/3/597?articleID=153901 Accessed Feb. 18 2015.

Do Rozario, Rebecca-Anne C. "Comic Book Princesses for Grown-Ups: Cinderella Meets the Pages of the Superhero." *Colloquy: Text Theory Critique* (2012): 191–206.

Duncan, Randy. "Fantasy." *Encyclopedia of Comics and Graphic Novels*. Ed. M. Keith Brooker. 2 Vols. Westport, CT: Greenwood, 2010. 200–209.

Duncan, Randy, Matthew J. Smith and Paul Levitz. *The Power of Comics: History, Form, and Culture*. 2nd Edition. London: Bloomsbury Academic, 2015.

Fineberg, Jessica. "Exposing the Traditional Marriage Agenda." *Northwestern Journal of Law & Social Policy* 7.2 (2012): 301–351.

Fischer, Craig. "Worlds Within Worlds: Audiences, Jargon, and North American Comics Discourse." *Transatlantica* 1 (2010). http://transatlantica.revues.org/4919. Accessed Jan. 4 2014.

Freud, Sigmund. *The Interpretation of Dreams*. Trans. Joyce Crick. Oxford: Oxford University Press, 1999.

Frisch, Mark-Oliver. "Collection Business." *Comiks Debris*. Nov. 28 2007. http://comiksdebris.blogspot.de/2007/11/collection-business.html. Accessed Nov. 4 2014.

_____. "Vertigo and Wildstorm Month-To-Month Sales: The Long View." *Comiks Debris*. Jun. 5 2012. http://comiksdebris.blogspot.ca/2012/06/vertigo-and-wildstorm-month-to-month.html. Accessed Nov. 4 2014.

Frus, Phyllis, and Christy Williams. "Introduction: Making the Case for Transformation." *Beyond Adaptation: Essays on Radical Transformations of Original Works*. Eds. Phyllis Frus and Christy Williams. Jefferson, NC: McFarland, 2010. 1–18.

Fuchs, Barbara. *Romance*. New York: Routledge, 2004.

Gardner, Jeanne. "'True-To-Life': Romance Comics and Teenage Desire, 1947–1954." *Forum for World Literature Studies* 3.1 (2011): 118–128.

Goldstein, Kalman. "Al Capp and Walk Kelly: Pioneers of Political and Social Satire in the Comics." *Journal of Popular Culture* 25.4 (1992): 81–95.

Grimm, Jacob, and Wilhelm Grimm. "Snow White and Rose Red." *The Great Fairy Tale Tradition*. Ed. Jack Zipes. New York: W.W. Norton, 2001. 774–778.

Hatfield, Charles. "Jack Kirby and the Marvel Aesthetic." *The Superhero Reader*. Eds. Charles Hatfield, Jeet Heer, and Kent Worcester. Jackson: University of Mississippi Press, 2013. 136–154.

Hatfield, Charles, Jeet Heer and Kent Worcester. "Introduction." *The Superhero Reader*. Eds. Charles Hatfield, Jeet Heer, and Kent Worcester. Jackson: University of Mississippi Press, 2013. xi–xxii.

Hill, Mark C. "Negotiating Wartime Masculinity in Bill Willingham's *Fables.*" *Fairy Tales Reimagined: Essays on New Retellings.* Ed. Susan Redington Bobby. Jefferson, NC: McFarland, 2009. 181–195.

Holquist, Michael. "Whodunit and Other Questions: Metaphysical Detective Stories in Post-War Fiction." *New Literary History* 3 (1972): 135–56.

Irvine, Alex. *The Vertigo Encyclopedia.* New York: DK Publishing, 2008.

Joosen, Vanessa. *Critical & Creative Perspectives on Fairy Tales.* Detroit, MI: Wayne State University Press, 2011.

_____. "Snow White." *The Greenwood Encyclopedia of Folktales and Fairy Tales.* Ed. Donald Haase. 3 Vols. Westport, CT: Greenwood, 2008. 884–886.

Justus, Dave, and Matthew Sturges. *The Wolf Among Us* #4. New York: DC Comics Vertigo, 2014. Digital Comic.

_____. *The Wolf Among Us* #5. New York: DC Comics Vertigo, 2014. Digital Comic.

_____. *The Wolf Among Us* #7. New York: DC Comics Vertigo, 2014. Digital Comic.

_____. *The Wolf Among Us* #8. New York: DC Comics Vertigo, 2014. Digital Comic.

_____. *The Wolf Among Us* #10. New York: DC Comics Vertigo, 2014. Digital Comic.

Kawan, Christine Shojaei. "A Brief Literary History of Snow White." *Fabula* 49 (2008): 325–342.

Kimmel, Michael. *Manhood in America: A Cultural History.* 3d Edition. New York: Oxford University Press, 2012.

Kleiman, Irit Ruth. "X Marks the Spot: The Place of the Father in Chrétien De Troyes *Conte Du Graal.*" *Modern Language Review* 103 (2008): 969–982.

Koh, Wilson. "Put Not Your Trust in Princes": *Fables* and the Problemitisation of Everyday Life." *Nebula: A Journal of Multidisciplinary Scholarship* 6.2 (2009): 142–154.

Kukkonen, Karin. *Contemporary Comics Storytelling.* Lincoln: University of Nebraska Press, 2013.

Landa, Ishay. "Slaves of the Ring: Tolkien's Political Unconscious." *Historical Materialism* 10.4 (2002): 113–133.

Lindahl, Carl. "Jacks: The Name, the Tales, the American Traditions." *Jack in Two Worlds: Contemporary North American Tales and Their Tellers.* Eds. William Bernard McCarthy, Cheryl Oxford, and Joseph Daniel Sobol. Chapel Hill: University of North Carolina Press, 1994. xiii-xxxiv.

Lynch, Andrew. "Archaism, Nostalgia, and Tennysonian War in the *Lord of the Rings.*" *Tolkien's Modern Middle Ages.* Eds. Jane Chance and Alfred K. Siewers. New York: Palgrave Macmillan, 2005. 77–92.

Madison, James. "The Federalist #10." *The Federalist: A Collection by Alexander Hamilton, James Madison, and John Jay.* Eds. George W. Carey and James McClellan. Indianapolis: Liberty Fund, 2001. 42–49.

Madsen, Deborah L. *Allegory in America: From Puritanism to Postmodernism.* Houndmills: Macmillan Press, 1996.

Malarte-Feldman, Claire L. "Adaptation." *The Greenwood Encyclopedia of Folktales and Fairy Tales*. Ed. Donald Haase. 3 Vols. Westport, CT: Greenwood, 2008. 2–3.

Martin, Laura. "The Kind and Unkind Girls." *The Greenwood Encyclopedia of Folktales and Fairy Tales*. Ed. Donald Haase. 3 Vols. Westport, CT: Greenwood, 2008. 533–535.

Marzolph, Ulrich. "*Arabian Nights*." *The Greenwood Encyclopedia of Folktales and Fairy Tales*. Ed. Donald Haase. 3 Vols. Westport, CT: Greenwood, 2008. 55–60.

Matsuuchi, Ann. "Wonder Woman Wears Pants: Wonder Woman, Feminism and the 1972 'Women's Lib' Issue." *Colloquy: Text Theory Critique* 24 (2012): 118–142.

McCarthy, William B. "Jack Tales." *The Greenwood Encyclopedia of Folktales and Fairy Tales*. Ed. Donald Haase. 3 Vols. Westport, CT: Greenwood, 2008. 509–510.

Naithani, Sadhana. "Politics." *The Greenwood Encyclopedia of Folktales and Fairy Tales*. Ed. Donald Haase. 3 Vols. Westport, CT: Greenwood, 2008. 754–756.

Nevins, Jess. *Fables Encyclopedia*. New York: DC Comics Vertigo, 2013.

Ó hÓgáin, Dáithí. "Animal Tale." *The Greenwood Encyclopedia of Folktales and Fairy Tales*. Ed. Donald Haase. 3 Vols. Westport, CT: Greenwood, 2008. 42–43.

O'Leary, Shannon. "My Little Pony Leads Kids' Comic Charge." *Publishers Weekly*. Apr. 12 2013. http://www.publishersweekly.com/pw/by-topic/industry-news/comics/article/56803-my-little-pony-leads-kids-comics-charge.html. Accessed Feb. 18 2015.

O'Shea, Tim. "'This is a wonderful job': An Orca Q&A with *Fables'* Bill Willingham." *Orca Fresh*. Aug. 18 2003. http://web.archive.org/web/20030818233108/http://www.orcafresh.net/interview/in020503.html Accessed Nov. 10 2014.

Parlevliet, Sanne. "Hunting Reynard: How Reynard the Fox Tricked His Way into English and Dutch Children's Literature." *Children's Literature in Education* 39 (2008): 107–120.

Parsons, Deke. *J.R.R. Tolkien, Robert E. Howard and the Birth of Modern Fantasy*. Jefferson, NC: McFarland, 2015.

Phillips. Nickie D., and Staci Strobl. *Comic Book Crime: Truth, Justice, and the American Way*. New York: New York University Press, 2013.

Propp, Vladimir. *Morphology of the Folktale*. 2nd Edition. Trans. Laurence Scott. Austin: University of Texas Press, 1968.

Pustz, Matthew. *Comic Book Culture: Fan Boys and True Believers*. Jackson: University Press of Mississippi, 1999.

Queenan, Bernard. "The Evolution of the Pied Piper." *Children's Literature* 7.1 (1979): 104–114.

Renaud, Jeffrey. "Carey and Willingham Explore 'The Unwritten Fables.'" *Comic Book Resources*. May 30 2013. http://www.comicbookresources.com/?page=article&id=45768 Accessed June 25 2015.

_____. "Willingham and Vertigo Announce 'Fables' Spinoff." *Comic Book Resources.* July 23 2011. http://www.comicbookresources.com/?page=article&id= 33508 Accessed August 26 2015.

Rhoades, Shirrel. *A Complete History of American Comic Books.* New York: Peter Lang, 2008.

Rifas, Leonard. "Funny Animal Comics." *Encyclopedia of Comics and Graphic Novels.* Ed. M. Keith Brooker. 2 Vols. Westport, CT: Greenwood, 2010. 234–242.

Robbins, Trina. "Feminism." *Encyclopedia of Comics and Graphic Novels.* Ed. M. Keith Brooker. 2 Vols. Westport, CT: Greenwood, 2010. 212–218.

Roberson, Chris. *Cinderella: Fables Are Forever.* New York: DC Comics Vertigo, 2012.

_____. *Cinderella: From Fabletown with Love.* New York: DC Comics Vertigo, 2010.

Robinson, Lillian. *Wonder Women: Feminisms and Superheroes.* New York: Routledge, 2004.

Robinson, Sally. *Marked Men: White Masculinity in Crisis.* New York: Columbia University Press, 2000.

Rogers, Vaneta. "A Fairy Tale Ending for Fables." Newsaramawww. 22 July 2015. http://www.newsarama.com/25309-a-fairy-tale-ending-for-fables-with-willingham-buckingham.html Accessed August 26 2015.

Round, Julia. "'Is this a book?' DC Vertigo and the Redefinition of Comics in the 1990s." *The Rise of the American Comics Artist.* Eds. Paul Williams and James Lyons. Jackson: University Press of Mississippi, 2010. 14–30.

Sanchez, Julian. "The Revolt of the Comic Books." *The American Prospect* (November 2007): 43–47.

Scully, Tyler, and Kenneth Moorman. "The Rise of Vigilantism in 1980s Comics: Reasons and Outcomes." *The Journal of Popular Culture* 47.3 (2014): 634–653.

Shathely Q. "The Long Game: Exclusive Interview with "Fables" Creator Bill Willingham." *PopMatters.* Jan. 25 2013. http://www.popmatters.com/feature/167612-the-long-game-exclusive-interview-with-fables-creator-bill-willingha/ Accessed Nov. 4 2014.

Shippey, Tom. "Rewriting the Core: Transformations of the Fairy Tale in Contemporary Writing." *A Companion to the Fairy Tale.* Eds. Hilda Ellis Davidson and Anna Chaudhri. Cambridge: D.S Brewer, 2003. 253–274.

Silver, Carole G. "Animal Bride, Animal Groom." *The Greenwood Encyclopedia of Folktales and Fairy Tales.* Ed. Donald Haase. 3 Vols. Westport, CT: Greenwood, 2008. 40–42.

Soper, Kerry. "From Jive Crows in 'Dumbo' to Bumbazine in 'Pogo': Walt Kelly and the Conflicted Politics Reracinating African American Types in Mid-20th Century Comics." *International Journal of Comic Art* 12.2/3 (2010): 125–149.

Spanos, William V. "The Detective and the Boundary: Some Notes on the Postmodern Literary Imagination." *Casebook on Existentialism.* Ed. William V. Spanos. New York: Crowell, 1976. 163–896.

Stableford, Brian. *Historical Dictionary of Fantasy Literature.* Lanham, MD: Scarecrow, 2005.

Stahl, Caroline. "The Ungrateful Dwarf." *The Great Fairy Tale Tradition.* Ed. Jack Zipes. New York: W.W. Norton, 2001. 772–773.

Stephens, John. "Woman Warrior." *The Greenwood Encyclopedia of Folktales and Fairy Tales.* Ed. Donald Haase. 3 Vols. Westport, CT: Greenwood, 2008. 1035–1037.

Taylor, Laurie N. "Snow White in the City: Teaching Fables, Nursery Rhymes, and Revisions in Graphic Novels." *Teaching the Graphic Novel.* Ed. Stephen E. Tabachnick. New York: Modern Language Association of America, 2009. 172–178.

Thompson, Stith. *The Folktale.* New York: Holt, Rinehart, and Winston, 1946.

Tondro, Jason. *Superheroes of the Round Table: Comics Connections to Medieval and Renaissance Literature.* Jefferson, NC: McFarland, 2011.

Waid, Mark. "Into the Woods." *JLA* 1.47 (2012): n.p.

Williams, Sean E. *Fairest 3: The Return of the Maharaja.* New York: DC Vertigo, 2014.

Willingham, Bill. *Fables 1: Legends in Exile* (new edition). New York: DC Comics Vertigo, 2012.

_____. *Fables 2: Animal Farm.* New York: DC Comics Vertigo, 2003.

_____. *Fables 3: Storybook Love.* New York: DC Comics Vertigo, 2004.

_____. *Fables 4: March of the Wooden Soldiers.* New York: DC Comics Vertigo, 2004.

_____. *Fables 5. Mean Seasons.* New York: DC Comics Vertigo, 2005.

_____. *Fables 6: Homelands.* New York: DC Comics Vertigo, 2005.

_____. *Fables 7: Arabian Nights (And Days).* New York: DC Comics Vertigo, 2006.

_____. *Fables 8: Wolves.* New York: DC Comics Vertigo, 2006.

_____. *Fables 9: Sons of Empire.* New York: DC Comics Vertigo, 2007.

_____. *Fables 10: The Good Prince.* New York: DC Comics Vertigo, 2008.

_____. *Fables 11: War and Pieces.* New York: DC Comics Vertigo, 2008.

_____. *Fables 12: The Dark Ages.* New York: DC Comics Vertigo, 2009.

_____. *Fables 13: The Great Fables Crossover.* New York: DC Comics Vertigo, 2010.

_____. *Fables 15: Rose Red.* New York: DC Comics Vertigo, 2011.

_____. *Fables 16: Super Team.* New York: DC Comics Vertigo, 2011.

_____. *Fables 17: Inherit the Wind.* New York: DC Comics Vertigo, 2012.

_____. *Fables 18: Cubs in Toyland.* New York: DC Comics Vertigo, 2013.

_____. *Fables 19: Snow White.* New York: DC Comics Vertigo, 2013.

_____. *Fables 20: Camelot.* New York: DC Comics Vertigo, 2014.

_____. *Fables 21: Happily Ever After.* New York: DC Comics Vertigo, 2015.

_____.*Fables 22: Farewell.* Burbank, CA: DC Comics Vertigo, 2015.

_____. *Fairest 1: Wide Awake.* New York: DC Comics Vertigo, 2012.

_____. *Fairest in All the Land.* New York: DC Comics Vertigo, 2013.

_____. *1001 Nights of Snowfall.* New York: DC Comics Vertigo, 2006.

_____. *Peter & Max: A Fables Novel.* New York: DC Comics Vertigo, 2009.

_____. *Werewolves of the Heartland.* New York: DC Comics Vertigo, 2012.

Willingham Bill, and Lauren Beukes. *Fairest 2: The Hidden Kingdom.* New York: DC Comics Vertigo, 2013.

Willingham, Bill, and Mark Buckingham. *Fairest 5: The Clamour for the Glamour.* Burbank, CA: DC Comics Vertigo, 2015.

Willingham, Bill, and Matthew Sturges. *Jack of Fables 1: The (Nearly) Great Escape.* New York: DC Comics Vertigo, 2007.

_____. *Jack of Fables 2: Jack of Hearts.* New York: DC Comics Vertigo, 2007.

_____. *Jack of Fables 3: The Bad Prince.* New York: DC Comics Vertigo, 2008.

_____. *Jack of Fables 4: Americana.* New York: DC Comics Vertigo, 2008.

_____. *Jack of Fables 5: Turning Pages.* New York: DC Comics Vertigo, 2009.

_____. *Jack of Fables 6: The Big Book of War.* New York: DC Comics Vertigo, 2009.

_____. *Jack of Fables 7: The New Adventures of Jack and Jack.* New York: DC Comics Vertigo, 2010.

_____. *Jack of Fables 8: The Fulminate Blade.* New York: DC Comics Vertigo, 2011.

_____. *Jack of Fables 9: The End.* New York: DC Comics Vertigo, 2011.

The Wolf Among Us. Telltale Games, 2013. Video Game.

Wright, Bradford W. *Comic Book Nation: The Transformation of Youth Culture in America.* Baltimore: Johns Hopkins University Press, 2001.

Ziolkowski, Jan. *Fairy Tales from Before Fairy Tales: The Medieval Latin Past of Wonderful Lies.* Ann Arbor: University of Michigan Press, 2007.

Zipes, Jack. *Breaking the Magic Spell: Radical Theories of Folk and Fairy Tales.* 2d edition. Lexington: University Press of Kentucky, 2002.

_____. "Cross-Cultural Connections and the Contamination of the Classical Fairy Tale." *The Great Fairy Tale Tradition.* Ed. Jack Zipes. New York: W.W. Norton, 2001. 845–869.

_____. *Fairy Tale as Myth / Myth as Fairy Tale.* Lexington: University of Kentucky Press, 1994.

_____. *Why Fairy Tales Stick: The Evolution and Relevance of a Genre.* New York: Routledge, 2006.

Zipes, Jack, ed. *The Great Fairy Tale Tradition.* New York: W.W. Norton, 2001.

Zolkover, Adam. "Corporealizing Fairy Tales: The Body, the Bawdy, and the Carnivalesque in the Comic Book *Fables.*" *Marvels & Tales: Journal of Fairy Tale Studies* 22.1 (2008): 38–51.

Index